Spatial Inequalities and Wellbeing

MULTIDISCIPLINARY MOVEMENTS IN RESEARCH

This high-quality series aims to publish reviews and original research in areas crossing the traditional boundaries between academic disciplines. As the value of multidisciplinary collaboration becomes clearer, the academic world is increasingly moving away from siloed research practices towards a more nuanced and open understanding of the challenges and complexity facing society today. Learning from and recognizing the values and insights of multiple disciplines can result in new and creative ways of thinking, and produce high-impact research to help address intractable problems.

For a full list of Edward Elgar published titles, including the titles in this series, visit our website at www.e-elgar.com.

# Spatial Inequalities and Wellbeing
## A Multidisciplinary Approach

*Edited by*

Camilla Lenzi

*Department of Architecture, Built Environment and Construction Engineering, Politecnico di Milano, Italy*

Valeria Fedeli

*Department of Architecture and Urban Studies, Politecnico di Milano, Italy*

MULTIDISCIPLINARY MOVEMENTS IN RESEARCH

Cheltenham, UK • Northampton, MA, USA

Published by
Edward Elgar Publishing Limited
The Lypiatts
15 Lansdown Road
Cheltenham
Glos GL50 2JA
UK

Edward Elgar Publishing, Inc.
William Pratt House
9 Dewey Court
Northampton
Massachusetts 01060
USA

A catalogue record for this book
is available from the British Library

Library of Congress Control Number: 2023951406

This book is available electronically in the **Elgar**online
Geography, Planning and Tourism subject collection
http://dx.doi.org/10.4337/9781802202632

ISBN 978 1 80220 262 5 (cased)
ISBN 978 1 80220 263 2 (eBook)

Printed and bound in Great Britain by
TJ Books Limited, Padstow, Cornwall

# Contents

# Contributors

**Dimitris Ballas,** Faculty of Spatial Sciences, Department of Economic Geography, University of Groningen, Groningen, the Netherlands.

**Daniel Behar,** Lab'URBA. École d'Urbanisme de Paris (EUP), Université Gustave Eiffel, Paris, France.

**Cristina Bernini,** Department of Statistical Sciences, University of Bologna, Bologna, Italy.

**Martijn J. Burger,** Erasmus Happiness Economics Research Organization, Erasmus University Rotterdam, Rotterdam, the Netherlands; Department of Organisation, Open University of the Netherlands, Heerlen, the Netherlands; School of Economics, University of Johannesburg, Johannesburg, South Africa.

**Valentina Vittoria Calabrese,** Universita degli Studi di Roma La Sapienza Dipartimento di Pianificazione Design Tecnologia dell'Architettura, Rome, Italy.

**Roberta Capello,** Politecnico di Milano, Department of Architecture, Built Environment and Construction Engineering, Milan, Italy.

**Silvia Cerisola,** Politecnico di Milano, Department of Architecture, Built Environment and Construction Engineering, Milan, Italy.

**Daniela De Leo,** Universita degli Studi di Roma La Sapienza Dipartimento di Pianificazione Design Tecnologia dell'Architettura, Rome, Italy.

**Arjen Edzes,** Faculty of Spatial Sciences, Department of Economic Geography, University of Groningen, Groningen, the Netherlands; School of Law, Hanze University of Applied Sciences, Groningen, the Netherlands.

**Silvia Emili,** Department of Statistical Sciences, University of Bologna, Bologna, Italy.

**Valeria Fedeli,** Politecnico di Milano, Department of Architecture and Urban Studies, Milan, Italy.

**Maria Rosaria Ferrante,** Department of Statistical Sciences, University of Bologna, Bologna, Italy.

**Franziska Görmar,** Leibniz-Institut für Länderkunde, Leipzig, Germany.

**Martin Graffenberger,** Leibniz-Institut für Länderkunde, Leipzig, Germany.

**Stefan Haunstein,** Leibniz-Institut für Länderkunde, Leipzig, Germany.

**Marloes Hoogerbrugge,** Erasmus Happiness Economics Research Organization, Erasmus University Rotterdam, Rotterdam, the Netherlands.

**Luise Koeppen,** Faculty of Spatial Sciences, Department of Economic Geography, University of Groningen, Groningen, the Netherlands.

**Sierdjan Koster,** Faculty of Spatial Sciences, Department of Economic Geography, University of Groningen, Groningen, the Netherlands.

**Thilo Lang,** Leibniz-Institut für Länderkunde, Leipzig, Germany.

**Camilla Lenzi,** Politecnico di Milano, Department of Architecture, Built Environment and Construction Engineering, Milan, Italy.

**Philip S. Morrison,** School of Geography, Environment and Earth Sciences, Victoria University of Wellington Te Herenga Waka, Wellington, New Zealand.

**Giovanni Perucca,** Politecnico di Milano, Department of Architecture, Built Environment and Construction Engineering, Milan, Italy.

# Introduction: the interplay among inequalities, wellbeing and space

## Camilla Lenzi and Valeria Fedeli

### NEW SPATIAL INEQUALITIES: THE NEED FOR A MULTIDISCIPLINARY PERSPECTIVE AND A NEW BOOK

The first two decades of the new century have been marked by a rapidly changing environment. Radical technological transformations coupled with an altered global landscape and a reorientation of international trade and value chains, emerging in response of the pandemic and of rising geopolitical tension and energy crisis, in fact, are inducing dramatic changes in the world economy, societies and territories.

A recurrent conclusion made by many scholars and commentators is that the combination of these megatrends has created rather unfavourable conditions for balanced growth and sociospatial resilience and this turbulence will likely amplify the chief paradox of our time: the co-occurrence of powerful technology (and accelerating technological change in the view of many) with stagnating median wages, increasing income inequalities and a generalised sentiment of discontent (McAfee and Brynjolfsson, 2017; McCann, 2020; Rodríguez-Pose, 2018).

Inequalities have been a long-standing issue and a terrain of theoretical and empirical discussions and debates in many disciplines (e.g. economics, social sciences, political sciences, geography and even philosophy), each proposing alternative perspectives, notions and interpretations. In most cases, the emphasis has been on the distributional aspects of inequalities, meaning the (unbalanced) allocation of resources and opportunities among individuals, social groups and places (Piketty and Saez, 2003; Piketty, 2014; Diemer et al., 2022).

Importantly, an abundance of empirical evidence has recently been produced showing that, in the past 40 years, a small percentage of individuals and communities did enjoy improved economic prosperity while the vast majority did not benefit from the rise of aggregate wealth. This unbalance has been particularly well-documented in the case of the US, starting in the past century, from the work of Piketty and Saez (2003) and confirmed also for the last years (Kemeny et al. 2022; Alvaredo et al., 2018; Chancel et al., 2022).

Many (concurrent) explanations have been advocated for describing this secular trend, with enhanced globalisation and super-fast technological change, both achieving peak levels in the last couple of decades, representing the best candidate explanations (Autor and Dorn, 2013). Starting from the early 2000s in fact, massive computerisation, global connectivity, robotisation and automation and, more recently, full-scale digitalisation, have in subsequent waves progressively eroded and exhausted the competitive advantage of human labour with respect to machines, with the displacement of low- and middle-skilled workers being amplified by the offshoring of (primarily) manufacturing activities (Brynjolfsson and McAfee, 2014; Acemoglu and Restrepo, 2019). The shrinking of a middle-income class has progressively produced a polarisation of wages, the stagnation of median wage and the widening of interpersonal inequalities, i.e. the great divergence (Moretti, 2012).

While reduction in inequalities (i.e. convergence) has been a distinctive feature of the post-WWII period, at least at the national level of analysis, the rise of inequalities taking off at the turn of the millennium has been marked by a novel spatial dimension (Kemeny and Storper, 2020). Specifically in the US case, the rise of spatial inequality since the 1980s (i.e. spatial divergence) has been driven by the increasing split between a small group of big, wealthy, resilient and high-income superstar city-regions and the remaining ones, which instead show more similar patterns and an intra-group (i.e. club) convergence. Similar conclusions apply to the UK case, where regional labour market disparities, measured in terms of wage differences, have been found to largely depend on the unbalanced concentration of high-skilled workers (Overman and Xu, 2022). This is evident all over OECD countries in years following the pandemic: 'Remote regions and those far from cities continue to lag behind metropolitan regions in terms of GDP per capita levels and growth' (OECD, 2022, p. 17).

The European Union (EU) context is no exception to these trends. Beside common megatrends, such as the digitalisation of the economy and the unbalanced patterns of globalisation, EU countries have been particularly hit by a series of shocks: the 2007–08 financial crisis, the 2011 debt crisis and the COVID-19 pandemic. Moreover, the EU is particularly exposed to climate- and energy-related threats as well as to the migration crisis. The emergence of these new drivers and dynamics, together with the EU enlargement and integration processes, have exercised multiple pressures on economic, social and spatial cohesion in Europe. In this respect, among the many implications of these megatrends and shocks, many scholars have highlighted a process of increasing socioeconomic disparities across and, especially, within EU countries, hitting particularly those regions suffering from a mix of stagnating and/

or low productivity, limited opportunities and economic development prospects and in which these disadvantageous conditions have frequently translated into a mounting resentment amongst the resident population (McCann, 2020; Rodríguez-Pose, 2018; Dijkstra et al., 2020).

The resurgence of spatial inequalities is, therefore, pushing new challenges for development and social policy and collective action in order to tackle their multiple sources and their socioeconomic and political consequences and to move beyond pure and simplistic redistribution logics and mechanisms (Dijkstra et al., 2020; McCann, 2020; Petrakos and Sotiriou, 2021; Los et al., 2017).

In fact, socioeconomic disparities are a relative and multilayered concept that can depend on the comparison between places across (or within) countries as well as on the comparison between people themselves in their reference communities, with important consequences in terms of inequalities across different kinds of (urban) settings. In short, socioeconomic disparities depend on multiple disadvantage conditions, in particular: (i) the disadvantage of each single place (e.g. city or region) in terms of socioeconomic opportunities, i.e. interregional inequalities; (ii) the disadvantage of each single individual in terms of unequal distribution of income and socioeconomic opportunities within his or her community and place of residence, i.e. intraregional inequalities; (iii) the combination of the two (Lenzi and Perucca, 2021; Overman and Xu, 2022).

Yet, inequalities are still too often conceptualised with predefined and bounded spatial imaginaries, which often hinder their interrelated, interdependent and multiscalar nature (Brenner and Schmid, 2015; Lang et al., 2015). The spatial frames through which policies try to cope with them often contribute, unwittingly, to generating further stigmatisation and marginalisation. Indeed, different forms of 'contingent, systemic, collateral and leveraged marginality' can coexist (Mehretu et al., 2000; Wacquant, 2008) and this asks for the capacity of policies to rely on a sounder theory (Behar, 2017). From this perspective, the debate on the failures of redistributive policies at national or regional levels (Mehretu et al., 2000) is still open, as well as the one on how cities and city-regions are not only responsible for generating further inequalities but can be a crucial pillar in leveraging them.[1]

What is more and more clear, however, is that a multiscalar, multidimensional, multitemporal and multidisciplinary perspective is especially relevant

---

[1]  See, among others, the EU Committee of the Regions, 2022, EU Annual report on the State of Regions and Cities, but also the debate fed by Eurocities, EMA and Metrex, some of the main networks representing cities and metropolitan areas in the European context, as well as by the United Cities and Local Governments at international and global level.

to understand the genesis and impacts of the newly emerging spatial inequalities on the wellbeing of individual and places. As suggested by transition theory, we are more and more in need of a nonlinear, multilevel, multidomain coevolutionary analysis of factors and effects of change, able to investigate the interplay between 'a variety changes at different levels, in different domains, whose interaction reinforces each other' (Loorbach et al., 2017). This means studying change across domains, taking into consideration a variety of technological, social, economic, ecological and institutional factors, focussing on coevolution and going beyond linear causalities: 'It is not a matter of asking what comes first or what causes what, but rather a matter of acknowledging how different phenomena shape and relate to each other over longer periods of time' (Loorbach et al., 2017).

This edited book tackles this challenge by enabling the convergence into a single volume of different disciplinary perspectives, ranging from regional economics to urban studies, from economic and urban geography to planning.

The book moves from the idea that this multidisciplinary perspective, at first sight, may look quite consolidated and agreed among scholars: several recent books in fact try to contribute to developing a thoroughly integrated approach to define, explore and even deal with the challenges related to spatial inequalities and wellbeing. Nevertheless, our premise is the perception that there is an urgent need, now more than ever, of opening and collecting a critical discussion between seminal contributions that too often remain embedded and siloed in their study fields (McCall, 2017; Segal, 2022).

The multidimensional nature of inequality, in fact, generates by definition what some authors call 'inequality interactions' (Segal, 2022, p. 942), i.e. interactions of either causal or analytical nature, making a specific type of inequalities change together with the level or change of a different type of inequalities. These interdependencies can be in principle both positive (i.e. reducing one type of inequalities contributes to reducing another dimension of inequalities) but also negative (i.e. reducing one type of inequalities amplifies other types of inequalities). The multidisciplinary perspective adopted in this volume, then, enables highlighting and understanding the existence of different types and sources of inequalities and, consequently, emphasizing the emergence of possible trade-offs and opportunities to mitigate them, if not identifying room for policy action to tackle different types of inequalities at once.

Accordingly, the different chapters present a selection of the most recent and advanced discussions on the topic, with each chapter addressing different dimensions of inequalities, also at different spatial scales, having the final goal of stimulating the interaction among contributions. This interdisciplinary dialogue, shaped, guided and illustrated in the conclusive section of this introduction, takes the form of an interface discussion highlighting convergences and divergences among authors, a relevant effort to advance research on inequalities and its multidimensional and multidisciplinary nature and consequences.

## INEQUALITIES AND WELLBEING

The rich evidence documenting the upsurge of inequalities within and across places is not only important to flag-up critical situations but also to warn about their socioeconomic consequences, namely wellbeing.

Debates on the conceptualisation and measurement of wellbeing have a long record and no definitive answer. In economics, measurement issues are sorted out by looking primarily at two main alternatives: objective measures, chiefly gross domestic product (GDP), or subjective measure, such as self-reported individual assessment of (un)happiness, conceptually intended as 'the degree to which a person (...) evaluates the overall quality of his/her life as a whole' (Veenhoven, 1996, p. 6), an approach that has been validated empirically by hundreds of studies (Diener et al., 2002; Easterlin, 2001).

Economists have long debated the impact of inequalities on objective measures of wellbeing such as economic growth and productivity without achieving a definitive consensus on the real and empirically detectable effects of the former on the latter.[2] It is of course out of the scope of this Introduction, if not impossible per se, to review this massive literature (for a recent attempt, see Ferreira et al., 2022). The lack of consensus is the outcome of both theoretical and empirical issues. On the conceptual side, there can be multiple factors and transmission channels through which inequalities can exert an effect on economic performance and productivity, operating simultaneously and, in some cases, in opposite directions. For example, deeply rooted inequalities can reduce educational opportunities, in terms of both enrolment and attainment, as well as health status, therefore depressing long-term economic performance. At the same time, however, inequalities may trigger savings and investments. Moreover, mediating factors can make these relationships subject to specific circumstance, e.g. the level of development of the country under study. Furthermore, the empirical verification of the actual transmission channels has been a source of controversy rather than a useful ground to set the dispute definitely, with results frequently depending on the samples examined and their heterogeneity in terms of temporal and geographical coverage.

---

[2] The debate is ongoing. For what concerns European economies, however, there seems to be some evidence of a detrimental effect of interpersonal inequalities for long-term aggregate economic growth and missed productivity advances (OECD, 2014).

When looking at the relationship between inequality and subjective meas-ures of wellbeing, the puzzle described above does not seem to weaken either. Difficulties in drawing solid conclusions are both on the conceptual and the empirical sides. In the effort to develop comprehensive surveys on the subject, many authors in fact conclude that results are not definitive but highly depend-ent on the conceptualisation and measurement of both the key constructs, inequalities and wellbeing, the time frame, the countries and the structure of data (see for reviews, Schneider, 2016; Ngamaba et al., 2018; Hopkins, 2008; Katic and Ingram, 2018).

Self-interest generally represents a good reason for inequality dislike. Specific characteristics and circumstances (e.g. turbulent economic and/or political periods and shocks) can facilitate the link between inequality and reduced opportunities and worse future outcomes, thus reducing tolerance for inequality. Disadvantaged individuals, therefore, can suffer from the comparison with more affluent and advantaged peers and experience lower life satisfaction and wellbeing (Ferrer-i-Carbonell and Ramos, 2014; Luttmer, 2005). At the same time, concerns and preferences for fairness can play a role. Furthermore, upper-income groups may dislike inequality and their happiness may be depressed by high level of disparities, with some authors providing evi-dence for preferences for more equitable distribution of wealth than currently exists (Alesina et al., 2004; Norton and Ariely, 2011).

Even if a positive link between inequality and wellbeing has been hypothe-sised by Hirschman and Rothschild (1973) as the foundation of the so-called tunnel effect, and proved under some circumstances (Alesina et al., 2004), evi-dence in this regard is less consistent. Conceptually speaking, in fact, upward mobility can represent a positive signal about improved future opportunities, at least from an individual perspective. More favourable prospects can raise the tolerance for existing inequalities. Yet, as claimed by some authors, perceived social mobility, rather than actual social mobility, is likely to influence the preferences and tolerability for inequality (Ugur, 2021).

Put briefly, results are highly heterogeneous and possibly dependent on several moderating factors, including the country's level of development and/ or income (Ferre-i-Carbonell and Ramos, 2014), the role of institutions and political preferences, social engagement and sense of community (Alesina et al., 2004). For example, evidence for Western economies is overall convergent in pointing out a negative association between inequalities and individual well-being, whereas this link appears far weaker, if not unreliable, for non-Western countries (Ferre-i-Carbonell and Ramos, 2014).

Moreover, very recent contributions highlight that compositional effects, i.e. individual heterogeneity, play an important role in the explanation of the so-called urban wellbeing paradox, i.e. the recurrent observation of lower levels of individual wellbeing in most urbanised settings (Morrison, 2021; Ballas and

Thanis, 2022; Hoogerbrugge et al., 2022; Hoogerbrugge and Burger, 2021). From this perspective, an important conclusion achieved is that inequalities are particularly suffered by those experiencing specific educational, occupational, technological and income disadvantage; these individual-level disadvantage conditions systematically hamper wellbeing and increase discontent (Lenzi and Perucca, 2021; Koeppen et al., 2021).

Importantly, the increased vulnerability of significant social groups and places has not only raised the discontent of people living in the (relatively) disadvantaged areas of the EU (Lenzi and Perucca, 2021). It has also triggered political discontent and populistic and antisystem electoral outcomes, raising serious concerns about the potentially disruptive (and risky) consequences of widened inequalities for the economy, society and democratic national and, especially, European institutions (Camagni et al., 2020). As noted by the Economist (2016), therefore, 'Regional inequality is proving too politically dangerous to ignore'.

In recent years, an interesting and widening line of research has documented a strong spatial association between interregional inequalities and anti-antisystem voting. The economic transformations of the past decades have widened the gaps among social groups, downgrading the socioeconomic conditions for many and generating a diffused feeling of being left behind, a general sentiment of unhappiness and a mounting frustration with their personal socioeconomic conditions. This process has been exemplified in the literature and in the press as the rise of the so-called geography of discontent (Los et al., 2017; Dijkstra et al., 2020; McCann, 2020). While expanding in very recent years, the origin of this political discontent, however, is not new and well precedes the Great Recession, the first big shock exacerbating disparities within EU countries and across EU regions, which has triggered discontent further and created a fertile soil for antisystem movements worldwide, with dramatic electoral and political outcomes in several countries (Gordon, 2018; Fetzer, 2019; Camagni et al., 2020). In short, political and electoral outcomes can be considered the consequence of what has been called the 'revenge of places that don't matter' (Rodríguez-Pose, 2018); citizens express their dissatisfaction with their personal socioeconomic disadvantage conditions and with the backwardness and/or decline of their places through the ballot box, by voting for those parties that place blame on those institutions (primarily the EU) judged as the most responsible for their condition of socioeconomic disadvantage (Lenzi and Perucca, 2021).

Critically, therefore, political and individual discontent (and, conversely, wellbeing) are intertwined, although conceptually distinct and not necessarily overlapping in reality (Dijkstra et al., 2020), and can produce both outcomes and spillover effects for the economy and society as a whole, both in positive ways by sustaining a sense of community and social engagement but also by nurturing antisystem resentment, supporting radical newcomers and, thus, threating political stability (Liberini et al., 2017; Ward, 2020; Rodríguez-Pose, 2018).

A deeper look at the determinants and interrelations, i.e. interactions (Segal, 2022), of the different sources of inequalities and their impacts is, therefore, increasingly relevant to raise appropriate and timely warnings so as to avoid the translation of individual discontent into political discontent as well as to devise adequate interventions aimed at mitigating the adverse effects of contextual and individual-level disadvantage factors (Lenzi and Perucca, 2021; Koeppen et al., 2021).

In the field of urban studies, the so-called 'spatial turn' of the social sciences has affirmed the centrality of space in the structure and functioning of the capitalist world. Starting from the seminal studies of Lefevbre and Foucault, the spatial turn has provided a critical reevaluation of the role of space and spatiality in social thought. The contribution of Harvey to the understanding of the transformation of time and space within a model of production has dramatically opened the way to studying how 'each round of capital circulation is successively territorialized, deterritorialized, and reterritorialized' in a complex interplay between 'fixity and motion' (Brenner, 1998), based on the need to stabilise a certain configuration of space to produce surplus value and the need to annihilate consolidated geographies and adapt to new logics of production. Moving from this perspective, not only has the 'spatial turn' of the social sciences been able to stress established urban theories on their fundamentals (as for example the traditional dualisms as city/countryside), but it has proved to be influential in conceptualising spatial justice as a crucial issue of current time, that is the role of space in producing inequalities and/or wellbeing. As such, as for the seminal work of Marcuse (2010), we are deeply immersed in a trilemma, according to which 'social injustices always have a spatial aspect, (...) social injustices cannot be addressed without also addressing their spatial aspect (..). Spatial remedies are necessary but not sufficient to remedy spatial injustices – let alone social injustice' (Marcuse, 2010).

Elsewhere, urban studies have also discussed the 'stochastic' vs the 'contextual' nature of wellbeing: as argued by Paba (2017), there is a challenging debate between the supporters of the first hypothesis (e.g. Lykken and Tellegen, 1996) and those of the second (e.g. Helliwell and Putnam, 2004). The first hypothesis basically states that the context can only limitedly change our destiny at birth while the second one highlights the role of the context in the perception of wellbeing and happiness. Urban and territorial conditions play a role in this, in terms, for example, of 'proximity relationships, the organisation of public space, citizens' participation in the urban life, the varying articulations of social and relational capitals' (Paba, 2017). Because of that, measuring wellbeing and happiness, as well as designing policies that can contribute to reducing inequalities and addressing wellbeing, are both challenging, yet unaccomplished, ventures.

In this respect, the collection of contributions in this volume can advance our understanding and offer new replies by complementing different spatial levels of analysis, different disciplinary backgrounds and different perspective of the multidimensionality of the concept of inequalities and wellbeing. The next section presents the structure of the volume and how it helps develop such bridges.

## STRUCTURE OF THE BOOK AND MAIN POLICY MESSAGES

The book is structured over three main parts, each dedicated to a specific issue.

The first section elaborates on the definition of inequalities by drawing on alternative but complementary perspectives on the issue. Regardless of the different starting points, the two contributions located in this part converge in highlighting the complexity and multifaceted nature of the concept of spatial inequalities and the innate trade-offs any action willing to narrow territorial gaps implies.

In Chapter 1, Capello and Cerisola propose an interregional (EU-wide) perspective on the notion of inequalities, understood as the EU capacity to narrow differentials in regional productivity growth according to alternative modernization strategies and scenarios. This perspective is relatively new and interestingly complements the traditional one based on the analysis of interregional differentials in terms of GDP per capita level or growth (Diemer et al., 2022; Dijkstra et al., 2020). In fact, the relaunch of productivity through a process of modern reindustrialization has received strong support by and a central position for the EU institutions in recent years, being intended as pivotal to narrow productivity and economic gaps. This centrality in the European policy debate, however, has not been accompanied by rich enough evidence in support of decision making. The work by Capello and Cerisola replies to this need by showing that modern and upgraded industrial policy can have some impact on balanced growth among different areas and conse-quently on spatial disparities. In particular, the authors stress the importance of specific forms of reindustrialization strategies, especially those centred on the modernization of manufacturing sectors. Importantly, the authors highlight how different reindustrialisation strategies can generate opposite effects on within- vs between-countries disparities, with the most advanced strategies, those which payoff the most in terms of regional productivity growth, raising challenges in terms of within-country inequalities.

In Chapter 2, Lang, Görmar, Haunstein and Graffenberger present an over-view of the conceptual debate on peripheralisation and governance in small and medium-sized towns in the German context, by addressing also the relations to issues of local democracy. The authors suggest that this perspective can be beneficial in understanding how smaller towns are tackling increasing sociospatial polarization and which are the political and societal implications, in particular regarding processes of local (but not only local) democracy.

The second section unpacks the relationship between inequalities and wellbeing by looking at selected individual- and place-specific aspects, which may contribute to explaining the spatial heterogeneity in this nexus, i.e. the role of education and the heterogeneity of the labour force, the quality and affordability of housing, and the degree of urbanisation in general.

Chapter 3, by Morrison, debates the so-called urban wellbeing paradox, the recurrent stylised fact that the largest agglomerations of developed, mainly Western, countries are characterised by inferior average subjective wellbeing of residents with respect to other parts of the country, in spite of the production and consumption economies available in the densest settings. Morrison proposes that the unbalances in the capacity to reap the benefits from urban concentration are not only the outcome of the (un)balance between agglomeration advantages and disadvantages (e.g. congestion, pollution, house prices and crime) but primarily due to the heterogeneity of the labour force. The higher productivity and wellbeing returns of education in dense settings depress the relative wellbeing of the less formally educated. Since better-educated individuals represent a minority in urban settings (despite their disproportionate location), the wellbeing of the less-educated majority may be reduced by their residence in poorer neighbourhoods, with longer commutes and lower levels of social engagement. Morrison concludes that this compositional effect gives rise to the urban wellbeing paradox and finds empirical support for this conclusion in an EU-wide analysis.

Hoogerbrugge and Burger's Chapter 4 adds a further dimension in the explanation of the urban wellbeing paradox documented especially for the Western world. In particular, they examine the role played by differences in the quality and affordability of housing between the largest cities and peri-urban and rural areas in the case of The Netherlands. Their main results highlight that housing tenure, housing and neighbourhood quality and housing affordability largely contribute to explain the observed differential in individual wellbeing between more and less urbanised settings.

In Chapter 5, Lenzi and Perucca address once more the urban wellbeing paradox, as in the chapters by Morrison and by Hoogerbrugge and Burger, by looking at the role of the degree of urbanisation. Based on data sourced from Eurobarometer survey on all EU27 countries plus the UK, this work shows that while both, on average, inequalities and discontent tend to be higher in denser settings, diffused urbanisation in regions missing a top-rank city can mitigate the negative effects of inequalities on societal wellbeing.

The last section aims at offering some reflections, if not warnings, on the outcomes of the complex interplay between inequalities and wellbeing, an issue already anticipated in the contributions by Lang et al. as well as Lenzi and Perucca.

In Chapter 6, Bernini, Emili and Ferrante address the complex nexus between poverty and wellbeing and the important role of mediating contextual and territorial characteristics. In fact, the poverty-wellbeing nexus finds, on average, strong empirical support, but its territorial heterogeneity is still poorly understood. In particular, the chapter offers a detailed geographical analysis of the poverty-subjective wellbeing nexus in the Italian case, by exploiting the multidimensionality in the concepts of both wellbeing and poverty. Their results indicate that the response of people's wellbeing to poverty varies across territories due to economic and social heterogeneity. Effects are particularly strong in the Northern regions of Italy, where people's level of satisfaction appears to be strongly affected by the fact of living below the poverty line.

De Leo and Calabrese contribute to the discussion, in Chapter 7, by introducing a specific perspective of experts from the sphere of spatial planning, a field often too biased and based on what Simone defines as 'politics of disappointment', that is the fact of basically pointing at what a city (neighbourhoods, areas) is not and should be and where some functions and practices are and shall be or not; despite aspirations and expectations of what a city shall be, often policies inspired by such a mood have generated less and less fair and more unequal cities. Particularly when experts trained in some countries try to apply their own (mostly Western) schemes. Based on this concern, they describe how an urban transformation project can become an experiment inclusive of different points of views and perspectives on wellbeing and happiness.

Chapter 8, by Koeppen, Ballas, Edzes and Koster, examines the relationship between inequalities, wellbeing and electoral outcomes, understood as a switch in voting patterns towards populist parties on both the right and left sides of the political spectrum. Based on an analysis of how the heterogeneity in levels of subjective wellbeing across European democracies is linked to different likelihoods of voting for radical parties, results confirm the existence of a geography of discontent across EU regions and highlight the importance of both contextual elements, i.e. the long-term socioeconomic decline of specific places, and individual-level elements such as strong regional community, cultural and emotional ties.

In Chapter 9, Behar's text, in the form of an interview, finally engages the readers from a policy-design perspective, by framing the issue of interregional disparities in terms of spatial justice and illustrating the aspirations and contradictions of public policies in addressing sociospatial inequalities. Drawing on the French experience, Behar links the notion of spatial justice to French constitutional principles of freedom, equality and cohesion and explains how equity among people requires equity across places (Estèbe, 2015). This tight link between social and territorial cohesion is strongly anchored to very specific public action models based on specific institutional and administrative arrangements boosting municipality political representativeness within legislative chambers. However, the legitimacy of the social and territorial cohesion pair has diluted over time, in concomitance with the emergence of the new millennium macrotrends, opening up the risks of political uncertainty and reduced consensus for public and territorial policies. Finally, the interview concludes by discussing the limits and fragilities of current political debates on policy-design.

## REFERENCES

Acemoglu, D. and Restrepo, P. (2019) Robots and Jobs: evidence from US Labor Markets. *Journal of Political Economy*, 128(6), 2188–244.
Alesina, A., Di Tella, R., and MacCulloch, R. (2004) Inequality and happiness: are Europeans and Americans different? *Journal of Public Economics*, 88(9–10), 2009–42.
Alvaredo, F., Chancel, L., Piketty, T., Saez, E., Zucman, G., et al. (2018) *World Inequality Report 2018*. World Inequality Lab.
Autor, D. H. and Dorn, D. (2013) The growth of low-skill service jobs and the polarization of the US labor market. *American Economic Review*, 103(5), 1153–597.
Ballas, D., and Thanis, I. (2022) Exploring the geography of subjective happiness in Europe during the years of the economic crisis: a multilevel modelling approach. *Social Indicators Research*, 164(1), 1–33.
Behar, D. (2017) Fracture territoriale. Le frisson qui rassure. In: Benbassa, E. and Assia, J.-C. (eds.) *Nouvelle relegations territoriales*. Paris: CNRS.
Brenner, N. (1998). Between Fixity and Motion: Accumulation, Territorial Organization and the Historical Geography of Spatial Scales. *Environment and Planning D: Society and Space*, 16(4), 459–81.
Brenner, N. and Schmid, C. (2015) Towards a new epistemology of the urban? *City*, 19(2–3), 15182.
Brynjolfsson, E. and McAfee, A. (2014) *The Second Machine Age: Work, Progress and Prosperity in a Time of Brilliant Technologies*. London: W.W. Norton & Company.
Camagni, R., Capello, R., Cerisola, S., and Fratesi, U. (2020) Fighting gravity: institutional changes and regional disparities in the EU. *Economic Geography*, 96(2), 108–36.
Chancel, L., Piketty, T., Saez, E., Zucman, G. et al. (2022) *World Inequality Report 2022*. World Inequality Lab.
Diemer, A., Iammarino, S., Perkins, R., and Gros, A. (2022) Technology resources and geography in a paradigm shift: the case of critical and conflict materials in ICTs. *Regional Studies*. doi: 10.1080/00343404.2022.2077326.
Diener, E., Lucas, R. E., and Oishi, S. (2002) Subjective well-being: the science of happiness and life satisfaction. In: Snyder, C. R. and Lopez, S. J. (eds.) *The Handbook of Positive Psychology*, 63–73. Oxford: Oxford University Press.
Dijkstra, L., Poelman, H., and Rodríguez-Pose, A. (2020) The geography of EU discontent. *Regional Studies*, 54(6), 737–53.

Easterlin, R. A. (2001) Income and happiness: towards a unified theory. *Economic Journal*, 111(473), 465–84.

Economist (2016), Place-based economic policies as a response to populism. Available at https://www.economist.com/finance-and-economics/2016/12/15/place-based-economic-policies-as-a-response-to-populism?fsrc=scn%2Ftw%2Fte%2Fbl%2Fed%2F.

Estèbe, P. (2015) *L'égalité des territoires, une passion française*. Paris: Presses Universitaires de France.

EU Committee of the Regions (2022) *EU Annual Report on the State of the Regions and Cities*. https://cor.europa.eu/en/our-work/Pages/State-of-Regions-and-Cities -2022.aspx.

Ferreira, I. A., Gisselquist, R. M., and Tarp, F. (2022) On the impact of inequality on growth, human development, and governance. *International Studies Review*, https://doi.org/10.1093/isr/viab058.

Ferrer-i-Carbonell, A. and Ramos, X. (2014) Inequality and happiness. *Journal of Economic Surveys*, 28, 1016–27.

Fetzer, T. (2019) Did austerity cause Brexit? *American Economic Review*, 109(11), 3849–86.

Gordon, I. R. (2018) In what sense left behind by globalisation? Looking for a less reductionist geography of the populist surge in Europe. *Cambridge Journal of Regions, Economy and Society*, 11(1), 95–113.

Helliwell, J. F. and Putnam, R. D. (2004) The social context of well-being. *Philosophical Transactions of The Royal Society B*, 359, 1435–46.

Hirschman, A. O. and Rothschild, M. (1973) The changing tolerance for income inequality in the course of economic development: with a mathematical appendix. *Quarterly Journal of Economics*, 87(4), 544–66.

Hoogerbrugge, M. and Burger, M. (2021) Selective migration and urban-rural differences in subjective well-being: evidence from the United Kingdom. *Urban Studies*. doi: 10.1177/00420980211023052.

Hoogerbrugge, M. M., Burger, M. J., and Van Oort, F. G. (2022) Spatial structure and subjective well-being in North-West Europe. *Regional Studies*, 56(1), 75–86.

Hopkins, E. (2008) Inequality, happiness and relative concerns: what actually is their relationship? *Journal of Economic Inequality*, 6, 351–72.

Katic, I., and Ingram, P. (2018) Income inequality and subjective well-being: toward an understanding of the relationship and its mechanisms. *Business & Society*, 57(6), 1010–44.

Kemeny, T., Petralia, S., and Storper, M. (2022) Disruptive innovation and spatial inequality. *Regional Studies*. doi: 10.1080/00343404.2022.2076824.

Kemeny, T. and Storper, M. (2020) The fall and rise of interregional inequality: explaining shifts from convergence to divergence. *Scienze Regionali*, 19(2), 175–98.

Koeppen, L., Ballas, D., Edzes, A., and Koster, S. (2021) Places that don't matter or people that don't matter? A multilevel modelling approach to the analysis of the geographies of discontent. *Regional Science Policy & Practice*, 13(2), 221–45.

Lang, T., Henn, S., Ehrlich, K., and Sgibnev, W. (2015) *Understanding Geographies of Polarization and Peripheralization: Perspectives from Central and Eastern Europe and Beyond*. Verlag: Palgrave Macmillan/Springer.

Lenzi, C. and Perucca, G. (2021) People or places that don't matter? Individual and contextual determinants of the geography of discontent. *Economic Geography*, 97(5), 415–45.

Liberini, F., Redoano, M., and Proto, E. (2017) Happy voters. *Journal of Public Economics*, 146(February), 41–57.

Loorbach, D., Frantzeskaki, N., and Avelino, F. (2017) Sustainability transitions research: transforming science and practice for societal change. *Annual Review of Environment and Resources*, 42(1), 599–626.

Los, B., McCann, P., Springford, J., and Thissen, M. (2017) The mismatch between local voting and the local economic consequences of Brexit. *Regional Studies*, 51(5), 786–99.

Luttmer, E. F. P. (2005) Neighbors as negatives: relative earnings and well-being. *Quarterly Journal of Economics*, 120(3), 963–1002.

Lykken, D. and Tellegen, A. (1996) Happiness is a stochastic phenomenon. *Psychological Science*, 7(4), 186–9.

Marcuse, P. (2010) Spatial justice: derivative but causal of social justice. In: Bret, B., Gervais-Lambony, P., Hancock, C., et al. *Justice et Injustices Spatiales*. Nanterre: Presses universitaires de Paris.

McAfee, A. and Brynjolfsson, E. (2017) *Machine, Platform, Crowd. Harnessing Our Digital Future*. London: W.W. Norton & Company.

McCall, L. (2017) Book review symposium: Ruth Milkman on gender labor and inequality by Lesli McCall. *Work, Employment and Society*, 31(5), 873–5.

McCann, P. (2020) Perceptions of regional inequality and the geography of discontent: insights from the UK. *Regional Studies*, 54(2), 256–67.

Mehretu, A., Pigozzi, B. W., and Sommers, L. M. (2000) Concepts in social and spatial marginality. *Geografiska Annaler. Series B, Human Geography*, 82(2), 89–101. http://www.jstor.org/stable/491067.

Moretti, E. (2012) *The New Geography of Jobs*. Boston, MA: Houghton Mifflin Harcourt.

Morrison, P. S. (2021). Wellbeing and the region. In: Fischer, M. M., and Nijkamp, P. (eds), Handbook of Regional Science. Berlin and Heidelberg: Springer, pp. 779–98.

Ngamaba, K. H., Panagioti, M., and Armitage, C. J. (2018) Income inequality and subjective well-being: a systematic review and meta-analysis. *Quality of Life Research*, 27(3), 577–96.

Norton, M. I. and Ariely, D. (2011) Building a better America – one wealth quintile at a time. *Perspectives on Psychological Science*, 6(1), 9–12.

OECD (2014) *Focus on Inequality and Growth – December 2014*. This document as well as figures and underlying data can be downloaded via www.oecd.org/social/inequality-and-poverty.htm.

OECD (2022) *OECD Regions and Cities at a Glance 2022*. Paris: OECD Publishing. https://www.oecd-ilibrary.org/urban-rural-and-regional-development/oecd-regions-and-cities-at-a-glance-2022_14108660-en (accessed June 2023).

Overman, H. G. and Xu, X. (2022) Spatial disparities across labour markets. *IFS Deaton Review of Inequalities*, pp. 1–66, available online at https://ifs.org.uk/inequality/spatial-disparities-across-labour-markets/.

Paba, G. (2017) Sulla felicità pubblica (e anche un po' privata), sul benessere collettivo e sulla qualità della vita nella città e nel territorio. *Società dei Territorialisti*. http://www.societadeiterritorialisti.it/wp-content/uploads/2011/10/111125_gpaba.felicit%20pubblica.pdf.

Petrakos, G. and Sotiriou, A. (2021) Grexit and Brexit: incidents, accidents and wake-up calls on the bumpy road of European (dis)integration. *European Urban and Regional Studies*, 28(1), 20–5.

Piketty, T. (2014) *Capital in the Twenty-First Century*. Cambridge, MA: The Belknap Press of Harvard University Press.

Piketty, T. and Saez, E. (2003) Income inequality in the United States, 1913–1998. *Quarterly Journal of Economics*, 118(1), 1–41.

Rodríguez-Pose, A. (2018) The revenge of the places that don't matter (and what to do about it). *Cambridge Journal of Regions, Economy and Society*, 11(1), 189–209.

Schneider, S. M. (2016) Income inequality and subjective wellbeing: trends, challenges, and research directions. *Journal of Happiness Studies*, 17, 1719–39.

Segal, P. (2022) Inequality interactions: the dynamics of multidimensional inequalities. *Development and Change*, 53(5), 941–61.

Ugur, Z. B. (2021) How does inequality hamper subjective well-being? The role of fairness. *Social Indicator Research*, 158, 377–407.

Veenhoven, R. (1996) The study of life-satisfaction. In: Saris, W. E., Veenhoven, R., Scherpenzeel, A. C., and Bunting, B. (eds.) *A Comparative Study of Satisfaction with Life in Europe*, 11–48. Budapest, Hungary: Eötvös University Press.

Wacquant, L. (2008) *Urban Outcasts: A Comparative Sociology of Advanced Marginality*. Cambridge: Polity Press.

Ward, G. (2020) Happiness and voting: evidence from four decades of elections in Europe. *American Journal of Political Science*, 64(3), 504–18. doi: 10.1111/ajps.12492.

# 1. Spatial inequalities in an era of modern reindustrialization

## Roberta Capello and Silvia Cerisola

## 1.1 INTRODUCTION

In the last thirty years, most advanced countries have experienced an overall process of deindustrialization. Although in part physiological (e.g. Rowthorn and Ramaswamy, 1997; Nickell et al., 2008; Rodrik, 2016; Škuflić and Družić, 2016; Dosi et al., 2021), according to a stage of development theoretical framework that implies the progressive shift of economies from agriculture to manufacturing and then to services (Fisher, 1933; Hoover, 1948; Kuznet and Murphy, 1966; Landesmann and Pichelmann, 1999), such evolution has been recently related with productivity stagnation and with the well-known productivity paradox and productivity gap between the EU and the USA (see, among others, Solow, 1987; Brynjolfsson, 1993; Acemoglu et al., 2014).

This association came out in particular after the 2008–09 economic crisis and in fact the European institutions became more vocal in calling for a modern reindustrialization process (European Commission, 2012, 2014, 2019), also considering that manufacturing is in fact intrinsically characterized by higher productivity growth compared to other sectors (see, for instance, Tregenna, 2009; European Commission, 2010a, 2010b; Dosi et al., 2021). The clear political interest towards reindustrialization, however, has not yet been followed by an equally rich corpus of academic analyses, and the related literature seems in fact to be quite scant (among the few exceptions we are aware of, the reader may refer to Christopherson et al., 2014).

In particular, the potential impact of a reindustrialization process on balanced growth among different areas and, consequently, on spatial disparities have not yet been explored. Therefore, the present chapter aims at addressing these topics at the regional level and at contributing to fill the existing gaps in the literature, first through the study of the relationship between reindustrialization and productivity growth – with a special focus on the role of modernization in the reindustrializing sectors – and subsequently, through the investigation of the relationship between such dynamics and spatial inequalities.

In more detail, our contribution refers to a conceptual and operational definition at a subnational level (NUTS2) of both reindustrialization and modernization in the reindustrializing manufacturing sectors, developed in a previous work of ours (Capello and Cerisola, 2022). In addition, the role played by modern reindustrialization at the regional level on spatial inequalities is originally investigated through a simulation procedure, making it possible to assess the potential impact on regional disparities in terms of wealth between and within European countries. This is, in fact, the specific perspective here considered on the overall reasoning about spatial inequalities. Thus, the present study allows us to draw some conclusions and make policy suggestions for an equitable and modern regional reindustrialization, which is, in effect, the final objective and the main value added of the contribution.

Accordingly, the chapter is organized as follows. Starting from the EU position on the reindustrialization process (Section 2), the chapter defines the concepts of reindustrialization and modernization in reindustrializing sectors and explains how they are empirically operationalized (Section 3). The econometric estimation strategy and the related results are presented in Section 4, followed by an illustration of the simulation procedure and the associated outcomes (Section 5). Finally, concluding remarks with summarized policy suggestions are presented in Section 6.

## 1.2    REINDUSTRIALIZATION PROCESSES AND THE EU POSITION

As anticipated in the introduction, after the 2008–09 economic crisis, the European Commission began to call explicitly for 'A stronger European industry for growth and economic recovery' (European Commission, 2012), to strengthen industrial competitiveness and reverse the declining role of manufacturing. In this sense, some priority action lines were identified, including, significantly, advanced manufacturing technologies. The rationale of such approach is in the belief that a strong industrial base is indeed essential for a wealthy and economically successful Europe. Therefore, the Commission urged new investments to bring innovation and new technologies back to European factories.

These overall reflections were also associated to the awareness that EU companies cannot compete on low price and low-quality products (European Commission, 2014); although such recognition was accompanied by the assumption that Europe's comparative advantage lies in high value-added goods and services.

In fact, the general idea that only a substantial increase in R&D and product innovation may, in the long run, drive overall productivity and growth characterizes the current debate about the perspectives of modern societies.

However, this conception of economic growth as mostly associated with research-intensive industries may result in a reductive and simplified picture of the complex nature of knowledge creation and its relation to inventive and innovative capability (see also Storper and Walker, 1989; Damanpour et al., 2009) and has been indeed labelled 'high-tech myopia' (Heidenreich, 2009). Our impression is indeed that disregarding different situations would lead to neglecting potentially important sources of efficiency and productivity in manufacturing industry.

   In reality, it is important to distinguish between product and process, organizational and marketing innovations. Even sectors characterized by no or low R&D expenditures can, in fact, be considered innovative in their own way if we take into account the adoption of new technologies in traditional activities, incremental changes, imitation and the combination of existing knowledge in new ways (Arundel et al., 2008; Hirsch-Kreinsen, 2008; Mendonça, 2009; Hansen and Winther, 2014). Modernization and the upgrading of production processes, as well as incremental innovations originating from learning by doing, can, in fact, reveal their importance in determining productivity gains (Ghosal and Nair-Reichert, 2009) and, in this sense, should be of interest in relation to policy.

   As per our knowledge, reflections on the importance of reindustrialization have been strongly put forward at the institutional level, but they have not yet been followed and clearly operationalized within the academic literature. The related role of modernization has also been scarcely investigated up to now and these lacks are even more evident at the regional level, which is, however, an important dimension, given the critical territorial differences and features we observe in reality. Within the present work, therefore, we try to fill these gaps in the literature. As a first step in this direction, a conceptually well-reasoned operational definition for reindustrialization and modernization at the subnational level is provided in the next section.

## 1.3   REINDUSTRIALIZATION AND MODERNIZATION: OPERATIONALIZING THE CONCEPTS

### 1.3.1   Operational Definition of Reindustrialization

To explore the role of a modern reindustrialization process at the regional level in affecting local productivity growth and, subsequently, spatial disparities, the first step to be made is, of course, defining reindustrialization itself in a way that allows its empirical operationalization. This is no easy task, since, as mentioned before, reindustrialization has not yet been studied in depth in the academic literature and, therefore, no specific and detailed reference is available in this respect.

Much more is available on deindustrialization; thus, one could think of exploiting the same measures to interpret the opposite phenomenon. However, most works refer to the trend (decrease) in manufacturing employment in absolute or relative terms. Such choice, nevertheless, may be considered disputable, since it could be associated with elements that, in fact, have nothing to do with a real reduction of the industrial value added (physiological processes, innovation and technological progress or wide restructuring all affect employment dynamics but do not capture a reduction in the industrial value added). Similarly, in the case of reindustrialization, a positive trend in employment in manufacturing could simply be the result of public assistance and sheltered development in particular sectors and this situation could easily coexist with a decrease in value added.

This limit may be overcome by using the change in manufacturing value added, again either in absolute or relative terms. However, when used in constant prices, this measure tends to catch changes in quantity of output rather than changes in quality, which are mostly left aside (see Aghion et al., 2019; Camagni et al., 2021). Furthermore, in this case, it would be highly debatable to exclude from the measurement of a 'reindustrialization' process regions that are able to sell their products at increasing prices, acquiring market share.

Taking all these considerations into account, the increase in the share of manufacturing value added over total at current prices is the measure we put forward. The share, rather than the absolute value, guarantees that the price effects are controlled for, while the value added at current prices contains the quality effect.[1]

According to these reflections, reindustrialization occurs (a NUTS2 region reindustrializes) when the change in the share of current manufacturing value added grows over time. In practical terms, here we compare the trend between a pre-crisis period (2000–07) and a post-crisis period (2013–17).[2] Data on manufacturing value added at NUTS2 subnational level are available from Eurostat.

However, the identification of an operational definition of regional reindustrialization is not enough to pursue the aim of the present work. In fact, a clear

---

[1]   This approach was first introduced in Capello and Cerisola, 2022.

[2]   To make the trends in the two periods perfectly comparable, the compound annual growth rate (CAGR) is used. This is computed below, where $t_0$ is the initial year and $t_n$ the final one:

$$\left[ \left( \frac{VA_{t_n}}{VA_{t_0}} \right)^{\frac{1}{t_n - t_0}} - 1 \right]$$

perspective on modernization in the manufacturing sector – and its translation in empirical terms – is also needed. This is provided in the next subsection.

### 1.3.2    Operational Definition of Modernization in Reindustrializing Sectors

As explained in Section 2, modernization does not take place exclusively in high-tech sectors. Therefore, R&D or new patent measures in high-tech sectors risk neglecting (and maybe excluding completely from the picture) some potentially very competitive medium- and low-tech manufacturing sectors, which could potentially show different – but possibly extremely effective – innovative strategies.

Following this reasoning, it is particularly important to devote special attention to the operational definition of 'modernization' in the reindustrializing sectors we here put forward.[3] The measure, in fact, needs to be representative of a type of innovation that is more wide-ranging with respect to the science-based perspective usually considered, and which involves a kind of progress that can be more suitable even for non-high-tech sectors.

To pursue our objective satisfactorily and to obtain a higher degree of understanding of the mechanisms associated with a modernization process, our database needed to be complemented by the addition of more sectorally disaggregated data on regional value added, in time series. In more detail, the information was mainly collected through interaction with the individual national statistical offices (NSOs) and estimated when necessary.

The result was a relevant and original sectoral–regional database, which allowed us to measure 'modernization' in the reindustrializing sectors. Reindustrializing sectors have been identified as those sectors showing a faster trend in their value-added (VA) shares over the period 2013–17 with respect to 2000–07, as explained above.

Instead, the 'modernization' of reindustrializing sectors was quantified by their degree of automation. Among reindustrialization sectors, we extracted those showing a higher adoption of robots per employee with respect to the adoption within the same sector in the country.[4] The comparison with the national sectoral adoption level allows us to control for national sectoral effects, which are rather strong (see also Storper and Walker, 1989; Graetz and Michaels, 2018).

---

[3]    Such operational definition was first proposed in Capello and Cerisola, 2023.

[4]    On the use of automation to maintain (or bring back) jobs in the home country the reader may refer to Arlbjørn et al., 2013; Arlbjørn and Mikkelsen, 2014.

As for the robots, the data source is the International Federation of Robotics. However, the information provided is in terms of count data (number of robots introduced every year) by country and sector. Therefore, the stock of robots was calculated through the permanent inventory method (PIM), with 2006 as the base year[5] and, due to the volatility of count data, a three-year average was considered. In addition, technological differences have been shown to be there between subnational regions and, in fact, these data are typically regionalized based on the local distribution of employment in the related sectors. However, we embrace a more sophisticated approach, which allows us to regionalize data through the use of three weights for which information is available at NUTS2 level, as in Capello and Lenzi (2021, 2022). In particular, the chosen weights are the regional share of population with broadband access (source: Eurostat), the regional share of blue-collar workers (plant and machine operators, source: EU Labour Force Survey (EU-LFS)), and the regional share of employment by sector (source: Structural Business Statistics (SBS)).

Making use of the operational definitions of reindustrializing regions and modernization in reindustrializing sectors explained above, the relationship between (modern) reindustrialization and productivity growth is estimated. The econometric model and the related results are presented in the next section.

## 1.4    REINDUSTRIALIZATION, MODERNIZATION AND PRODUCTIVITY GROWTH: ESTIMATION STRATEGY

### 1.4.1    The Model

The aim of this section is to explore empirically the association between reindustrialization and modernization at the regional level and aggregate productivity growth. To do this, the following OLS econometric specifications are estimated on European NUTS2 regions:[6]

$$
\begin{aligned}
prod\,growth_{r,13-19} &= \alpha + \beta_1 reind_r + \beta_2 modern_r + \beta_3 hc_{r,2013} + \\
&\quad \beta_4\,popdensity_{r,2013} + \beta_5\,prod_{r,2013} + \beta_6\,share\,agr_{r,2013} \\
&\quad + \beta_7\,share\,serv_{r,2013} + \beta_8 east_r + \varepsilon_r
\end{aligned}
\tag{1.1}
$$

$$
\begin{aligned}
prod\,growth_{r,13-19} &= \alpha + \beta_1\,reind_r + \beta_2\,modern_r + \\
&\quad \beta_3\,reind_r x\,modern_r + \beta_4 hc_{r,2013} + \beta_5\,popdensity_{r,2013} \\
&\quad + \beta_6\,prod_{r,2013} + \beta_7\,share\,agr_{r,2013} + \beta_8\,share\,serv_{r,2013} + \beta_9 east_r + \varepsilon_r
\end{aligned}
\tag{1.2}
$$

---

[5]    2006 was chosen as the first year for which the information was available for all countries. This is also consistent with Caselli et al., 2021.

[6]    Data for Germany are at NUTS1 level, as well as the city of London (UKI).

where prod growth is labor productivity (measured as GDP PPS per worker) growth between 2013 and 2019 in region (NUTS2) *r*, computed as compound average growth rate. Since the final aim of the present work is to assess the impact of different determinants of productivity growth on regional disparities, traditionally measured in PPS even by the EU when designing the cohesion policy, data chosen were GDP in PPS. The explanatory variables are entered for year 2013 (beginning of the period).

As for the main variables of interest, *reind* is a dummy variable equal to one if the region reindustrialized, according to the definition provided above; *modern* is instead our measure of modernization, i.e. the share of VA in reindustrializing sectors in which the region has more robots per employee with respect to its country average in those sectors (see previous section).

Additional traditional controls, expected to affect productivity dynamics, are included, namely: human capital (*hc*), to consider its well-known function in determining and enhancing economic growth; population density (*popdensity*), to take into account the expected positive role played by agglomeration economies; the level of productivity at the beginning of the period (*prod*), to highlight potential convergence; the share of employment in agriculture and in services (*share agr* and *share serv*, respectively), to control for sectoral composition; and a dummy variable (*east*), equal to one if the region belongs to a Central Eastern European Country, since we do anticipate likely different growth patterns and performance in those areas. Finally, the errors are clustered by country.

Equation (1.2) further explores the role of modernization in reindustrializing regions, through the inclusion of an interaction term between the two variables of interest.

The data, their sources and timespans are thoroughly described in Table 1.1, while the results obtained by running the regressions presented above are displayed and discussed in the next subsection.

### 1.4.2    Reindustrialization, Modernization and Productivity Growth: the Estimation Results

The estimation of the models presented in the previous subsection led to the outcomes displayed in Table 1.2. In the first regression (column 1), the non-significant coefficients of our variables of interest, when related to aggregate productivity growth, are, in fact, no big surprise. The effects are expected to be strong within sectors, while they lose significance at aggregate level, since positive repercussions from the reindustrializing manufacturing sectors to the whole economy would need to be particularly efficient and a longer time span with respect to the sectoral effects is necessary for those transmission mechanisms to occur (Capello and Cerisola, 2022).

*Table 1.1*     *Variables' description*

| Variable name | Description | Data source | Time |
|---|---|---|---|
| Productivity growth | Labor productivity (GDP PPS/ employment) compound growth rate (authors' computation) | Cambridge Econometrics* | 2013–19 |
| Reindustrialization | Dummy var = 1 if the region reindustrializes (authors' computation – see text for details) | Eurostat | 2000–17 |
| Modernization | Share of VA in reindustrializing sectors in which the region has more robots per employee with respect to its country average in those sectors (authors' computation) | International Federation of Robotics and Eurostat (for the regionalization of data) | Avg 2012–14 |
| Human capital | Human capital measured as the share of tertiary educated over total employment | Eurostat | 2013 |
| Population density | Population per square km | Eurostat | 2013 |
| Productivity | Labor productivity (GDP PPS/ employment) | Cambridge Econometrics | 2013 |
| Share of agriculture employment | Share of employment in agriculture over total | Cambridge Econometrics | 2013 |
| Share of service employment | Share of employment in services over total | Cambridge Econometrics | 2013 |

*Note*:     * Cambridge Econometrics was preferred as a data source with respect to Eurostat, since it made it possible to cover all the countries (including UK) at NUTS2 level up to 2019.

As for modernization, in particular, many contributions in the existing literature have already pointed out how such mechanisms require a long time to be effective, longer than our period of analysis. Moreover, it should be accompanied by related managerial and organizational changes (e.g. Brynjolfsson and Hitt, 2000; Hervas-Oliver et al., 2015; Chaminade et al., 2018; Cirillo et al., 2021).

As for the second specification, instead, the results are interesting since the positive and statistically significant coefficient associated with the interaction term between reindustrializing regions and modernization shows how modernization is in fact capitalized through the overall reindustrializing environment characterizing the region. This means that reindustrializing regions are able to grasp the advantages from their reindustrialization only when this is carried out with modernizing strategies. These positive effects do not remain confined within the sector where they take place. Regional (aggregate) productivity growth takes in fact advantage from the presence of sectors reindustrializing in a modern way.

Finally, looking at the control variables, as expected human capital and agglomeration economies are positively and significantly associated to aggregate productivity growth, while also the specialization in service activities plays a role, being negatively correlated to productivity growth. This result may capture the lower productivity growth associated to higher stages of development economies.

Drawing on the regression results presented above, a simulation on regional disparities is performed to highlight the implications of a modern reindustrialization on spatial inequalities. The simulation strategy – its rationale and methodology, together with its results – is explained in the next section.

## 1.5    MODERN REINDUSTRIALIZATION AND REGIONAL DISPARITIES: SIMULATION STRATEGY

### 1.5.1    The Rationale

This section is devoted to the presentation of the rationale behind our simulation strategy, aimed at highlighting the role of a modern reindustrialization in regional disparities. In order to compute the impact of reindustrialization, and of modern reindustrialization in particular, on spatial inequalities, in fact, we perform a simulation exercise in which the coefficients obtained from the second regression presented in the previous section are exploited. The simulation works by assuming:

- firstly, that reindustrialization becomes a common strategy in all regions in Europe, i.e. all the NUTS2 regions reindustrialize; and
- secondly, that modern reindustrialization becomes a common strategy in all regions in Europe, i.e. all the NUTS2 regions reindustrialize in a modern way.

All this is operationalized by re-calculating productivity growth under the two assumptions above, i.e. by

- assuming all regions to be reindustrializing regions, for the first simulation, and
- assuming all regions to be reindustrializing regions with an average level of modernization for the second one.[7]

---

[7]    Robustness checks have been performed by setting the modernisation variable at its maximum level. Results do not change.

*Table 1.2     Relationship between reindustrialization, modernization, and productivity growth: estimation results*

|  | (1) | (2) |
|---|---|---|
| Reindustrialization | -0.004 | -0.010** |
|  | -0.003 | (0.003) |
| Modernization | 0.003 | -0.005 |
|  | (0.003) | (0.004) |
| Reindustrialization *modernization |  | 0.010* |
|  |  | (0.006) |
| Human capital | 0.025* | 0.025* |
|  | (0.014) | (0.014) |
| Population density | 0.000* | 0.000* |
|  | (0.000) | (0.000) |
| Productivity levels | -0.000 | -0.000 |
|  | (0.000) | (0.000) |
| Share of agriculture employment | -0.000 | 0.003 |
|  | (0.034) | (0.035) |
| Share of service employment | -0.054** | -0.049** |
|  | (0.021) | (0.019) |
| Eastern countries | 0.099 | 0.010 |
|  | (0.006) | (0.006) |
| Constant | 0.050*** | 0.051*** |
|  | (0.012) | (0.012) |
| No. Of obs. | 237 | 237 |
| Prob > F | 0.000 | 0.000 |
| R-squared | 0.399 | 0.409 |

*Note*:     Dependent variable: aggregate labor productivity growth (2013–2019). Independent variables are measured at the beginning of the period. Robust standard errors clustered by country are in parentheses. Significance levels as follows: *** 1%, ** 5%, * 10%.

These assumptions have been applied to obtain a new (simulated) productivity growth 2013–19. Starting from the actual productivity level in 2013, the simulated growth is used to retrieve a simulated productivity level in 2019 and the corresponding simulated GDP level. This was considered in per capita terms to calculate an indicator of spatial imbalances, consistently with the traditional measurement of regional disparities performed by the European Commission itself in planning the cohesion policy.

Finally, the simulated index of regional disparities is compared with the real one, used as a benchmark.

The indicator of spatial inequalities applied here is the Theil index. The reason for such a choice is that it has the advantage of being decomposable in two or more layers (Akita, 2003; Butkus et al., 2018). This peculiarity is important because it allows to disentangle between- and within-country disparities. The Theil index has been computed on GDP PPS per head according to the following formula, which also shows the decomposition in two components, adding up to the total:

where Y stands for GDP PPS, P for population and the indexes EU, C and r stand, respectively, for Europe (total sample), Country, and region. As can be clearly seen in Equation (3), the total Theil index (the first element) can be decomposed into a 'between-country' index and a 'within-country' index.

The results derived according to the methodology presented above are reported and discussed in the next sub-section.

### 1.5.2    Reindustrialization, Modernization and Regional Disparities: Simulation Results

The outcomes of the simulations explained above are presented in Figure 1.1, where panel (a) shows the effects of the first exercise, assuming that all regions do reindustrialize, and panel (b) of the second one, assuming that all regions reindustrialize in a modern way. The results are displayed on the total Theil index and on its two components, i.e. between and within countries. In more detail, in order to favor an immediate reading of the results, in the graphic

$$T = \sum_r \frac{Y_r}{Y_{EU}} \ln \frac{Y_r/P_r}{Y_{EU}/P_{EU}} = \underbrace{\sum_c \frac{Y_c}{Y_{EU}} \ln \frac{Y_c/P_c}{Y_{EU}/P_{EU}}}_{\text{Between-country}} + \underbrace{\sum_c \frac{Y_c}{Y_{EU}} \sum_{r \in c} \frac{Y_r}{Y_C} \ln \frac{Y_r/P_r}{Y_C/P_C}}_{\text{Within-country}}$$

Total Theil Index

(1.3)

representation the actual values are standardized to 1, while the bars display the levels recomputed according to the simulation procedures.[8]

When we simulate a situation where all the regions reindustrialize (panel (a) in Figure 1), the total Theil index decreases, although this overall positive outcome is entirely due to the reduction of between-countries disparities.

These results tell us that a reindustrialization strategy favors a country as a whole when it moves from a non-reindustrialization to a reindustrialization

---

[8]    Due to the normalization of results, in the graphic representation the two components of the Theil index do not sum up to the total.

situation. Instead, within countries, disparities remain stable, showing that reindustrialization is a strategy applied at the national level, with very limited within-country heterogeneity.

When, instead, we consider a situation where all the regions reindustrialize through a modernization strategy (panel (b) in Figure 1.1), the decrease in total regional disparities is only moderate and, again, exclusively due to the contraction of between-countries spatial inequalities. We interpret this result as a signal of increased advantage for weaker countries that at present do not reindustrialize.

Instead, within countries, disparities increase, in a manner consistent with some reasoning already widely present in the existing literature.[9] This result is probably due to the fact that, within each country, a modern reindustrialization strategy favors the strongest regions.

All these results underline that the structural changes in the direction of a modern reindustrialization imply critical challenges when a cohesion perspective is taken. In particular, understanding whether modernization through technological change can be detrimental or beneficial for productivity is not straightforward and unequivocal, and fundamentally depends on the specific sectors and occupations considered and on the particular compensation mechanisms at play (see, among others, Acemoglu et al., 2014; Vivarelli, 2014; Autor, 2015; Calvino and Virgillito, 2018).

Therefore, these processes should be guided by relevant associated policies in order to avoid, as much as possible, potential negative consequences in terms of widening the gap between stronger and weaker areas in the same country. A modern reindustrialization, in fact, although effective for general growth, clearly risks developing in the more advanced regions, typically better endowed with skilled human capital and economic and social infrastructures suitable for promoting and supporting this type of activity and innovation. Of course, positive spillovers from core to less developed areas can be envisaged and – in fact – even expected, but they do take time to occur, and by the time they happen, more advanced areas could already be experiencing the next modernization step, moving further onward and basically leaving less dynamic regions behind. This type of mechanism would clearly push towards greater disparities and, therefore, the whole process should be carefully planned and monitored.

---

[9]    See e.g. Brynjolfsson and McAfee, 2014; Autor, 2015; Graetz and Michaels, 2018; Dosi and Virgillito, 2019; Montobbio et al., 2022.

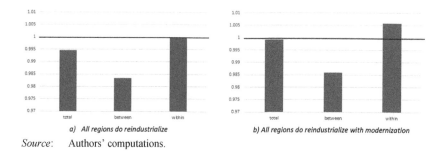

*a) All regions do reindustrialize*                  *b) All regions do reindustrialize with modernization*

*Source*:     Authors' computations.

*Figure 1.1      Modern reindustrialization and spatial disparities:*
*              simulations results (actual values standardized to 1)*

## 1.6    CONCLUSIONS

The present chapter aimed at exploring the potential effects of a modern reindustrialization process on regional disparities. Starting by investigating the relationship between (modern) reindustrialization and productivity growth, a simulation exercise was performed, and interesting reflections emerged on the possible impact of this kind of mechanism on spatial inequalities.

A modern reindustrialization seems, in fact, to be a useful tool for seeking regional growth and appears indeed as a fruitful and promising path to be pursued, although we must be aware that, in order to get the most out of modernization processes, modernization should be accompanied by related managerial and organizational innovation.

Even if potentially encouraging, the positive dynamic described above risks concealing some more complex side effects in terms of cohesion. According to the results here presented, in fact, overall regional disparities would not be importantly affected, but this would hide a situation where between-countries disparities could decrease quite substantially, but within-country inequality would rise. This brings along important considerations on the most appropriate ways and policy approaches to guide these processes, in order to avoid as much as possible a situation where a supportive economic trend is accompanied by increasing regional disparities and widening of the gap between stronger and weaker areas. Specific redistributive/employment/industrial policies, as well as focused education and training programs, should, therefore, be carefully planned.

According to these considerations, there seems to be room for further exploration and important future research. First, a focus on the effectiveness of modernization depending also on accompanying managing and organizational innovation could be extremely useful. These aspects definitely go beyond the scope of the present work, but the intuitions in this direction could certainly be refined and taken into account in further developments of the topic. In particular, the use of firm-level data could be a suitable way to investigate this specific subject.

Second, the potential trade-off between modernization and employment has rightly gained more and more attention in the existing research, and the possible and actual polarization of the labor market, in which wage gains appear to go disproportionately to those at the top or at the bottom of the income and skill distribution, has been studied. In many cases, machines seem to both substitute for and complement human labor and, even if automation does not reduce the quantity of jobs, it may greatly affect the quality of jobs available. On the whole, the situation is certainly extremely complex and understanding of all these aspects needs to be deepened in the immediate future.

Finally, the overall picture has unquestionably been further complicated and blurred by the Covid-19 pandemic, which has had a significant effect on all realms of social and economic activity globally since the beginning of 2020, and, more recently, by the war in Ukraine, which has dramatically changed the socioeconomic relationships between countries all over the world. The interplay of these worldwide challenges with reindustrialization and modernization processes, as well as, very clearly, their impact on inequality, are still to be investigated, but will certainly represent dramatically important aspects that future research will have to focus on.

## REFERENCES

Acemoglu D., D. Autor, D. Dorn, G. Hanson and B. Price (2014) Return of the Solow Paradox? IT, Productivity, and Employment in US Manufacturing, *American Economic Review*, vol. 104(5), pp. 394–9.

Aghion P., A. Bergeaud, T. Boppart, P. J. Klenow and H. Li (2019) Missing Growth from Creative Destruction, *American Economic Review*, vol. 109(8), pp. 2795–822.

Akita T. (2003) Decomposing Regional Income Inequality in China and Indonesia Using Two-Stage Nested Theil Decomposition Method, *Annals of Regional Science*, vol. 37(1), pp. 55–77.

Arlbjørn J. S. and O. S. Mikkelsen (2014) Backshoring Manufacturing: Notes on an Important but Under-Researched Theme, *Journal of Purchasing & Supply Management*, vol. 20, pp. 60–2.

Arlbjørn J. S., T. Lüthje, O. S. Mikkelsen, J. Schlichter and L. Thoms (2013) Danske Producenters Udflytning og Hjemtagning af Produktion. Kraks Fond Byforskning, Institut for Entreprenørskab og Relationsledelse, Syddansk Universitet.

Arundel A., C. Bordoy and M. Kanerva (2008) Neglected Innovators: How Do Innovative Firms That Do Not Perform R&D Innovate?, Innometrics Thematic Paper.

Autor D. (2015) Why Are There Still So Many Jobs? The History and Future of Workplace Automation, *The Journal of Economic Perspectives*, vol. 29(3), pp. 3–30.

Brynjolfsson E. (1993) *The Productivity Paradox of Information Technology*, Communications of the ACM, vol. 36(12), pp. 66–77.

Brynjolfsson E. and L. M. Hitt (2000) Beyond Computation: Information Technology, Organizational Transformation and Business Performance, *Journal of Economic Perspectives*, vol. 14(4), pp. 23–48.

Brynjolfsson E. and A. McAfee (2014) *The Second Machine Age: Work, Progress, and Prosperity in a Time of Brilliant Technologies*, New York: W. W. Norton & Company.

Butkus M., D. Cibulskiene, A. Maciulyte-Sniukiene, and K. Matuzeviciute (2018) What Is the Evolution of Convergence in the EU? Decomposing EU Disparities up to NUTS3 Level, *Sustainability*, vol. 10, pp. 15–52.

Calvino F. and M. E. Virgillito (2018) The Innovation–Employment Nexus: A Critical Survey of Theory and Empirics, *Journal of Economic Surveys*, vol. 32(1), pp. 83–117.

Camagni R., R. Capello and G. Perucca (2021) Towards an Interpretation of Labour Productivity Growth: Patterns of Regional Competitiveness in European Regions, paper presented at the RSAI Webconference, May.

Capello R. and S. Cerisola (2022) Regional Reindustrialization Patterns and Productivity Growth in Europe, *Regional Studies*, DOI: 10.1080/00343404.2022.2050894.

Capello R. and S. Cerisola (2023) Regional Transformations Processes: Reindustrialization and Technological Upgrading as Drivers of Productivity Gains, in R. Capello and A. Conte (eds.) Cities and Regions in Transition, p. 19-38, Milano: Franco Angeli.

Capello R. and C. Lenzi (2021) Industry 4.0 and Servitisation: Regional Patterns of 4.0 Technological Transformations in Europe, *Technological Forecasting and Social Change*, DOI: 10.1016/j.techfore. 2021.121164.

Capello R. and Lenzi C. (2022) *The Regional Economics of 4.0 Technological Transformations. Industry 4.0 and Servitisation in European Regions*, Oxford: Routledge.

Caselli M., A. Fracasso, S. Scicchitano, S. Traverso, and E. Tundis (2021) Stop Worrying and Love the Robot: An Activity-Based Approach to Assess the Impact of Robotization on Employment Dynamics, Global Labour Organization (GLO) Discussion Paper, No. 802.

Chaminade C., B. Å. Lundvall, and S. Haneef (2018) *Advanced Introduction to National Innovation Systems*, Cheltenham: Edward Elgar.

Christopherson S., R. Martin, P. Sunley, and P. Tyler (2014) Reindustrialising Regions: Rebuilding the Manufacturing Economy?, *Cambridge Journal of Regions, Economy and Society*, vol. 7, pp. 351–8.

Cirillo V., M. Rinaldini, J. Staccioli, and M. E. Virgillito (2021) Technology vs. Workers: The Case of Italy's Industry 4.0 Factories, *Structural Change and Economic Dynamics*, vol. 56, pp. 166–83.

Damanpour F., R. M. Walker, and C. N. Avellaneda (2009) Combinative Effects of Innovation Types and Organizational Performance: A Longitudinal Study, *Journal of Management Studies*, vol. 46(4), pp. 650–75.

Dosi G. and M. E. Virgillito (2019) Whither the Evolution of the Contemporary Social Fabric? New Technologies and Old Socio-Economic Trends?, *International Labour Review*, vol. 158(4), pp. 593–625.

Dosi G., F. Riccio, and M. E. Virgillito (2021) Varieties of Deindustrialization and Patterns of Diversification: Why Microchips Are Not Potato Chips, *Structural Change and Economic Dynamics*, vol. 57, pp. 182–202.

European Commission (2010a) *An Integrated Industrial Policy for the Globalisation Era – Putting Competitiveness and Sustainability at Centre Stage*, COM(2010) 614 final.

European Commission – DG Enterprise and Industry (2010b) *EU Manufacturing Industry: What are the Challenges and Opportunities for the Coming Years?*, accessed 17 March 2022 at https://op.europa.eu/en/publication-detail/-/publication/6b1472cf-3084-4a97-ac3b-a6b250288011.

European Commission (2012) *A Stronger European Industry for Growth and Economic Recovery*, COM(2012) 582 final.

European Commission (2014) *For a European Industrial Renaissance*, SWD(2014) 14 final.

European Commission (2019) *A Vision for the European Industry until 2030, Final Report of the Industry 2030 High-Level Industrial Roundtable*, accessed 14 January 2022 at https://op.europa.eu/it/publication-detail/-/publication/339d0a1b-bcab-11e9 -9d01-01aa75ed71a1.

Fisher A. (1933) Capital and the Growth of Knowledge, *The Economic Journal*, vol. 43, n. 171, pp. 379–89.

Ghosal V. and U. Nair-Reichert (2009) Investments in Modernization, Innovation and Gains in Productivity: Evidence from Firms in the Global Paper Industry, *Research Policy*, vol. 38, pp. 536–547.

Graetz G. and G. Michaels (2018) Robots at Work, *Review of Economics and Statistics*, vol. 100(5), pp. 753–68.

Hansen T. and L. Winther (2014) Competitive Low-tech Manufacturing and Challenges for Regional Policy in the European Context – Lessons from the Danish Experience, *Cambridge Journal of Regions, Economy and Society*, vol. 7, pp. 449–70.

Heidenreich M. (2009) Innovation Patterns and Location of European Low- and Medium-Technology Industries, *Research Policy*, vol. 38, pp. 483–94.

Hervas-Oliver J. L., F. Sempere-Ripoll, C. Boronat-Moll, and R. Rojas (2015) Technological Innovation without R&D: Unfolding the Extra Gains of Management Innovations on Technological Performance, *Technology Analysis & Strategic Management*, vol. 27(1), pp. 19–38.

Hirsch-Kreinsen H. (2008) 'Low-Tech' Innovations, *Industry and Innovation*, vol. 15(1), pp. 19–43.

Hoover E. M. (1948) *The Location of Economic Activity*, New York: McGraw-Hill.

Kuznet S. and J. T. Murphy (1966) *Modern Economic Growth: Rate, Structure, and Spread*, New Haven: Yale University Press.

Landesmann M. and K. Pichelmann (1999) Employment Patterns and the Welfare Services Sector, in Landesmann M. and K. Pichelmann (eds.), *Unemployment in Europe*, London: Macmillan, pp. 205–31.

Mendonça S. (2009) Brave Old World: Accounting for 'high-tech' Knowledge in 'low-tech' Industries, *Research Policy*, vol. 38, pp. 470–82.

Montobbio F., J. Staccioli, M. E. Virgillito, and M. Vivarelli (2022) Robots and the Origin of Their Labour-Saving Impact, *Technological Forecasting & Social Change*, vol. 174, 121122.

Nickell S., S. Redding, and J. Swaffield (2008) The Uneven Pace of Deindustrialization in the OECD, *The World Economy*, pp. 1154–84.

Rodrik D. (2016) Premature Deindustrialization, *Journal of Economic Growth*, vol. 21, pp. 1–33.

Rowthorn R. and R. Ramaswamy (1997) *Deindustrialization: Causes and Implications*, International Monetary Fund, WP/97/42.

Škuflić L. and M. Družić (2016) Deindustrialization and Productivity in the EU, *Economic Research – Ekonomska Istraživanja*, vol. 29(1), pp. 991–1002.

Solow R. (1987) We'd Better Watch Out, *New York Times Book Review*, 12 July, p. 36.

Storper M. and R. Walker (1989) Technological Change and Geographical Industrialization, in Storper M. and Walker R. (eds.), *The Capitalist Imperative – Territory, Technology, and Industrial Growth*, New York: Basil Blackwell.

Tregenna F. (2009) Characterizing Deindustrialization: An Analysis of Changes in Manufacturing Employment and Output Internationally, *Cambridge Journal of Economics*, vol. 33, pp. 433–66.

Vivarelli M. (2014) Innovation, Employment and Skills in Advanced and Developing Countries: A Survey of Economic Literature, *Journal of Economic Issues*, vol. 48(1), pp. 123–54.

# 2. Left behind places and local democracy: German small towns under the conditions of peripheralisation

**Thilo Lang, Franziska Görmar, Stefan Haunstein and Martin Graffenberger**

## 2.1 INTRODUCTION[1]

Against the backdrop of continuing sociospatial polarisation, a lively discourse has emerged in politics and the media in recent years about the state and development prospects of rural peripheral areas in Germany. While large cities and agglomerations are growing, many rural peripheral areas are struggling with multiple challenges. It is not uncommon to hear talk of 'disconnected regions' (Deutschlandfunk, 2017). The FAZ (2018) writes of a 'divided country' and draws the dividing line, not between the old and new federal states, but between 'globalisation winners' (big cities) and 'globalisation losers' (rural peripheral areas) and predicts: 'The gap is growing' (ibid.). Der Spiegel (2016) takes a look at the voting behaviour of people living in 'peripheries' and notes that 'frustration reigns in the countryside'. Behind such statements lies the assumption that rural peripheral areas are not only lagging behind the developments of big cities and agglomerations in economic and demographic terms, but that a lack of perspective is also spreading among the population living there, making it difficult to embark on new paths of development.

When we talk about rural peripheral areas, we are not only referring to villages but also to small and medium-sized towns located there. On the one hand, these have to struggle frequently with population losses, tight public

---

[1]  This chapter is based on the final report (Görmar et al. 2020) of the research project 'Local democracy in small and medium-sized cities under the conditions of peripheralization', run by the Leibniz Institute for Regional Geography on behalf of the vhw-Bundesverband für Wohnen und Stadtentwicklung e. V. from 2018–2020.

coffers and functional losses in the areas of administration and services of general interest (Bode and Hanewinkel, 2018). On the other hand, small and medium-sized towns take on important central functions and – especially in the polycentric system of the Federal Republic of Germany – still have a central position for balanced spatial development, which makes them important sources of impetus and focal points for their surrounding areas (Gatzweiler and Joswig-Erfling, 2012; Ries, 2019). Small and medium-sized towns are also very important in that more than half of the people in Germany live in them. According to the Federal Institute for Research on Building, Urban Affairs and Spatial Development (BBSR), there are about 24.3 million inhabitants in small towns and about 23.6 million in medium-sized towns (BBSR, 2018a: 3).

Against this background, in the following sections, we present an overview of the conceptual debate on peripheralisation and governance in small and medium-sized towns in Germany in relation to issues of local democracy. We suggest that this perspective helps to better understand the current challenges of smaller towns in the context of increasing sociospatial polarization and their political and societal implications, in particular regarding processes of local democracy and their wider consequences for the democratic system of our society overall. We conclude with a discussion of current tensions in participatory governance in small and medium-sized towns under the conditions of peripheralisation.

## 2.2  PERIPHERALISATION, URBAN GOVERNANCE AND LOCAL DEMOCRACY

### 2.2.1  Peripheralisation of Small and Medium-sized Towns

Spaces develop unequally. This observation is not new but has a long tradition in spatial science research. The cornerstone for this was laid by Myrdal (1957) and Hirschman (1958), who, in their contributions to polarisation theory, gave economic reasons for the fact that disparities between areas increase in a circular manner and do not even out over time, as assumed in neoclassical arguments (e.g. Solow, 1956; Borts and Stein, 1964). The (historically justified) formation of economic centres and growth poles leads to specific local advantages and, thus, to further concentration processes. Growth centres are strengthened – so-called peripheries fall further behind. While the attention of economic studies in Germany is currently primarily focused on the centres and agglomeration areas, which are understood as 'engines of growth' (DIW, 2018), a very lively debate has developed in the social sciences in recent years, which has turned to their spatial counterparts: peripheries (as status) or peripheralisation (as process) (Fischer-Tahir and Naumann, 2013; Lang and Görmar, 2018; inter alia).

These terms are conceptually underpinned by three frameworks of thought. Firstly, the emphasis is on the fact that 'peripheries' are not bound to a specific spatial category (such as rural areas) or defined as such due to their spatial distance from complementary centres. Instead, it takes into account the fact that they are constituted at very different scales (global, national, regional, local). Following such a multiscalar understanding, a small town, for example, can be understood as a 'periphery' within a region, which, in turn, is itself a 'periphery' within a country (cf. Kühn, 2015; Lang, 2015). Secondly, spaces are not peripheral simply because of specific features. They are only made peripheral through a variety of social processes. In this context, complementary 'centres' must always be considered, which ultimately have a great influence on the scope for the actions of the actors in the so-called peripheries (Kühn et al., 2017). Nevertheless, such influences do not force these spaces into a rigid corset: 'peripheries' always remain spaces of possibility with specific potentials (see below). Thirdly, the concept of peripheralisation moves away from a static, temporally fixed view in favour of a dynamic understanding of peripheralisation as a process creating 'peripheries'. Therefore, the question of why 'peripheries' have been constituted must always consider past events, since the past can continue to have an effect into the present (although not in a deterministic sense).

Various dimensions need to be taken into account to gain a better understanding of the constitution (and perpetuation) of peripheralised spaces. In the following, with reference to Kühn and Weck (2013), four dimensions are addressed (political, economic, demographic and discursive) and placed within the development contexts of small and medium-sized towns in Germany.

### 2.2.1.1 Political dimensions

The political dimension of peripheralisation encompasses the diminishing leeway of actors in 'peripheries' to exert self-determined influence on developments and position themselves against deficits and challenges. Neu (2006: 13) describes an inherent powerlessness as: 'Not being able to defend oneself (any more) against disadvantages, that is what periphery means.' Decisions about local developments are often made at other levels and in other places than those that have to bear the consequences of these decisions. This means that there are dependencies on external decision-makers, who ultimately also decide what decision-making and organisational leeway they grant or deny to the 'peripheries' (Kühn et al., 2017). In this context, municipal area reforms, which were implemented in the 1960s and 1970s in many states of the Federal Republic of Germany (FRD) and from 1990 onwards also on a large scale in the new states, had a particular influence. In North Rhine-Westphalia (NRW), for example, the number of municipalities was reduced from 2277 in 1968 to 396 today. In Saxony-Anhalt, the number declined from 1349 in

1990 to 218 today (Bogumil and Holtkamp, 2013: 27). This meant for small and medium-sized towns that numerous villages were assigned to them and that municipal councils, henceforth, had to balance various interests specific to local areas. The effects of such municipal area reforms are controversial. Blesse and Rösel (2017) presented a summary of previous studies on the topic, showing that the hoped-for fiscal savings of such reforms mostly did not materialise, but that they were often associated with an erosion of local democratic participation.

Which municipal infrastructures and services of general interest are (or can be) maintained depends not only on the municipalities' own financial resources, but is often also determined by the extent to which municipal political actors have the basic decision-making power to maintain the corresponding services. Bogumil and Holtkamp (2013: 77) speak of the 'overall decreasing capacity of municipalities to act'. Schools are an example of this. The decision as to whether a municipality can continue to maintain a school is less within its own sphere of influence, but is primarily taken at district and state level. Austerity measures – coupled with declining pupil numbers – have led to schools being merged or abandoned in many places (Walde, 2019). Schools have closed in 35 per cent of all shrinking municipalities since 1995, with small and medium-sized towns being particularly affected (BMU 2016: 18). The latter have experienced a loss of functions in numerous fields even beyond that of education. Bode and Hanewinkel (2018) used the example of 522 small towns to examine changes in the central functions in the areas of administration, culture, education and medical care between 2001 and 2017. They come to the conclusion that one-third of the small towns have lost their importance, whereas only one in ten has gained in importance. It becomes clear that small towns, which have already had to cope with great economic and demographic challenges, are the ones that have been deprived of functions. More than half of the small towns in Mecklenburg-Vorpommern and Brandenburg, for example, have lost importance (ibid.).

### 2.2.1.2  Economic dimensions

Large towns and agglomeration areas are considered to be engines of economic development and innovation (e.g. Shearmur, 2012; DIW, 2018). Large companies, technology-oriented small and medium-sized enterprises (SMEs), high-tech industries, universities and research institutions, private research and development (R&D) resources, patent applications, highly qualified employees and value creation are concentrated in large towns (Meng, 2012; Lentz, 2014; Henn and Werner, 2016). Economic geography literature refers primarily to agglomeration advantages to explain this concentration. Accordingly, large towns are characterised by advantages of both specialisation and diversification. Both mechanisms induce specific advantages in terms of transaction and coordination costs or knowledge flows (van der Panne, 2004). In addition, it is argued that the spatial proximity between companies, research institutions and institutional organisations, and proximity to sales markets, promotes local/regional exchange potentials and also creates specific local advantages that can be reinforced in the long term (Moulaert and Sekia, 2003). Large cities and agglomerations are, therefore, considered particularly conducive to the creation of innovations (Florida, 2005; Shearmur, 2012; Florida et al., 2017). The European Commission also states: 'Cities play a crucial role as engines of the economy, as places of connectivity, creativity and innovation (…)' (European Commission, 2011: vi).[2] Notably, the public focus on the centres as essential business and science locations has manifested such notions. In this context, Stein and Kujath (2013: 173) were able to show in their studies on peripherised medium-sized towns that they often find it difficult to assert themselves as business locations in the (global) knowledge economy, for example, because they do not have direct access to universities, or the institutions are only small or have little relevance for the regional economy in terms of their orientation.

To date, only a few studies have questioned the idea in this discourse that 'peripheries' (and their actors) are not able to produce innovations, or are only able to do so to a reduced extent (Graffenberger and Vonnahme, 2019). The example of German global market leaders has shown that they are not only located in agglomerations, but are also competitive and produce innovations in peripheral locations (Ermann et al., 2012). Such companies can shape their location, especially in small and medium-sized towns, and contribute significantly to local development (Vonnahme et al., 2018). It is becoming increasingly apparent in the discourse on innovation and space that, in addition to spatial proximity, other forms of proximity (and distance) between economic actors, such as cognitive, social, institutional and organisational proximity, also have a beneficial effect on innovation and economic development processes (Boschma, 2005; Ibert, 2011; Vonnahme and Lang, 2017).

In principle, it is essential for municipalities to retain existing companies and attract new ones, as trade taxes and proportional income taxes are among the most important sources of revenue for municipalities (Destatis, 2019). If there is a lack of potent companies, this ultimately also affects the fiscal leeway of the municipalities.

### 2.2.1.3 Demographic dimensions

According to the Urban Development Report 2016, 47 per cent of all medium-sized towns and 60 per cent of all small towns in Germany shrank

---

2   Cities are defined in the document as settlements with more than 50 000 inhabitants (European Commission, 2011: 3). Hence, no attention is paid to small towns.

between 2004 and 2014. Only 16 per cent of medium-sized towns and 13 per cent of small towns were able to show stable population figures (BMU, 2016: 16). In the spatial planning report from 2018 it is noted that, 'the central medium-sized and small towns as well as rural communities in both eastern and western Germany show a more favourable development than their counterparts in peripheral locations' (BBSR, 2018b: 12f.). While small and medium-sized towns in agglomerations often benefit from immigration and the influx of young families, the situation in small and medium-sized towns far from the centre is more precarious: 'Shrinking small and medium-sized towns outside the metropolitan regions now have the lowest proportion of children and young people, at 15.2 per cent, due to this ongoing bloodletting' (BMU, 2016: 16). The decline in young people is particularly problematic from the perspective of the affected municipalities from two points of view. On the one hand, demographic developments are intensifying due to the (expected) low fertility; and on the other hand, the accompanying dwindling demand for childcare facilities ultimately leads to the reduction or abandonment of corresponding offers and, thus, to a loss of attractiveness and function (Kroismayr et al., 2016). The reduction in the number of young people contrasts with an increase in the number of older and retired people. This leads to local services of general interest becoming particularly important so that immobile people can continue to manage their everyday lives locally. Additionally, this also means that the people who have alternative ideas about the provision of public services and can actively participate in urban development processes are becoming fewer and older (Nadler, 2017). Beyond this deficit discourse, however, there are also voices that argue that the involvement of older people creates opportunities for meaningful participation (Alisch et al., 2018: 117) and options in urban development, especially in strengthening services of general interest, for example, through citizens' aid associations.

### 2.2.1.4  Discursive dimensions

'Peripheries' are not only constituted by objective (i.e. statistically ascertainable) characteristics, but are also created and reproduced through discourses. Negative attributions can shape the view of such spaces from the outside (cf. Bürk and Beißwenger, 2013) and, thus, for example, undermine immigration potentials. Additionally, such external attributions can also settle in the minds of the people living there. A feeling of being left behind can contribute to the undermining of democratic structures and the strengthening of antidemocratic forces (Bürk, 2012). Furthermore, stigmatisation can become effective in local and regional political contexts, for example, when local decision-makers, who actually have a pioneering role in the context of spatial transformation processes, find it difficult to create the necessary impetus in the face of a deeply internalised narrative of peripheralisation (e.g. Willett, 2019).

## 2.2.2 Urban Development, Participatory Governance and Local Democracy

A central guiding principle of urban development policy in Germany is related to the paradigm of integrated development. It is based on the broad participation of different groups of actors and citizens and, consequently, on cooperative and participatory process design (Deutscher Städtetag, 2013). Local politics is attributed a moderating role, although it must be emphasised that the final decision-making right remains with local politics (Holtkamp and Bogumil, 2007). Integrated urban development is, thus, closely interwoven with local governance and local democracy.

The term governance encompasses nonhierarchical forms of control and decision-making, emphasising voluntary forms of regulation (Benz, 2004; Heinelt, 2018).[3] The network-like forms of cooperation and interaction underlying the governance concept transcend the sectoral boundaries between the public and private sectors (Schwalb and Walk, 2007; Schuppert, 2011; Burdack and Kriszan, 2013). In the context of integrated urban development, governance can be seen as a local coordination and orientation framework in which urban development processes are initiated, negotiated and implemented. In the course of such local governance, it is necessary to coordinate specialist topics, actors and their different positions, taking into account existing hierarchical levels (Kuder, 2011). The participation and involvement of citizens are essential elements of local governance (Schwalb and Walk, 2007). Consequently, they play an important role in the implementation of urban development and the design of urban development policy. The creation of specific governance structures in the field of urban development is also explicitly called for in the Leipzig Charter, a central orientation framework for urban development policy:

> Integrated urban development policy is a process. In this process, the coordination of central urban policy fields takes place in spatial, factual and temporal terms. The involvement of economic actors, interest groups and the public are indispensable in this process. (Leipzig Charta, 2007: 2)

The concept of local governance is used quite differently in current debates on participation in urban development. Three basic dimensions can be identified.

---

[3]    The term governance must be distinguished from the term government. Therefore, '(...) the term government means governing through forms of direct control emanating from the political centre, while governance encompasses forms of context control and indirect influence on and co-operation with a wide variety of actors in a differentiated system of political arenas' (Haus, 2010: 210).

Local governance can be understood descriptively as changes in the content of political control: away from isolated state intervention towards the inclusion of social, economic and political actors. In this context, new interaction, cooperation and coordination structures become evident. The analytical task is to uncover the effects that result from the inclusion of these groups of actors and interests on governance systems. In addition, governance can be understood normatively – in the sense of good governance – as how political coordination and governance should change in a specific direction (Holtkamp and Bogumil, 2007: 231f.).

Participatory governance structures can make an important contribution to strengthening local democracy. Schuppert (2011), for example, emphasises that the involvement of citizens and their interests in urban development processes should not be seen as an end in itself. Participation is essential for the functioning of local democracy. Local governance can increase the social reach of decisions through the broad involvement of urban society actors and citizens from different milieus – and ultimately contribute to strengthening local democracy (Walk, 2014). Against this background, a variety of participation formats are already used in urban development policy practice (e.g. citizens' forums, elaboration of integrated urban development concepts) to establish a dialogue within the heterogeneous urban societies and lay the foundation for goal-oriented communication, trust and joint learning (see, inter alia, Dehne, 2018). These include open formats geared to the entire citizenry and special actor-focused forums, which are usually composed according to thematic aspects. In this way, participation can contribute to democratic decision-making 'bottom-up' – and, thus, strengthen local democracy in principle. Commitment in the urban development process chain (preparation–decision–implementation) is considered a central factor in generating and securing the communicative resonance of political decisions and legitimacy in urban society in the long term (Holtkamp and Bogumil, 2007; Schuppert, 2011).

In practice, local democracy is exposed to diverse challenges. It is becoming evident that a growing number of people and groups feel less and less represented in the political structure, which leads ultimately to an increase in the much-discussed 'disenchantment with politics' (Vortkamp, 2007: 146). This is also expressed in the fact that often only a few social groups, and mostly members of specific social milieus, get actively involved in urban development policy processes at all (e.g. Holtkamp and Bogumil, 2007; Rohland and Kuder, 2011). This selectivity is confirmed in recent studies: a project on cooperative small town development in Loitz (Mecklenburg-Vorpommern) found it difficult to win over excluded groups, such as the long-term unemployed, for participation processes (Wegner and Klie, 2018). The same applies to young families (Dehne, 2018). In addition, men generally participate more often than women, not least because women often have more involvement in their close social environment or are tied down by care work (Eckes et al., 2019). It is true that formats geared towards participation are regarded as (idealised) elements of cooperative democracy building. However, it is clear that the increased use of participatory approaches can also lead to already active citizens and urban society groups being offered an additional platform for their issues and, thus, tend to reinforce one-sided and dominant views (Holtkamp and Bogumil, 2007). Walk (2014: 205) points out that it is often mainly those interest groups that 'have a good connection to the state actors', i.e. have relationships through which they can channel their interests, that get involved. Another challenge concerns effectiveness. Broad participation can make finding solutions more difficult, especially when it comes to complex and demanding contexts of urban development that are difficult for laypeople to grasp and are not explained in a clear and comprehensible way. Thus, there is also the danger that the consequences of the formerly democratically negotiated decisions can go in a different direction than previously envisaged.

## 2.3 LOCAL GOVERNANCE AND LOCAL DEMOCRACY UNDER CONDITIONS OF PERIPHERALISATION

Against the background of the dimensions of peripheralisation of small and medium-sized towns described above, questions arise about the design, potential and limits of local governance and its significance for local democratic processes. Two things need to be considered here: the specificity of small-town local structures on the one hand and the influences and effects of peripheralisation on the other.

Regarding the specifics of small-scale structures, it should first be emphasised that local institutions, such as municipal and city administrations and mayors, are important reference points for political trust. Local politics is often evaluated more positively by citizens in numerous fields of action than politics at higher levels, which can be attributed, inter alia, to the comparatively close proximity between decision-makers and citizens (Rohland and Kuder, 2011). This is particularly true for small municipalities. The results of a Forsa survey show that trust in local political institutions tends to increase as the size of the municipality decreases (Güllner, 2019). In this context, there is reason to believe that the size of the municipal reference unit is relevant for local democratic processes. While the scope for citizen influence is sometimes narrowly limited, especially in large municipalities (due to complexities and bureaucratic hurdles in administrative processes, among other things), the conditions for more direct influence are significantly better in small-town arenas due to closer communication networks (Maaß, 2018). The probability of being heard regarding concrete concerns is thus greater. The consequences of negotiated decisions, in turn, can be perceived more quickly. If direct influence can be exerted on urban development, this can also have identity-forming effects – as Wegner and Klie (2018) have emphasised in their studies in the Mecklenburg town Loitz (Peenetal). Regarding the future design of infrastructural services in peripheral areas, Naumann and Reichert-Schick (2012: 41) formulate: 'The co-design of infrastructure provision by the inhabitants, as long as it does not represent a withdrawal of the state from the provision of public services, can certainly serve the empowerment and identification of the people with their region.'

However, it should not be overlooked that peripheralisation processes pose particular challenges for the establishment of sustainable local governance and a broad democratic involvement of citizens. Borsig et al. (2010) found in their studies on post-Soviet (including East German) small towns in peripheral locations a low level of participation of citizens in urban development processes. It remained unclear whether this was due to a lack of interest (as local political decision-makers assessed it) or whether it was due to a lack of opportunities to exert influence, as voices from the citizenry suggested (ibid.: 94f.). A study on 'democratic integration' at the regional level (Klie, 2019) points out that this is also related to regional structural characteristics.[4] According to the study, high demographic adjustment needs, relative social disadvantage and low economic performance have a negative impact on democratic integration at the regional level. The study concludes that 'structural conditions at the regional and local level are important for a vital civil society, for engagement as a prerequisite for social cohesion and for democracy as a lived and valued form of state' (Klie, 2019: 48).

Looking at the political dimension of peripheralisation, Blesse and Rösel (2017) examined the effects of municipal area reforms. They came to the conclusion that the merger of independent localities into larger municipalities was generally associated with 'a decline in democratic satisfaction, voter turnout, the number of candidates in local elections, and a strengthening of populist currents'. Since small and medium-sized towns were frequently affected by municipal reorganisation (e.g. through the allocation of new local districts), it can be assumed that such developments also have an impact. Bernt (2013) examined the fiscal side of political peripheralisation and its effect on local governance arrangements. In the context of the medium-sized municipalities studied, he found that they often have major problems in fulfilling their com-

---

[4]   In the context of the study, the concept of 'democratic integration' is defined by the indicators of voter turnout, voluntary engagement and sociopolitical orientations/ perceptions.

pulsory public duties at all in the face of scarce budgetary resources. They are dependent on financial support from a higher political level in order to embark on new and development paths, which, in turn, are linked to narrow specifications by the resource providers – and, thus, hinder the self-determined finding of a local strategy (ibid.: 80). Bernt points out that 'fashionable calls for more co-operation, more vision and more innovation can have little success in the context of peripherized cities if they are not accompanied by better basic financial resources' (ibid.: 81).

In addition, demographic developments are limiting the capacity of active citizenship in many places. Various studies suggest that the areas that are exposed to major structural challenges are those in which both the capacity and the willingness to get involved in local issues are below average. Hameister and Tesch-Römer (2017: 549) came, on the basis of a survey of volunteers, to the conclusion: 'In regions with a high unemployment rate, the proportion of volunteers is significantly lower.' Nadler (2017) speaks of a 'geographical dilemma' in this context. On the one hand, there is selective migration and a decreasing number of people who are able and willing to get involved in local development and can reconcile this with their everyday lives (empirically proven by Kummel and Nadler, 2018, for the example of Weißwasser; for the Altenburger Land, see Schwarzenberg et al., 2017). On the other hand, there is a particularly strong need for participation in these areas, as the private sector and the public sector often do not (or cannot) meet local needs adequately (for a detailed consideration of this problem, see the metastudy by Eckes et al., 2019).

Citizens are increasingly becoming involved in urban development processes with their knowledge and skills, especially in problematic areas. At the same time, citizens are subject to certain expectations that they are often unable to meet (ibid.: 109). Using the example of the involvement of citizens in public planning in the area of services of general interest, Elbe and Müller (2015) see the danger of excessive demands, as citizens may not be able to meet the requirements that have been set. This is especially true when it is not only a matter of being able to co-decide on certain developments but also of providing and maintaining specific services (of general interest) in coproduction (e.g. through financial participation). In this context, Walk (2014: 197) points to the danger that 'co-operation with civil society is misunderstood as an alternative to compensate for empty public coffers and the increasing deterioration in the quality of state services'.

## 2.4    CONCLUSIONS AND DISCUSSION

Peripheralisation generally has a negative connotation in the literature – as a process that restricts the scope for action and paralyses the activities of local actors. Clinging to traditional structures, coupled with resignation about one's own powerlessness, can lead to a blockade against new things and even to the strengthening of antidemocratic forces. On the other hand, there are also voices that argue that shrinking can introduce new opportunities. A downward spiral that has been discursively mapped out can be counteracted by strengthening personal responsibility and social capital (Porsche et al., 2019; Ročak, 2019). 'Spaces of possibility' (Willett and Lang, 2018) or 'windows of opportunity' (Matthiesen, 2013) are created. This means that derelict sites and areas offer a variety of starting points and perspectives for use beyond the pressure of commercial exploitation, which actors from civil society, local politics and business can develop and maintain in coproduction (Schlappa, 2017). From a governance perspective, this also means that opportunities arise to rethink participation and make self-efficacy tangible through the involvement of citizens. Because hierarchical top-down formats often only capture the needs of local people insufficiently, joint action – based on the knowledge of local people – can set new stimuli in favour of local development (Böcher et al., 2008). Such considerations follow on from debates on resident-led interventions and performative citizen participation: 'Through the use of performative participation, the use and design of an urban place by residents is no longer mentally at the end of a planning process, but forms a central element of the planning itself' (Mackrodt, 2014). This goes hand in hand with the fact that civic participation can counteract the disenchantment with politics that can often be observed in peripherised areas, resulting in a stronger bond between people and their locality and, thus, offering a new perspective to considerations of staying (cf. Burdack and Kriszan, 2013). Making a virtue out of necessity would then mean not taking local governance seriously (only) out of considerations of fiscal austerity, but recognising in it a structure for a living democracy.

However, certain preconditions are needed for this to succeed. Eckes et al. (2019) have identified four factors in their literature review on the triangle of issues, 'Promoting engagement – strengthening democracy – rural areas', that promote engagement and participation. These are (1) places of social participation,[5] (2) central key figures (mostly mayors or leading administrative staff, see above), (3) sufficient financial resources that are also available in the long term, and (4) communication, connecting and networking. If one or, in the best case, several of these prerequisites are met, participation can succeed and local democracy can be strengthened.

---

[5]   Cf. the social-place concept that is currently being developed in a research project at the Sociological Research Institute (SOFI) at the Georg August University Göttingen (also see Kersten et al., 2017).

Peripheralisation processes operate in different dimensions (political, economic, demographic and discursive) in individual cities, which influence participation and local democracy in specific ways. Urban development and local governance are always dependent on structural framework conditions and local actors. Despite the specific framework conditions, the actors have a variety of instruments and possibilities to shape local democracy cooperatively. These actors (administration, politics, civic activists, business) operate not only in different areas of tension with specific challenges but also with room for manoeuvre. Dealing with these areas of tension has a decisive influence on how civic engagement is exercised and shaped, and how local democracy is filled with life in the local structure.

It has been shown that local democracy in small and medium-sized towns under the conditions of peripheralisation is characterised not only by various challenges but also spaces of opportunity, which are based on both structural conditions and specific actor constellations.

In this chapter, we have offered a new framework to understand left-behind places in Germany. We suggest the importance of looking into processes of peripheralisation producing characteristics leading to large parts of a local population feeling 'left behind'. Against the backdrop of demographic shrinkage, cuts in local services and central functions, combined with economic stagnation or decline and partly physical decay of central areas, these places are increasingly characterized by dominant perceptions of loss and drawbacks in the local quality of life. It seems increasingly difficult to maintain local democratic cultures and practices under these conditions.

It is of immense importance for the development of municipalities whether the relationship between the individual actors is conflictual or harmonious and to what extent they have a relationship of trust with each other. This concerns the relationship between the administration and the municipal parliament, between the administration and civil society or economic actors, and the relationship between the core municipality and its districts. It also appears important to what extent voluntary local politicians are in good contact with their fellow citizens, for example, through memberships in associations or presence at important events, such as city festivals, and not just waiting to be addressed by their electorate. The fewer resources (financial, but also human) available, the more relevant it is to join forces and create synergies. If there is no will to cooperate, this can lead to resources and forces being unnecessarily tied up in conflicts and blockades of action.

In view of tight budgets, voluntary tasks of the municipalities (e.g. support of clubs, sports and youth work, cultural facilities) have been limited in the past or partially handed over to voluntary initiatives. The need for voluntary commitment, therefore, seems to be growing and is increasingly taken for granted. However, this brings the danger of an overuse of civic engagement.

This is sometimes expressed in the fact that, although short-term projects are initiated and carried out, the sustainable maintenance of facilities such as playgrounds or green spaces and long-term projects are often no longer possible and are either discontinued or transferred back to the municipality. This can then lead to a certain reluctance on the part of the municipality to engage in civic activities, which, in turn, creates frustration on the part of the community about a perceived lack of support. This then reinforces the tendency for engagement potential to decline under conditions of peripheralisation – in part due to demographic change, partially due to resignation after years of experiencing loss.

In the past, both civil society actors and local administrations have expressed the wish for more participation. However, municipalities often have limited human and financial resources to implement such processes adequately. There is evidence that, where the field of action participation is explicitly anchored in the task profile of certain functions/offices, a greater variety of participation formats tends to be implemented. Participation processes are often organised and moderated by external service providers, for example, in the course of preparing an integrated development concept. In such cases, it also depends on their competence to what extent such a process is successful and involves the citizens. Moreover, participation is often used to develop something new, to move the municipality forward. Financial or infrastructural cuts, on the other hand, are less often moderated, although this is precisely where an opportunity for a new orientation of the respective municipality lies.

Small and medium-sized towns under conditions of peripheralisation are dependent on funding (e.g. from the federal and state governments), especially for investment. However, the success of applications in increasingly competitive programmes depends to a large extent on the capacities and competencies of local staff. If an administration, for example, is fully occupied with day-to-day business, there is often no time to develop well-thought-out applications. The chances of success are, therefore, sometimes very uncertain, depending on how much money is available and how large the field of applicants is. In addition, the availability of funding for certain topics or construction measures sometimes seems to determine the strategic development of a municipality. In addition, funding is always secured only for the project period, whereas long-term funding would be necessary, especially for personnel-intensive projects.

The scope for actively shaping urban development processes is sometimes quite limited, especially in municipalities affected by peripheralisation processes. This is often expressed by the administration and citizens through the impression that it is primarily a matter of managing a state of shortage – instead of actively shaping it.

Comprehensive decisions in this respect often lie outside municipal decision-making competences. This concerns both the influence on the financial possibilities (e.g. due to high expenditures for compulsory tasks, there is often only room for manoeuvre by raising the assessment rates or local fees) and the legal responsibilities (e.g. for infrastructure projects, monument protection, water protection, facilities of general interest, such as schools and cultural facilities, that are borne by the state). Here, it is also important to communicate decisions made at higher levels (district, state, federal) transparently to the urban community and to involve local residents.

## REFERENCES

Alisch, M., Ritter, M., Boos-Krüger, A., Schönberger, C., Glaser, R., Rubin, Y. and Solf-Leibold, B. (2018): 'Irgendwann brauch' ich dann auch Hilfe ...!' Selbstorganisation, Engagement und Mitverantwortung älterer Menschen in ländlichen Räumen. Opladen, Berlin and Toronto (= Beiträge zur Sozialraumforschung 17).

BBSR (Ed.) (2018a): Kleinstädte in Deutschland – Statistiken und generelle Trends In: BBSR (Ed.): Kleinstädte in Deutschland. Urbanität. Vielfalt. Perspektiven. Online: http://www.kleinstaedteindeutschland.de/hintergrundinformationen_zum_kongress.pdf.

BBSR (Ed.) (2018b): Raumordnungsbericht 2017. Daseinsvorsorge sichern. Bonn.

Benz, A. (Ed.) (2004): Governance – Regieren in komplexen Regelsystemen. Wiesbaden: VS Verlag für Sozialwissenschaften.

Bernt, M. (2013): Governanceprozesse und lokale Strategiebildung. In: Bernt, M. and Liebmann, H. (Ed.): Peripherisierung, Stigmatisierung, Abhängigkeit? Deutsche Mittelstädte und ihr Umgang mit Peripherisierungsprozessen. Wiesbaden, 65–82.

Blesse, S. and Rösel, F. (2017): Gebietsreformen: Hoffnungen, Risiken und Alternativen. München (= ifo Working Papers 234).

BMU – Bundesministerium für Umwelt, Naturschutz und nukleare Sicherheit (Ed.) (2016): Stadtentwicklungsbericht der Bundesregierung 2016: Gutes Zusammenleben im Quartier. Berlin.

Böcher, M., Krott, M. and Tränkner, S. (2008): Regional Governance und integrierte ländliche Entwicklung. In: Böcher, M., Krott, M. and Tränkner, S. (Ed.): Regional Governance und integrierte ländliche Entwicklung. Ergebnisse der Begleitforschung zum Modell und Demonstrationsvorhaben 'Regionen Aktiv'. Wiesbaden, 11–22.

Bode, V. and Hanewinkel, C. (2018): Kleinstädte im Wandel. In: Nationalatlas aktuell 12 (03.2018). Leipzig. Online: http://aktuell.nationalatlas.de/Kleinstaedte.01_03–2018.0.html.

Bogumil, J. and Holtkamp, L. (2013): Kommunalpolitik und Kommunalverwaltung. Eine praxisorientierte Einführung. Bonn.

Borsig, A., Burdack, J. and Knappe, E. (2010): Small towns in Eastern Europe: local networks and urban development. Leipzig (= Beiträge zur regionalen Geographie 64).

Borts, G.H. and Stein, J.L. (1964): Economic Growth in a Free Market. New York: Columbia University Press.

Boschma, R. (2005): Proximity and Innovation: A Critical Assessment. Regional Studies 39(1), 61–74.

Burdack, J. and Kriszan, A. (2013): Kleinstädte in Mittel- und Osteuropa: Perspektiven und Strategien lokaler Entwicklung. Leipzig (= Forum IfL 19).

Bürk, T. (2012): Gefahrenzonen, Angstraum, Feindesland. Stadtkulturelle Erkundungen zu Fremdenfeindlichkeit und Rechtsradikalismus in ostdeutschen Kleinstädten. Münster (= Raumproduktionen: Theorie und gesellschaftliche Praxis Band 14).

Bürk, T. and Beißwenger, S. (2013): Stigmatisierung von Städten. In: Bernt, M. and Liebmann, H. (Ed.): Peripherisierung, Stigmatisierung, Abhängigkeit? Deutsche Mittelstädte und ihr Umgang mit Peripherisierungsprozessen. Wiesbaden, 125–45.

Dehne, P. (2018): Kooperative Kleinstadtentwicklung. Eine Annäherung. In: Informationen zur Raumentwicklung 6/18, 86–101.

Der Spiegel (2016): Auf dem Land regiert der Frust. 31.07.16. Online: http://www.spiegel.de/wirtschaft/soziales/stadt-und-land-wo-afd-donald-trump-le-pen-und-co-stark-sind-a-1105526.html.

Destatis (Ed.) (2019): Kommunen mit 9,8 Milliarden Euro Finanzierungsüberschuss im Jahr 2018. Pressemitteilung Nr. 127 vom 2. April 2019. Online: https://www.destatis.de/DE/Presse/Pressemitteilungen/2019/04/PD19_127_71137.html.

Deutscher Städtetag (2013): Integrierte Stadtentwicklungsplanung und Stadtentwicklungsmanagement – Strategien und Instrumente nachhaltiger Stadtentwicklung. Berlin and Köln.

Deutschlandfunk (2017): Reihe 'abgehängten Regionen' im September 2017. Online: https://www.deutschlandfunk.de/abgehaengte-regionen.3378.de.html.

DIW – Deutsches Institut für Wirtschaftsforschung (2018): Industrie in der Stadt: Wachstumsmotor mit Zukunft: Editorial. Berlin (= DIW Wochenbericht 47/2018).

EC – European Commission (Ed.) (2011): Cities of Tomorrow. Challenges, Visions, Ways Forward. Online: https://ec.europa.eu/regional_policy/sources/docgener/studies/pdf/citiesoftomorrow/citiesoftomorrow_final.pdf.

Eckes, C., Piening, M.-T. and Dieckmann, J. (2019): Literaturanalyse zum Themendreieck 'Engagementförderung – Demokratiestärkung – Ländlicher Raum'. Ed. Von Bundesnetzwerk Bürgerschaftliches Engagement Berlin.

Elbe, S. and Müller, R. (2015): Gleichwertigkeit als Bürgeraufgabe. Partizipation der Zivilgesellschaft = Überforderung der Zivilgesellschaft? In: Informationen zur Raumentwicklung 1/2015, 57–69.

Ermann, U., Lang, T. and Megerle, M. (2012): Weltmarktführer abseits der Agglomerationsräume. In: Nationalatlas aktuell 6 (10.2012). Leipzig: Leibniz-Institut für Länderkunde. Online: http://aktuell.nationalatlas.de/wp-content/uploads/12_11_Weltmarktfuehrer.pdf.

FAZ – Frankfurter Allgemeine Zeitung (2018): Das geteilte Land. 28.02.18. Online: https://www.faz.net/aktuell/wirtschaft/deutschland-ein-geteiltes-land-15456747.html.

Fischer-Tahir, A. and Naumann, M. (Ed.) (2013): Peripheralization. The Making of Spatial Dependencies and Social Injustice. Wiesbaden: Springer.

Florida, R. (2005): Cities and the Creative Class. New York: Routledge.

Florida, R., Patrick, A. and Mellander, C. (2017): The city as innovation machine. In: Regional Studies 51(1), 86–96.

Gatzweiler, H.P. and Joswig-Erfling, A. (2012): Klein und Mittelstädte in Deutschland – eine Bestandsaufnahme. Stuttgart (= Analysen Bau.Stadt.Raum 10).

Görmar, F., Graffenberger, M., Haunstein, S. and Lang, T. (2020): Lokale Demokratie in Klein- und Mittelstädten unter den Bedingungen von Peripherisierung. Abschlussbericht im Auftrag des vhw – Bundesverband für Wohnen und Stadtentwicklung e. V. Berlin: vhw-Schriftenreihe Nr. 18, 95 S.

Graffenberger, M. and Vonnahme, L. (2019): Questioning the 'Periphery Label' in Economic Geography: Entrepreneurial Action and Innovation in South Estonia. In: ACME – An International Journal for Critical Geographies 18(2), 529–50.

Güllner, M. (2019): Hohes Vertrauen in die Kommunalpolitik. Online: https://kommunal.de/forsa-kommunalwahlen?utm_medium=email&utm_source=newsletter&utm_campaign=20191402.

Hameister, N. and Tesch-Römer, C. (2017): Landkreise und kreisfreie Städte: Regionale Unterschiede im freiwilligen Engagement. In: Simonson, J., Vogel, C. and Tesch-Römer, C. (Ed.): Freiwilliges Engagement in Deutschland. Wiesbaden, 549–71.

Haus, M. (2010): Von government zu governance? Bürgergesellschaft und Engagementpolitik im Kontext neuer Formen des Regierens. In: Olk, T., Klein, A. and Hartnuß, B. (Ed.): Engagementpolitik. Die Entwicklung der Zivilgesellschaft als politische Aufgabe. Wiesbaden, 210–32.

Heinelt, H. (2018): Handbook on Participatory Governance. Cheltenham: Edward Elgar.

Henn, S. and Werner, P. (2016): Erfinderaktivitäten in Deutschland – Patente, Gebrauchsmuster, Marken und Design. In: Nationalatlas aktuell 10(9). Leipzig.

Hirschman, A.O. (1958): The Strategy of Economic Development. New Haven: Yale University Press.

Holtkamp, L. and Bogumil, J. (2007): Bürgerkommune und Local Governance. In: Schwalb, L. and Walk, H. (Ed.): Local Governance – mehr Transparenz durch Bürgernähe? Wiesbaden, 231–50.

Ibert, O. (2011): Dynamische Geographien der Wissensproduktion – Die Bedeutung physischer und relationaler Distanzen in interaktiven Lernprozessen. In: Ibert, O. and Kujath, H.J. (Ed.): Räumer der Wissensarbeit. Zur Funktion von Nähe und Distanz in der Wissensökonomie. VS Verlag. Wiesbaden.

Kersten, J., Neu, C. and Vogel, B. (2017): Das Soziale-Orte-Konzept. Ein Beitrag zur Politik des sozialen Zusammenhalts. In: Umwelt und Planungsrecht 2/2017, 50–6.

Klie, T. (2019): Demokratische Integration. Strukturbedingungen von Regionen und ihr Einfluss auf Wahlbeteiligung und freiwilliges Engagement. In: Aus Politik und Zeitgeschichte, 46/2019, S.41–8.

Kroismayr, S., Hirzer, P. and Bittner, M. (2016): Schulschließungen im ländlichen Raum. Beginn oder Endpunkt einer demografischen, wirtschaftlichen und sozialen Abwärtsspirale? In: Egger, R. and Posch, A. (Ed.): Lebensentwürfe im ländlichen Raum. Wiesbaden, 139–65.

Kuder, T. (2011): Governance und Dialog in der Integrierten Stadtentwicklung. In: vhw (Ed.): Dialog: Zur Stärkung lokaler Demokratie. Berlin, 53–60 (= vhw Schriftenreihe 3).

Kühn, M. (2015): Peripheralization: Theoretical Concepts Explaining Socio-Spatial Inequalities. In: European Planning Studies 23, 367–78.

Kühn, M., Bernt, M. and Colini, L. (2017): Power, Politics and Peripheralization: Two Eastern German Cities. In: European Urban and Regional Studies 24(3), 258–73.

Kühn, M. and Weck, S. (2013): Peripherisierung – ein Erklärungsansatz zur Entstehung von Peripherien. In: Bernt, M. and Liebmann, H. (Ed.): Peripherisierung, Stigmatisierung, Abhängigkeit? Deutsche Mittelstädte und ihr Umgang mit Peripherisierungsprozessen. Wiesbaden, 24–46.

Kummel, O. and Nadler, R. (2018): Die Grenzen des Ehrenamts. In: Informationen zur Raumentwicklung 6/18, 102–11.

Lang, T. (2015): Socio-Economic and Political Responses to Regional Polarisation and Socio-Spatial Peripheralisation in Central and Eastern Europe: A Research Agenda. In: Hungarian Geographical Bulletin 64, 171–85.

Lang, T. and Görmar, F. (Ed.) (2018): Regional and Local Development in Times of Polarisation. Re-Thinking Spatial Policies in Europe. Berlin, Heidelberg and New York (= New Geographies of Europe).

Leipzig Charta (2007): Leipzig Charta zur nachhaltigen europäischen Stadt. Angenommen anlässlich des Informellen Ministertreffens zur Stadtentwicklung und zum territorialen Zusammenhalt in Leipzig am 24./25. Mai 2007. Online: https://www.bmu.de/fileadmin/Daten_BMU/Download_PDF/Nationale_Stadtentwicklung/leipzig_charta_de_bf.pdf.

Lentz, S. (2014): Außeruniversitäre Forschung in Deutschland. In: Nationalatlas aktuell 8(2). Leipzig.

Maaß, A. (2018): (Aktivierende) Stadtplanung und Governance. In: Informationen zur Raumentwicklung 6/18, 112–17.

Mackrodt, U. (2014): Bürgerbeteiligung im urbanen öffentlichen Raum: Reflexionen über eine Neuerung in der Beteiligungspraxis. In: Küpper, P., Levin-Keitel, M., Maus, F., Müller, P., Reimann, S., Sondermann, M., Stock, K. and Wiegand, T. (Ed.): Raumentwicklung 3.0 – Gemeinsam die Zukunft der räumlichen Planung. Hannover, 235–45.

Matthiesen, U. (2013): Raumpioniere und ihre Möglichkeitsräume. In: Faber, K. and Oswalt, P. (Ed.): Raumpioniere in ländlichen Regionen. Neue Wege der Daseinsvorsorge. Dessau, 153–60 (= Edition Bauhaus 35).

Meng, R. (2012): Verborgener Wandel: Innovationsdynamik in ländlichen Räumen Deutschlands – Theorie und Empirie. Mannheim.

Moulaert, F. and Sekia, F. (2003): Territorial Innovation Models: A Critical Survey. In: Regional Studies 37(3), 289–302.

Myrdal, G. (1957): Economic Theory and Underdeveloped Regions. London: Gerald Duckworth.

Nadler, R. (2017): The Elephant in the Room. Über das Verhältnis von demographischem Wandel, Daseinsvorsorge und zivilgesellschaftlichem Engagement in Deutschland. In: Raumforschung und Raumordnung 75(6), 499–512.

Naumann, M. and Reichert-Schick, A. (2012): Infrastrukturelle Peripherisierung: Das Beispiel Uecker-Randow (Deutschland). In: disP. The Planning Review 48(1), 27–45.

Neu, C. (2006): Territoriale Ungleichheit – eine Erkundung. In: Aus Politik und Zeitgeschichte 37, 8–15.

Porsche, L., Steinführer, A. and Sondermann, M. (Ed.) (2019): Kleinstadtforschung in Deutschland – Stand, Perspektiven und Empfehlungen. Arbeitsberichte der ARL 28. Hannover.

Ries, E.J. (2019): Mittelstädte als Stabilisatoren ländlich-peripherer Räume. In: Arbeitspapiere zur Regionalentwicklung. Elektronische Schriftenreihe des Lehrstuhls Regionalentwicklung und Raumordnung. Band 20. Kaiserslautern. Online: https://regionalentwicklung-raumordnung.de/wp-content/uploads/2019/04/AzR_Band20_Ries.pdf.

Ročak, M. (2019): Perspectives of Civil Society on Governance of Urban Shrinkage: The Cases of Heerlen (Netherlands) and Blaenau Gwent (Wales) Compared. In: European Planning Studies 27(4), 699–721.

Rohland, P. and Kuder, T. (2011): Stärkung lokaler Demokratie durch bürgerorientierte integrierte Stadtentwicklung. In: vhw (Ed.): Dialog: Zur Stärkung lokaler Demokratie. Berlin, 3–7 (= vhw Schriftenreihe 3).

Schlappa, H. (2017): Co-Producing the Cities of Tomorrow: Fostering Collaborative Action to Tackle Decline in Europe's Shrinking Cities. In: European Urban and Regional Studies 24(2), 162–74.

Schuppert, G.F. (2011): Bürgerdialog, lokale Demokratie und Urban Governance aus kommunikationstheoretischer Perspektive. In: vhw (Ed.): Dialog: Zur Stärkung lokaler Demokratie. Berlin, 43–53 (= vhw Schriftenreihe 3).

Schwalb, L. and Walk, H. (2007): Blackbox Governance – Lokales Engagement im Aufwind? In: Schwalb, L. and Walk, H. (Ed.): Local Governance – mehr Transparenz durch Bürgernähe? Wiesbaden, 7–20.

Schwarzenberg, T.; Miggelbrink, J.; Meyer, F. (2017): 'Nicht für Erich Honecker früher oder heute für Angela Merkel, sondern für sich selber' – Eine Fallstudie zu ehrenamtlichen Engagementformen im ländlichen Raum zwischen gesellschaftspolitischen Ansprüchen und individuellen Wahrnehmungen. In: Raumforschung und Raumordnung, 75(6), 563–86.

Shearmur, R. (2012): Are Cities the Font of Innovation? A Critical Review of the Literature on Cities and Innovation. In: Cities 29(2), s9–18.

Solow, R.M. (1956): A Contribution to the Theory of Economic Growth. In: The Quarterly Journal of Economics 70(1), 65–94.

Stein, A. and Kujath, H.-J. (2013): Peripherisierte Städte im Wettbewerb der Wissensgesellschaft. In: Bernt, M. and Liebmann, H. (Ed.): Peripherisierung, Stigmatisierung, Abhängigkeit? Deutsche Mittelstädte und ihr Umgang mit Peripherisierungsprozessen. Wiesbaden, 148–77.

van der Panne, G. (2004): Agglomeration Externalities: Marshall versus Jacobs. In: Journal of Evolutionary Economics 14(5), 593–604.

Vonnahme, L. and Lang, T. (2017): Rethinking Territorial Innovation: World Market Leaders outside of Agglomerations. Leipzig (= Working paper series des SFB 1199 an der Universität Leipzig 6).

Vonnahme, L., Graffenberger, M., Görmar, F., and Lang, T. (2018): Kaum beachtet, gemeinsam stark. Versteckte Potenziale von Kleinstädten mit Hidden Champions. In: Informationen zur Raumentwicklung, 6, 38–49.

Vortkamp, W. (2007): Gesellschaftliche Integration und Vertrauensbildung durch Partizipation in Vereinen – Ergebnisse einer empirischen Untersuchung in Ostdeutschland. In: Schwalb, L. and Walk, H. (Ed.): Local Governance – mehr Transparenz durch Bürgernähe? Wiesbaden, 131–66.

Walde, A. (2019): Schulpolitik in Städten mit Schülerrückgang. Eine Governance-Analyse am Beispiel von Leipzig und Timişoara. Wiesbaden.

Walk, H. (2014): Veränderungen lokaler Governance. In: Zimmer, E. and Simsa, R. (Ed.): Forschung zu Zivilgesellschaft, NPOs und Engagement. Quo vadis. Wiesbaden, 197–207.

Wegner, M. and Klie, T. (2018): Verantwortung und Identität vor Ort. In: Klie, T and Klie, A.W. (Ed.): Engagement und Zivilgesellschaft. Expertisen und Debatten zum Zweiten Engagementbericht. Wiesbaden, 547–67.

Willett, J. (2019): The Periphery as a Complex Adaptive Assemblage: Local Government and Enhanced Communication to Challenge Peripheralising Narratives. In: ACME – An International Journal for Critical Geographies 18(2), 496–512.

Willett, J. and Lang, T. (2018): Peripheralisation: A Politics of Place, Affect, Perception and Representation. In: Sociologia Ruralis 58(2), 258–75.

# 3. Resolving the urban wellbeing paradox: the role of education and social contact

**Philip S. Morrison**

## 3.1   INTRODUCTION

The term urban paradox has been employed in several different contexts to refer to apparent contradictions: 'The lonely city' is one example (Liang, 2016) as is 'Uncivilized genes: human evolution and the urban paradox' (Milne, 2017). Another version addresses 'social disparities, exclusion and poverty' (OECD, 2010). In this chapter I refer to the urban wellbeing paradox as the tendency of the very largest urban centres in developed countries to return lower wellbeing than the rest of the country.[1] Although subject to considerable discussion in the scholarly and popular press, the reasons for the urban wellbeing paradox remain poorly understood. Very few studies have tried to explain the process, either theoretically or empirically, as opposed to simply describing the phenomenon.[2]

Wellbeing is the experience of health, happiness and prosperity. It includes having good mental health, high life satisfaction and a sense of meaning or purpose. However, social indicators alone do not define quality of life (Diener and Suh, 1997). People react differently to similar circumstances and they evaluate conditions based on their own unique expectations, values and previous experiences (Diener et al., 1999: 277). The attraction of the subjective measure of wellbeing I use below is that people act on the basis of what they perceive (Diener, 1984).

---

[1]   I use the following terms interchangeably: cities, agglomerations, conurbations and metropolitan centres, notwithstanding specialist differences in interpretation.

[2]   Several international reviews have also kept this issue in front of policy makers. See for example: (Albouy, 2008; European Commission, 2013; Lagas et al., 2015; OECD, 2014).

I begin with an idea familiar to regional economists – that spatial agglomeration increases the returns to skill. Increasing market size permits greater specialization, which induces greater productivity, which in turn gets reflected as higher incomes (Betz et al., 2015; Duranton, 2019; Duranton and Puga, 2004; Tabuchi, 2008; Vives, 2017; Zheng, 2016). In this chapter I show that while the proportion of skilled/educated workers rises with urban size, their minority status means they only reduce rather than reverse the lower wellbeing returned by the absolutely larger number of less skilled workers. Recognising this heterogeneity largely resolves the urban wellbeing paradox.[3]

I support this argument with three less familiar ideas. The first is the positive effect of education on social engagement (Fischer, 1982), the second is the role of cities in promoting social interaction (Wellman, 1999), and the third is the spatial clustering of the educated within large cities (Berry and Glaeser, 2005). I provide empirical support by applying a multivariate ordinary least squares (OLS) model to the 2012 European Social Survey.

I begin by reviewing the literature documenting the negative association between metropolitan size and subjective wellbeing in developed economies. An alternative conceptual framework is outlined in Section 3.3, which argues that the lower wellbeing found in large cities is a function of the three-way interaction between social engagement, education and city residence. Section 3.4 introduces the variables from the 2012 European Social Survey. Section 3.5 presents the multivariate model and the main empirical estimates are reported in Section 3.6, followed by interaction results in Section 3.7. Conclusions are presented in Section 3.8. An appendix to the chapter offers several robustness checks based on the distinction between paid and unpaid work and the influence of monetary and subjective or felt income.

## 3.2    URBAN AGGLOMERATION AND WELLBEING

Designed to make us all richer, the city has more than demonstrated its case (Glaeser, 2011). As the World Bank's impressive assembly of evidence reminded us, the route to higher per capita incomes rests heavily on urbanisation (The World Bank, 2009). Despite many examples of the diseconomies of agglomeration (Campos, 2016), people in the developing world continue to flock to the megacity (those over 10 million population), which governments view as key instruments in their quest for economic growth (United Nations,

---

[3]    Certain features of this argument, originally presented at the 16th annual meeting of the International Society for Quality-of-Life Studies (ISQOLS) conference in Hong Kong, 14–16 June 2018, have now been recognised and applied by others in the case of Oslo by Carlsen and Leknes (2022a, 2022b) and across Europe by Lenzi and Perucca (2022).

2016). Given the existing and anticipated material benefits of the conurbation, it is therefore paradoxical that the average life satisfaction of its residents should sit below those of smaller settlements.[4]

Almost as soon as questions on the life satisfaction (and happiness) of individuals were added to large sample surveys of labour, economists familiar with the study of job satisfaction began exploring life satisfaction – see for example Layard (1980) and Clark et al. (2006). Their models drew on national data sets, which usually included city size and other attributes of place; however, city size variables were usually included in their wellbeing functions so their contextual effects could be removed – in order to focus on the role played by personal attributes such as income. Meanwhile their disciplinary neighbours, including regional scientists and economic geographers, viewed urban residence and urban size not as something to be removed but as a feature intrinsic to understanding subjective wellbeing.

The size of cities began to receive attention in the wellbeing literature once their lower average levels of subjective wellbeing came to light. Initially, the evidence came from a range of 'new settler' countries including the USA (Berry and Okulicz-Kozaryn, 2009, 2011; Glaeser et al., 2016; Valdmanis, 2015), Canada (Helliwell et al., 2019; Lu et al., 2015), Australia (Cummins et al., 2005; Shields and Wooden, 2003), and New Zealand (Morrison, 2007, 2011). This evidence complemented patterns observed in Britain (Ballas, 2010; Ballas and Tranmer, 2012; Smarts, 2012), Ireland (Brereton et al., 2008) and Scotland (Dunlop et al., 2016) as well as continental Europe (Aslam and Corrado, 2012; European Commission, 2013; Lenzi and Perucca, 2016a, 2016c; Piper, 2014; Pittau et al., 2010) and Central and Eastern Europe (Rodriguez-Pose and Maslauskaite, 2012). Several European countries have received particular attention, including Germany (Botzen, 2016), Italy (Lenzi and Perucca, 2019; Loschiavo, 2019) and Romania (Lenzi and Perucca, 2016b).

---

[4]    The point I develop here is quite distinct from the observation made by Edward Glaeser, who says, 'Across countries, reported life satisfaction rises with the share of the population that lives in cities, even when controlling for the countries' income and education' (Glaeser, 2011: 8). Glaeser is addressing the impact of urbanization per se – the fact that the average level of wellbeing of the country rises with the proportion living in cities. In contrast, my focus is on the differences in average wellbeing of those in metropolitan centres compared to the rest of the country. Therefore, there is no contradiction between the two observations; average wellbeing can rise with urbanisation at the same time as the wellbeing gap between metropolitan and nonmetropolitan areas widens (see Figure 3.1).

As an example, the European Commission Flash Eurobarometer Perception Survey interviewed 41 000 people in 79 cities and four urban agglomerations and concluded that,

> The size of the city seems to play an important role regarding life satisfaction, with respondents in cities of over 1 million inhabitants least likely to be satisfied (European Commission, 2013: 14). Among the 28 cities with a level of satisfaction below 90%, they found 14 EU capitals and 9 cities with between 1 and 5 million inhabitants (Ibid p. 20). In Europe at least it seemed as if a 'happiness penalty' had been imposed on the largest cities. (Piper, 2014)[5]

More recently, we have seen increasing attention paid to the lower average subjective wellbeing in several of the largest cities in China (Chen et al., 2015; Dang et al., 2020), some of which have only been published in Chinese (Luo, 2006; Sun et al., 2014). While the phenomena in many parts of the developed world still have to be explored, there appear to be relatively few exceptions to the urban wellbeing paradox.[6]

For many decades, urban size differentials in wellbeing were simply an accepted feature of society. As sociologist Robert Campbell noted, 'City life has suffered a bad reputation among social critics for many years' because '… the anonymity and stress of the large urban centres compared unfavourably with the human neighbourly qualities of the small communities' (Campbell, 1981: 148–9). Few put the issue more clearly than sociologist Claude Fischer, who asked 'Does the likelihood of an individual expressing malaise increase with an increase in the urbanism of his place of residence (indexed by the size of community)?' (Fischer, 1973: 221). After reviewing the survey evidence available at the time, he concluded that, 'What small association there is may not be an urban malaise, but a "great city" malaise' (Ibid: 228), and he went on to speculate that, 'The very largest cities may be too large and may contribute modestly to unhappiness' (Ibid: 234).

Possible reasons have been ventured, not only by sociologists, including Ogburn and Duncan (1964), Simmel (1976) and Wirth (1969), but also by

---

[5]    In a more recent exercise, I sought evidence for the possibility that the negative wellbeing effect of residence in the largest city of three European countries would be more severe for those in the lower quantiles of the city's wellbeing distribution (Morrison, 2021). The results varied over the three case studies (Austria, Czech Republic and Slovenia).

[6]    I am aware of only a few studies which have been unable to identify negative effects of metropolitan living on wellbeing, notably Albouy (2008) and Itaba (2016). The first was based on 'objective' quality of life estimates (in US cities) rather than subjective wellbeing and, while the second study was based on subjective measures of happiness across Japanese cities, it was unable to separately identify the influence of the largest cities, where much lower levels of life satisfaction are typically detected.

urban economists, such as Hoch (1987), Richardson (1973) and Tolly (1974). In one of the few systematic treatments of urban size by an economist, Harry Richardson pointed to two characteristics of very large cities: their higher than average wages and their more extensive negative externalities (Richardson, 1973). Specialisation is a function of the size of the market, as Glaeser and Maré (2001) remind us, and higher incomes reflect the higher productivity that comes with agglomeration. The demand for the skills of the tertiary educated therefore rises with the specialisation of firms, as does the level of human capital (Betz et al., 2015; Vives, 2017). At the same time, their higher wages may also include a compensating payment for the negative externalities and other disutilities of big city life (Richardson, 1973), an argument that was repeated by Hoch (1987) with supporting evidence.

In the early 1970s another economist, George Tolly, was also exploring the implications of the joint presence of higher wages and negative externalities:

> If labour moves in response to externalities making real wages everywhere the same, money wages will reflect differences in externalities between cities. The presence of increasing negative externalities will make externalities greater in larger cities, giving a further reason for higher money wages there. Furthermore, the increasing negative externalities will make the marginal externality greater than the average externality. The full effects of hiring extra resources will not be taken into account in private decisions. A major conclusion is that externalities such as pollution and congestion tend to make large cities too large. (Tolly, 1974: 344)

Buried in these early ideas is the key to resolving the urban wellbeing paradox. The lower average subjective wellbeing expressed by residents of the large urban centres of developed economies is rooted in the joint processes of agglomeration, economic growth and structural transformation that accompany urban growth. The central idea is captured in Figure 3.1, which is based on a study by Easterlin et al., who drew on over 80 countries to show how the average subjective wellbeing of cities rose with economic growth largely as a result of industrial growth and then slowed relative to non-urban areas as similar occupational and educational profiles spread into smaller settlements and rural areas (Easterlin et al., 2011).

Figure 3.1 expresses the stylised fact that, while the average subjective wellbeing in all settlement types grows during the early stages of economic development, the gap between average wellbeing in urban and rural areas diminishes as a result of urbanization's role in the process of growth, phase A. In phase B the relationship then reverses and the average wellbeing begins to decline in the very largest centres absolutely and relatively compared to the

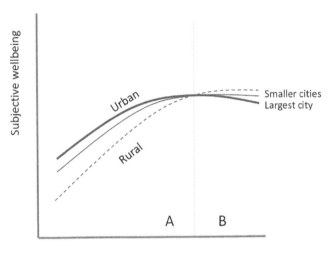

*Source*: Figure 2 in Morrison (2020: 791) and Figure 4.1 in Burger et al. (2020: 68).

*Figure 3.1*    *The urban wellbeing paradox*

average of smaller towns and cities. The generalisation is supported empirically by data from the Gallup World Poll (Burger et al., 2020).[7]

While Figure 3.1 is a convenient representation of the general thesis, it suffers from a major weakness – namely the implicit assumption of a homogeneous population and hence on the fiction of the average resident.[8] In what follows, I argue that a reliance on the average masks the tensions present in the socioeconomic inequalities of the large city, which are a major source of the urban wellbeing paradox. Resolving the urban paradox, therefore, requires

---

[7]   Cities also experience a fall in subjective wellbeing when they are in population decline. Examples include the US (Glaeser et al., 2016) and Central and Southern Italy (Lenzi and Perucca, 2019). This is because urban populations grow primarily by attracting young, educated workers, whose wellbeing is enhanced by metropolitan residence (Carlsen and Leknes, 2021). Any reduced capacity to attract lowers a city's average wellbeing, the more so if educated workers are discouraged.

[8]   A similar point has been made with respect to reported differences in the average wellbeing of countries: 'a country may be in the midst of a major social upheaval, with a large group of dispossessed and disadvantaged individuals, yet this fact is completely hidden by the arithmetical average' (Ovaska and Takashima, 2010: 205).

explicit recognition of the diversity of large centres, their heterogeneity and associated inequalities.

The academy demonstrated quite early on that, past some materially adequate standard of living, further consumption of material goods has less and less influence on our wellbeing.[9] After a certain material standard of living has been reached, our subjective wellbeing depends more on the degree and quality of our social engagement (Helliwell and Putnam, 2004). What has been less appreciated in this shift of attention from the material to the social is the role played by higher education, which, together with its associated affluence, creates opportunities and motivations for deeper and wider social interaction (Buryi and Gilbert, 2014). Apart from its direct income effect, higher education facilitates wellbeing by helping people maintain high-quality social connections with others (Pichler and Wallace, 2009). In addition to their more open and metropolitan worldview, those who have secured a tertiary education are able to accrue more social capital in both private and public networks (Gesthuizen et al., 2008; Pichler and Wallace, 2009; Rodriguez-Pose and Maslauskaite, 2012).[10] As Chen found in a comparative study on four East Asian societies, interpersonal networks and the degree of cosmopolitanism, net of monetary factors, account for a considerable proportion of the association between education and happiness (Chen, 2012).[11]

---

[9]   At root are the negative effects of prioritizing extrinsic values (Kasser and Ryan, 1996).

[10]   As Pichler and Wallace point out, 'social stratification is an important element in understanding social capital both at the country and individual level. They note how upper layers of society have higher levels of social capital, especially through associational networks (formal social capital), although informal contacts are not so clearly stratified by class. Countries with high levels of inequality magnified these differences between classes, giving the upper classes further advantages' (Pichler and Wallace, 2009: 319).

[11]   Not all studies support a positive relationship between education and happiness. For a contrary view see Nikolaev and Rusakov (2016) and Ferrante (2009). One possible reason may be that, 'happiness is more likely to depend on situational relevance abilities' (Veenhoven and Choi, 2012: 7). Another could be supply outgrowing demand, for when tertiary education spreads, so the supply of qualified graduates begins to exceed demand resulting in over education in certain sections of the job market. This can lead to a diminished sense of achievement, leading to the identification of so-called 'frustrated achievers' (Graham and Pettinato, 2002). Evidence from data collected in urban China, for example, points to a declining trend in the average enhancing effect of a college credential on subjective wellbeing as well as a growing heterogeneity in this relationship (Hu, 2015). These market factors may account for the findings of Salim (2008), who found upper-level education not to be significantly associated with life satisfaction. Han also found that satisfaction with the standard of living in China was negatively correlated with education (Han, 2012) and an insignificant association was documented by Salinas-Jimenez et al., (2013).

In addition to enjoying the wider and deeper social networks that specialization brings, tertiary level workers enjoy higher incomes, which enables them to harness the positive features of the large city and offset many of the negative environmental features. Those without a tertiary qualification, however, have less choice as to where to live, who they live next to and the range of activities they can engage in. One of the reasons the tertiary educated are advantaged is that they are more likely to work in the tradeables sector and to access national and international markets in contrast to those without a degree who are more reliant on the smaller, local, nontradeables sector.[12] Many nontertiary educated workers are employed in personal services and, therefore, must work in close physical proximity to their customers, the majority of whom work in the central business districts of large centres. However, the relatively lower wages of those workers means they have to find housing at the other end of the rent gradient, often on the urban periphery (Loschiavo, 2019). The net result can be a much longer commute.

While commuting can be enjoyed in certain circumstances (Ory et al., 2004), it is the negative effects of long commutes on wellbeing that prevail (Koslowsky et al., 1995; Morris et al., 2020). While monetary costs of the commute can often be off-set by lower rents, this may not be possible in the case in other domains such as physical activity, relaxation and social participation (Juster and Stafford, 1991). To the costs of the long commute we should add interpersonal conflict (road rage) as well as social comparison effects (Abou-Zeid and Ben-Akiva, 2011; Abou-Zeid et al., 2012; Chng et al., 2016). Most important from a wellbeing perspective are the restrictions long commutes impose on family time and social interaction (Voydanoff et al., 1988).

Many have also argued that income inequality is negatively associated with wellbeing (Berg and Veenhoven, 2010; Wilkinson and Pickett, 2009; Zagorski et al., 2014), although there remains considerable uncertainty over the nature of that relationship and its pathways (Katic and Ingram, 2017; Ngamaba et al., 2018; Reyes-Garcia et al., 2019; Senik, 2009). The argument is relevant for this chapter because social inequalities rise with city size (Behrens and

---

[12] The relationship between wellbeing and employment in the tradeable and nontradeable sectors has yet to receive much attention by the academy. However, recent work in New Zealand suggests workers in the tradeable sector get paid about $3700 more on average than workers in the nontradeable sector. Women account for 40 per cent of the tradeable sector workforce, compared to 57 of the nontradeable sector and 21 per cent of tradeable sector workers are employed in firms with less than 10 employees, compared to 18 per cent for the nontradeable sector (NZIER, 2018: i). The distinction between employment in the tradeables and nontradeables sectors may be viewed as an extension of the positive relationship between the size of the workers' labour catchment and their wage, as outlined in Morrison (2005) and Martin and Morrison (2003).

Robert-Nicoud, 2014; Bolton, 1992; Glaeser et al., 2009) and its physical form (Lee et al., 2018), as well as the greater tendency of the skilled to live among other skilled people (Garcia-Lopez and Moreno-Monroy, 2018; Kawachi, 2002; Ross et al., 2001).[13]

In summary, there is reason to believe, conceptually and empirically, that the wellbeing benefits that accrue to the educated minority as a result of living in large metropolitan centres are outweighed numerically by the less positive effects experienced by the much larger number without tertiary education. The numerical dominance of the latter lowers the average wellbeing of large cities.[14]

## 3.3    CONCEPTUAL FRAMEWORK

The importance of social engagement for wellbeing is undeniable, as the extensive literature on loneliness demonstrates (Cacioppo and Patrick, 2008; Fu et al., 2017; Morrison and Smith, 2018; Oshio and Kan, 2019).[15] The relationship between wellbeing and the frequency of social contact is nonlinear; the first few social contacts increase wellbeing considerably, with successive contacts yielding diminishing returns, as suggested in Figure 3.2.

Despite its importance in accounting for wellbeing, the role of social engagement has been largely overlooked in the urban wellbeing paradox literature. For example, in their recent paper, Lenzi and Perucca only consider education, occupation and income (Lenzi and Perucca, 2022), as do two recent papers showing, respectively, how urban scale interacts with education and

---

[13]    Greater individual inequality in more segregated areas is mainly due to positive impacts of segregation for more advantaged groups, rather than negative impacts for the most disadvantaged (Gordon and Monastiriotis, 2006: 213) because the extent to which households concentrate in specific neighbourhoods tends to increase with their income levels (OECD, 2018: 11). There is evidence that large cities promote stronger comparison effects (Cheung and Lucas, 2016) and that this may even be related to assortative mating (Maré and Schwartz, 2006) and lower social cohesion (Kawachi et al., 1997). The causation may even be two-way, since inequality may affect urban growth itself (Escurra, 2007; Oshi and Kesebir, 2015; Royuela et al., 2014).

[14]    More specifically, respective average wellbeing scores of the tertiary and nontertiary groups (w) times their share of the population (subscript $_T$ = tertiary and $_N$ = nontertiary) determines the average level of wellbeing: $\bar{w} = (\bar{w}_T \times n_T) + (\bar{w}_N \times n_N)$. I make no attempt to consider possible trade-offs here; for example, the way one might reduce social connection in order to clear time for gaining higher qualifications. For a discussion of the role of trade-offs in subjective wellbeing theory, see Ormel et al. (1999).

[15]    The relationship is well documented in the wellbeing literature (Pichler, 2006; Powdthavee, 2008; Helliwell and Barrington-Leigh, 2010; Leung et al., 2011). There is now a growing recognition of the importance of social contact within economics, where the phenomenon has been recast as a relational good (Uhlaner, 1989) and (Becchetti et al., 2008).

*Figure 3.2      Wellbeing as a function of social contact*

income in accounting for life satisfaction (Carlsen and Leknes, 2022b) and why unhappy cities continue to receive migrants (Carlsen and Leknes, 2022a). The role of social engagement is also largely absent from an earlier inquiry into the relationship between education and city size (Migheli, 2016).

The lack of contemporary attention given to social engagement in the literature on the urban wellbeing paradox is somewhat surprising given its well established role in social psychology. For example, well into his 1969 classic, 'The structure of psychological well-being', Norman Bradburn draws our attention to, 'one of the best-established relationships in sociological literature... between socio-economic status (SES) and social participation' (Bradburn, 1969: 123). As an individual moves up the socioeconomic ladder, Bradburn explains, they experience a greater intensity and range of social activities, both formal and informal. Although the wellbeing literature that developed a half century later recognised the fundamental role of social engagement in accounting for wellbeing, this link to socioeconomic status has yet to be incorporated.[16]

---

[16]   Note in passing, however, the way Lee's quantile regression study picks up on the relationship between socioeconomic status and social engagement: '...we observe a *decreasing* importance [*sic*] of physical environments (leisure, green spaces, pedestrian spaces, public transit, public amenities, and community pride) and a increasing

The primary source of variation in socioeconomic status is education, particularly the distinction between those with tertiary (T) and nontertiary (N) qualifications. On the basis of Bradburn's evidence, if the population was partitioned into these two groups, the wellbeing function of the tertiary educated would experience a larger number of social contacts and the average wellbeing returns per contact would be higher. I invoke this relationship in Figure 3.3, which argues that at any given frequency of social contact, individuals with a graduate degree would enjoy a higher level of subjective wellbeing, a > b, *ceteris paribus*.

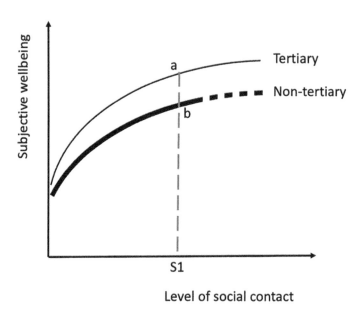

*Figure 3.3        Wellbeing as a function of social contact and education*

Although the proportion of the population holding a degree is rising globally, it is still well below half in developed economies.[17] The tertiary educated are,

importance of socio-relational characteristics of the environment (trust, altruism, and safety) with increasing quantiles of happiness' (Lee et al., 2022: p. 127) – my emphasis. Also, see Ruiu and Ruiu (2018).
    [17]   Glaeser has estimated that, 'As the share of the population with college degrees increases by 10 per cent, per capita gross metropolitan product rises by 22 per cent' (Glaeser, 2011: 27).

therefore, a minority, a feature which I represent stylistically by the relative thickness of the two curves in Figure 3.3. Those without a degree typically experience fewer social contacts and I represent this difference by their transition to a dashed line.

The urban wellbeing paradox thesis also rests on a third distinction, the difference between the metropolitan and nonmetropolitan parts of the country. With their higher incomes, the tertiary educated can enhance their wellbeing in large urban centres by leveraging proximity and increased social contact with each other both at home and at work. Their quest for intergenerational transfers, both of human capital and real estate capital, creates a demand for access to the best schools and an avoidance of relatively disadvantaged groups. The net result is their higher degree of geographical clustering, not only in the main centres, but in neighbourhoods within them (Morrison, 2015). In summary, the educated obtain greater wellbeing benefits from residence in metropolitan centres due to their higher income, enhanced social interaction and spatial clustering. The relationships are depicted schematically in Figure 3.4.

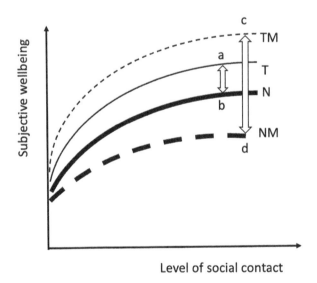

*Note*:     T = tertiary educated, N= nontertiary educated, TM = tertiary in metropoli, NM = nontertiary in metropoli.

Figure 3.4     *Wellbeing as a function of social contact, education and Big City residence*

The argument behind Figure 3.4 is that wellbeing rises at a decreasing rate with social contact, but higher wellbeing returns to any given level (frequency) of social contact are accrued by the tertiary educated (a > b). Metropolitan residence enhances both material and nonmaterial returns to the tertiary educated but reduces the relative wellbeing of the much larger number of nontertiary residents (c > d).

While these three arguments – social contact, education and spatial clustering – have been connected pairwise in previous studies, there have been few attempts to connect all three in order to account for the urban wellbeing paradox. The literature in positive psychology tells us that social contact promotes wellbeing (Diener et al., 1999), the sociological literature shows how education is associated with higher levels of social contact (Fischer, 1982) and human geographers have drawn attention to the spatial sorting and segregation characteristics of the large city (Bayer and McMillan, 2012; Clark and Morrison, 2012). A multidisciplinary approach is, therefore, required and the propositions in Figure 3.2 will now be tested using returns from the European Social Survey.

## 3.4    EUROPEAN SOCIAL SURVEY

The European Social Survey (ESS) is an academically driven multicountry survey, which has been administered in over 30 countries to date.[18] The 2012 survey (ESS6) has been selected because it carries the four variables of interest: subjective wellbeing, education, social engagement and settlement size, as well as a range of demographic attributes in 20 countries: Austria, Belgium, Czech Republic, Denmark, Estonia, Finland, France, Germany, Hungary, Ireland, Lithuania, Netherlands, Norway, Poland, Portugal, Slovenia, Spain, Sweden, Switzerland and the United Kingdom.[19]

---

[18]   The sixth round of the ESS6 survey used here was fielded in 2011 and covers 21 countries (as listed below, excluding Israel). The survey involved strict random probability sampling, a minimum target response rate of 70 per cent and rigorous translation protocols. Unlike many other surveys, which rely on postal or telephone interviews, the ESS is based on hour-long face-to-face interviews, which is especially important in gathering measures of social contact. Details on the ESS6 (2012) may be found in https://www.europeansocialsurvey.org/search?q=travel%20to%20work& rows=25&fq=round_facet:%22ESS6%202012%22 and for latter surveys in the series see https://www.europeansocialsurvey.org. .For a copy of the questionnaire in English see: https://www.europeansocialsurvey.org/docs/round6/fieldwork/ireland/ESS6_main _and_supplementary_questionnaire_IE.pdf.

[19]   For a validation of this 2012 European Social Survey's measurement of wellbeing in seventeen of the European countries, see Charalampi et al. (2020).

Wellbeing is captured by the following standard life satisfaction question (E31, Card 36, p. 50):[20] *All things considered, how satisfied are you with how your life has turned out so far?* Possible answers range from '*Extremely dissatisfied (0)*' to '*Extremely satisfied (10)*'. The negative or left-skewed distribution in Figure 3.5 is typical of the responses to this question in developed countries.[21]

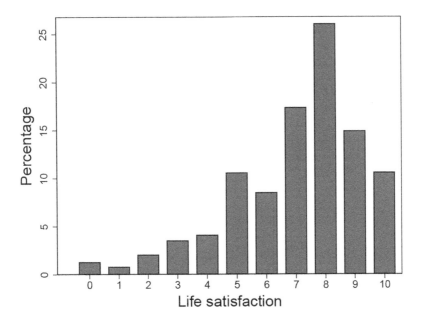

*Notes*:   Life satisfaction: 0 = Extremely Dissatisfied through 11 = Extremely Satisfied. Mean 7.07, median 8, SD 2.17, N=37,517. Missing 106 (0.28 per cent).
*Source*:   European Social Survey, 2012.

*Figure 3.5*   *The distribution of life satisfaction – 20 countries in Europe, 2012*

---

[20]   While there is strong support for this single variable as a valid proxy for wellbeing (Diener et al., 2002) others have pointed to its limitations as a measure of psychological wellbeing (Ryff and Keyes, 1995). I discuss this debate in the context of a typology of wellbeing in (Morrison, 2020).
[21]   For comparisons based on the two other social engagement questions over a wide range of countries, see Chapter 2 in Helliwell et al. (2016).

The main advantage of the 2012 European Social Survey over competing surveys is the presence of the following question on social engagement (C2, CARD 18 p. 12):[22] *Using this card, how often do you meet socially with friends, relatives or work colleagues? Never (01) Less than once a month (02) Once a month (03) Several times a month (04) Once a week (05) Several times a week (06) Every day (07) (Don't know).* 'Meet socially' implies meeting by choice rather than for reasons of either work or duty. It also implies face-to-face contact, which means that these ties are local, or at least that respondents can travel easily to other locations to meet. For both labelling and the generation of means I have converted the categorical responses to a frequency of meeting per month so that meeting every day becomes 30, several times a week becomes 12, once a week is 4, several times a month is 3, once a month is 1, less than once a month is 0.5 and no social meeting is 0.

When it comes to education, respondents were asked (F15, CARD 52, p. 39): *What is the highest level of education you have successfully completed?* Participants are presented with a country-specific card. The first five categories into which country-specific educational qualifications are grouped are 'less than lower secondary', 'lower secondary', 'lower and upper tier secondary' and 'advanced vocational' and I refer to these as non-tertiary qualifications. Those with qualifications labelled 'tertiary' include BA level, and higher tertiary, MA and above, which together make up about 22 per cent of the sample.

As in previous rounds, the 2012 survey relied on the respondent to select from a list of settlement types in which they live (F14, CARD 51, p. 38): *Which phrase on this card best describes the area where you live? A big city 1, The suburbs or outskirts of a big city 2, A town or a small city 3, A country village 4, A farm or home in the countryside 5 (Don't know).*[23] It is on the basis

---

[22]　Remarkably similar results also hold if one uses C3 or C4. The C3 CARD 19 reads: *How many people, if any, are there with whom you can discuss intimate and personal matters?* ['Intimate' implies relationships involving sex or family matters; 'personal' could include work or occupational issues as well]. *Choose your answer from this card. None 00–10 or more 06 (Don't know) 88* (page 13 questionnaire). The second is C4 CARD 20, which reads *Compared to other people of your age, how often would you say you take part in social activities?* [Events/encounters with other people, by choice and for enjoyment rather than for reasons of work or duty.] *Please use this card. Much less than most 1 Less than most 2 About the same 3 More than most 4 Much more than most 5 (Don't know) 8* (page 14 questionnaire).

[23]　This question is a subjective indication of the kind of environment the respondent considers they live in and as such has an ill-defined geographical footprint. For a recent attempt to assess the correlation between subjective and objective classification of urban and rural areas, see Dijkstra and Papadimitriou (2020). Their method is called 'Degree of urbanisation' and uses three classes to capture the urban-rural continuum: 1) cities, 2) towns and semi-dense areas and 3) rural areas. Their results are based on 115 countries covered by the Gallup World Poll where face-to-face interviews were used,

of these European Social Survey categories that I use the term Big City when referring to urban agglomeration. At the same time, most Europeans live in medium to small cities many of which have relatively high levels of accessibility to large cities.[24] Nearly a third live in small cities or towns (32.9 per cent), over a quarter in villages (29.23 per cent) and those living in the country make up less than ten per cent (6.64 per cent). Over the full sample of over 37 thousand responses, 19.2 per cent said they live in a Big City and a further 11.8 per cent live in its suburbs.

The variation in wellbeing across individuals is usually estimated after controlling for a set of largely exogenous characteristics, such as gender, age, country of birth and country of residence, as listed in Table 3.1.[25] Three slightly less exogenous characteristics also have an influence on the respondent's wellbeing: marital status, self-assessed physical health and the person's sense of personal security (Jabareen et al., 2017).

The ESS6 survey includes two questions on physical health, the first being the respondent's rating of their perceived mental and physical health (C7 and C8). Both are correlated with subjective wellbeing as well as sharing socioeconomic status in common. In order not to conflate the influence of the two, I only use the following more objective question (C8, p. 12): *Are you hampered in your daily activities in any way by any longstanding illness, or disability, infirmity or mental health problem? Yes, a lot (1), Yes, to some extent (2) and No (3). Don't Know.* Personal security is captured in this survey by the question (C6 p. 13): *How safe do you – or would you – feel walking alone in this area after dark? Do – or would – you feel: Very safe(1) safe(2), unsafe (3), or very unsafe(4).*

From Table 3.1 we learn that respondents return an average score of just over 7 on the 0 to 10 life satisfaction scale and experience an average of 8.8 social contacts per month, just over two a week. Over one fifth hold

---

and reveals that 80 per cent of the people who say they live in a large city fell within the urban classification. Of the people who say they live in rural areas or on a farm, 75 per cent were classified as in a rural area by the Degree of Urbanisation, see their Figure A1, P. 148, and for a related discussion involving these urban definitions, see Morrison (2021) Appendix 1.

[24]  The expansion of urban areas not only incorporates surrounding rural areas but brings more distant settlements within commuting distance allowing many to 'borrow' their much larger size (Alonso, 1973; Burger et al., 2015).

[25]  I also considered adding the body mass index (bmi), which is also available for this survey, but it is subject to a high proportion of missing values on both numerator and denominator, $kg/m^2$. I have also avoided including variables such as 'own mental health' given the possibility of common method bias. The same argument applies to another variable on the file, loneliness, which has a strong negative relationship with social contact.

*Table 3.1*        *The main variables. Selected statistics – 20 countries in Europe, 2012*

| Variable | Number of Categories | Categories | Mean | S.D. |
|---|---|---|---|---|
| Life satisfaction | 11 | (0) Extremely dissatisfied…, (10) Extremely satisfied. See Figure 3.3. | 7.07 | 2.17 |
| Social contact | 7 | (0) Never, (0.5) Less than once a month, (1) Once a month, (3) Several times a week, (4) Once a week, (12) Several times a week, (30) Every day. | 8.80 | 9.38 |
| Education | 2 | (1) Bachelor's degree and over (0) Less than Bachelor's degree | 0.22 | 0.42 |
| Settlement | 2 | (1) Big city (0) Other settlements | 0.19 | 0.39 |
| Gender | 2 | (1) Male (0) Female | 0.47 | 0.50 |
| Age | | Continuous. Min (14) Max (100) | 49.30 | 18.62 |
| Born in country | 2 | (1) Yes (0) No | 0.90 | 0.30 |
| Marital status | 2 | (1) Legally married or civil union (0) Other | 0.50 | 0.50 |
| Health hampered | 2 | (1) Yes a lot and to some extent (0) No | 0.27 | 0.44 |
| Security | 2 | (1) Very safe or Safe (0) Other | 0.79 | 0.41 |
| Country | 20 | Austria, Belgium, Czech Republic, Denmark, Estonia, Finland, France, Germany, Hungary, Ireland, Lithuania, Netherlands, Norway, Poland, Portugal, Slovenia, Spain, Sweden, Switzerland, United Kingdom | | |

*Source*:    European Social Survey, 2012.

a Bachelor's degree or higher and a similar proportion say they live in a Big City (up to a third if the suburbs are included – see appendix). The average age of those in the sample is just under 50 years old and there is a slight majority of females. Despite relative freedom of migration, ninety per cent of Europeans still live in their country of birth. Almost half say they are married or in civil union. Slightly over 27 per cent report they are physically hampered to some degree in their daily life and almost 80 per cent feel safe in their city after dark.

Meeting frequency is highest in the suburbs of the Big City, 9.2 per month, followed by those living in the country (8.9), the Big City and small city and town (8.8). Contrary to folklore, the average number of social contacts (meetings) per month is lowest in the 'village' category (8.6).[26] Despite their less

---

[26]   Similar findings have been reported from the Gallup World Poll: 'Despite the image of rural life being more closely knit, fewer people in rural areas than in cities say they have relatives or friends they can count on to help them when they are in trouble… More city dwellers feel they can rely on family or friends for help, meet people, and

frequent social contact, average life satisfaction is highest in the countryside at 7.57, falls to 7.28 in the suburbs of a Big City, and to 7.14 in the village, 6.95 in small city and towns and is lowest at 6.88 in the Big City.[27]

The distribution of the life satisfaction variable also varies by settlement type: the least negatively skewed are those who live in the country and the most negative skewed are those who live in the Big Cities, the later result being consistent with the higher inequality in larger centres. There are also marked differences in average life satisfaction across the 20 countries in the sample, ranging from a low of 5.80 per cent in Portugal to a high of 8.36 per cent in Denmark.[28]

In summary, the 2012 European Social Survey opens a window on those patterns of social contact that have an important influence on people's wellbeing as well as offering the necessary arguments and controls. By covering 20 countries and a representative sample of each, the ESS6 survey allows each of the hypotheses advanced above to be tested empirically.

## 3.5    THE MODEL

I test for the three main effects set out in Section 3.3: that subjective wellbeing rises with social contact, H1, with tertiary education, H2, and falls with residence in the Big City, H3. These are followed by three further hypotheses about their pairwise interactions: that the wellbeing of the tertiary educated is subject to more rapidly rising returns to social contact, H4, and that the relative wellbeing of the tertiary educated is enhanced by residence in the Big City, H5. Of particular relevance to the urban wellbeing paradox is the hypothesis of a three-way interaction, H6: the assertion that wellbeing of the tertiary

---

make friends than people living in rural areas' (Dijkstra and Papadimitriou, 2020: 149). 'The difference between cities and rural areas for the share of people satisfied with the opportunities to meet people and make friends is biggest in high-income countries, in which 79 per cent of the people living in cities are satisfied compared to 68 per cent in rural areas. Towns and semi-dense areas score almost as well as cities in all the four income groups' (Ibid). Note, however, that only 11 of the 115 countries in the Dijkstra and Papadimitrious sample are developed economies.

[27]    . A more sophisticated way of realising these differences is to regress life satisfaction against the settlement types while controlling for the suite of personal characteristics listed in Table 3.1. The predicted margins from this controlled regression are 6.96 compared to the uncontrolled average of 6.88. Controls lower the village mean from 7.14 to 7.08 and countryside means from 7.57 to 7.5 but induce few other changes. The personal characteristics of residents therefore appear to have only a limited influence on the settlement effect.

[28]    Geographic variations in subjective wellbeing are regularly summarized in the World Happiness Reports (Helliwell et al., 2012, 2013, 2015). Only in Chapter 4 of the 2020 edition have rural-urban differences been addressed (Helliwell et al., 2020).

educated will rise more rapidly as a result of social interaction and residence in the Big City.[29]

The model without the interactions is as follows and includes adjusting for spatial clustering at the country level.[30]

$$W_{ijk} = \alpha_o + \beta C_{ijk} + \gamma T_{ijk} + \varsigma B_{ijk} + \delta X_{ijk} + \lambda N_{ijk} + \varepsilon_{ijk} \qquad (3.1)$$

My measure of subjective wellbeing is the standard 'satisfaction with life' question as reported by the ith person living in the jth sized settlement in the kth country, $W_{ijk}$. Social engagement is measured by the number of social contacts reported per month, $C_{ijk}$. The level of education is captured by the binary variable $T_{ijk}$, which equals 1 if the respondent holds a tertiary qualification and 0 otherwise. The third main argument is agglomeration, residence in the Big City, $B_{ijk}$, which equals 1 if the respondent says they live in a Big City and 0 otherwise. A suite of personal attributes make up the vector $X_{ijk}$ and the vector $N_{ijk}$ identifies each country of residence.

The first hypothesis, H1, was that subjective wellbeing would rise at a diminishing rate with the level of social contact ($\beta > 0$), as expressed graphically as Figure 3.2. The second hypothesis, suggested that those holding a tertiary degree would not only report higher life satisfaction but respond more positively to social contact ($\gamma > 0$), as depicted in Figure 3.3. The third hypothesis, drawn as Figure 3.4, was that life satisfaction would reflect a three-way interaction between education, social contact *and* metropolitan residence.

---

[29]  Robustness checks in the appendix to this chapter present the results of four additional hypotheses: that residence in the suburbs of the city would not reduce the negative effect of the metropolis on average wellbeing, H7; that the positive association between tertiary education, social contact and residence in the Big City will be more keenly felt by those in paid work, H8, and that the same three-way relationships will hold for those in the top as well as the bottom household income distribution H9; and will not vary with perceived ability to cope on existing incomes, H10.

[30]  I follow the convention in wellbeing research of treating life satisfaction as a continuous variable even though it is ordinal (Helliwell and Putnam, 2004). Methodological justifications include Ferrer-i-Carbonell and Frijters (2004) and Kristoffersen (2010). While rarely a problem in the study of life satisfaction, the above practice ignores the possibility that the dependent variable is bounded, and that marginal effects cannot be constant, which can potentially lead to predictions outside the admissible range (Studer and Winkelmann, 2016: 2).

## 3.6 ESTIMATION

A separate column in the estimates Table 3.2 is devoted to testing the hypotheses, H1 through H9. The relative impacts of successive levels of social contact are given in column H1. The influence of tertiary education is tested in H2, the metropolitan effect in H3, and their joint presence in H4. The same comparisons are made with social contact present in models H5 through H7; demographic controls are added in model H8 and country controls in model H9.[31]

While this table of coefficients (Table 3.2) tests hypotheses, it does not easily convey the magnitude of the effect combinations of different predictors have on wellbeing, which is why the reporting of effect sizes is advocated (Geerling and Diener, 2020).[32] An alternative approach is to compare the predicted margins graphically. The mean wellbeing predicted by a selection of models is plotted against the frequency of social contact in Figure 3.6.

Estimates from the first of the equations in Table 3.2 (H1) support my expectation that wellbeing would increase at a decreasing rate with social contact (the base is meeting every day of the month).[33] The plot of predicted life satisfaction from this first model is displayed as the H1 curve in Figure 3.6 and shows how the average wellbeing of the European population rises from a mean life satisfaction of only 5, in the case of those reporting 'never' meeting socially over the course of the previous month, up to a maximum life satisfaction of 7.45 among those meeting socially every day. This difference is a substantial increase of nearly two and a half units on the wellbeing scale and confirms the importance attributed to social contact in the literature (Cacioppo and Patrick, 2008; Oshio and Kan, 2019).

Estimates from model H2 in Table 3.2 show that holding a tertiary qualification is associated with a rise in life satisfaction of over half a unit, a result

---

[31]   The variables used in model 1 are parameterized so that the reference person is a female of almost 50 years old living in Austria. She is legally married or in a civil union, is born in her country of residence and is not hampered in daily activities by illness, disability, infirmity or mental problems. She holds a tertiary qualification, does not live in a Big City, feels safe walking home alone in her local area after dark and meets socially with others several times a week.

[32]   Such an approach has been employed, for example, by Feng et al. (2018).

[33]   The social contact coefficient, -2.4, on factor 1 of the social contract variable represents the estimated reduction in wellbeing associated with the difference between no social contacts per month (less than one per cent of the sample) and the base of one contact per day. The second coefficient in the same column, -1.47 (over 8 per cent of the sample) indicates the reduction in units of life satisfaction relative to the base for those meeting socially once every two months (0.5/month). The remaining social contact coefficients are interpreted in the same way.

*Spatial inequalities and wellbeing*

*Table 3.2*     *The effect of social contact, tertiary education and Big City residence on life satisfaction controlling for demographic characteristics – 20 countries in Europe, 2012*

| | (H1) | (H2) | (H3) | (H4) | (H5) | (H6) | (H7) | (H8) | (H9) |
|---|---|---|---|---|---|---|---|---|---|
| **Social contact** | | | | | | | | | |
| 0 | -2.401*** | | | | -2.333*** | -2.414*** | -2.334*** | -1.948*** | -1.618*** |
| | (.302) | | | | (0.298) | (0.293) | (0.29) | (0.278) | (0.13) |
| 0.5 | -1.467*** | | | | -1.454*** | -1.464*** | -1.448*** | -1.248*** | -1.001*** |
| | (0.202) | | | | (0.202) | (0.199) | (0.197) | (0.186) | (0.055) |
| 1 | -0.798*** | | | | -0.799*** | -0.798*** | -0.799*** | -0.703*** | -0.605*** |
| | (0.145) | | | | (0.143) | (0.144) | (0.14) | (0.155) | (0.065) |
| 3 | -0.363*** | | | | -0.383*** | -0.363*** | -0.384*** | -0.348** | -0.365*** |
| | (0.126) | | | | (0.124) | (0.126) | (0.123) | (0.143) | (0.048) |
| 4 | -0.259* | | | | -0.274** | -0.263* | -0.278** | -0.235 | -0.276*** |
| | (0.134) | | | | (0.13) | (0.134) | (0.129) | (0.15) | (0.055) |
| 12 | 0.029 | | | | 0.004 | 0.03 | 0.004 | 0.03 | -0.11*** |
| | (0.113) | | | | (0.108) | (0.113) | (0.108) | (0.12) | (0.037) |
| | | | | | | | | | |
| Tertiary | | 0.62*** | | 0.659*** | 0.538*** | | 0.575*** | 0.489*** | 0.403*** |
| | | (0.082) | | (0.082) | (0.072) | | (0.072) | (0.064) | (0.063) |
| Big City | | | -0.244*** | -0.331*** | | -0.238** | -0.313*** | -0.202** | -0.043 |
| | | | (0.075) | (0.072) | | (0.086) | (0.082) | (0.076) | (0.086) |
| Male | | | | | | | | -0.079** | -0.11*** |
| | | | | | | | | (0.036) | (0.029) |
| Age | | | | | | | | -0.079*** | -0.076*** |
| | | | | | | | | (0.008) | (0.009) |
| Age$^2$ | | | | | | | | 0.001*** | 0.001*** |
| | | | | | | | | (0) | (0) |
| | | | | | | | | | |
| Born in country | | | | | | | | 0.058 | 0.215*** |
| | | | | | | | | (0.094) | (0.046) |
| | | | | | | | | | |
| Legally married | | | | | | | | 0.603*** | 0.592*** |
| | | | | | | | | (0.04) | (0.035) |
| | | | | | | | | | |
| Health hampered | | | | | | | | -0.774*** | -0.836*** |
| | | | | | | | | (0.057) | (0.035) |
| Unsafe after dark | | | | | | | | -0.665*** | -0.489*** |

| | (H1) | (H2) | (H3) | (H4) | (H5) | (H6) | (H7) | (H8) | (H9) |
|---|---|---|---|---|---|---|---|---|---|
| Social contact | | | | | | | | | |
| | | | | | | | | (0.068) | (0.035) |
| Country controls | No | No | No | No | No | No | No | No | Yes |
| cons | 7.442*** | 6.936*** | 7.119*** | 6.99*** | 7.333*** | 7.488*** | 7.385*** | 9.071*** | 9.14*** |
| | (0.201) | (0.175) | (0.165) | (0.174) | (0.206) | (0.202) | (0.205) | (0.169) | (0.199) |
| Observations | 37,399 | 37,280 | 37,429 | 37,212 | 37,170 | 37,314 | 37,102 | 37,014 | 37,014 |
| R-squared | 0.055 | 0.014 | 0.002 | 0.018 | 0.066 | 0.057 | 0.07 | 0.135 | 0.21 |

*Notes*:    Standard errors are in parentheses. *** p<.01, ** p<.05, * p<.1.
*Source*:   European Social Survey, 2012.

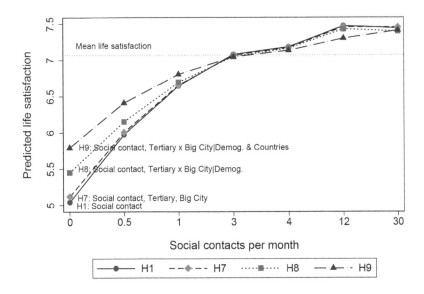

*Source*:   The European Social Survey, 2012.

*Figure 3.6*    *Predicted wellbeing effects of social contact in the presence of successive demographic, education, city and country controls – 20 countries in Europe, 2012*

consistent with most, if not all, of the evidence assembled elsewhere.[34] The estimates in column H3 of Table 3.2 show that, in the absence of any further controls, residence in the Big City lowers the predicted average wellbeing by almost a quarter of a unit on the life satisfaction scale – the predicted mean being 7.12 outside the Big City and 6.8 inside.

The estimated wellbeing (life satisfaction) based on any one of the three main predictors is not expected to be independent of other possible predictors. For example, we see in Table 3.2 that the negative wellbeing effect of living in the Big City in equation H3 (-0.244) is exceeded by a more highly significant negative coefficient (-0.331) in H4 after removing the presence of the tertiary educated. When the influence of social contact is controlled for in H5, the positive wellbeing effect of a tertiary education declines slightly (from 0.66 to 0.54), reflecting the fact that the tertiary educated are more socially engaged than the rest of the population (they enjoy an average of 4.92 social contacts per month compared to only 4.77 among the rest of the population).

When the effect of social contact is removed, we find the negative life satisfaction effect of living in the Big City diminishes slightly, from -0.244 (in H3) to -0.238 (in H6). When I further control for tertiary education in H7, the negative influence of Big City is largely reinstated (especially at low levels of social contact, as the accompanying plot for H7 shows in Figure 3.6).

### 3.6.1    Demographic and Country Controls

Model H8 in Table 3.2 includes the demographic controls listed in Table 3.1. As previous studies of life satisfaction have shown, recognising the way people differ demographically raises the proportion of the variance explained, and in Table 3.2, the coefficient of determination rises from 0.07 in H7 to 0.134 in

---

[34]   Estimates from Central and Eastern Europe show very strong life satisfaction returns to tertiary education even with income present (Rodriguez-Pose and Maslauskaite, 2012, Table 1 page 84). Chen draws on four East Asian countries and, using the happiness question and years of education with demographic controls, shows that individuals who receive more education have more extensive social networks as well as greater involvement with the wider world. However, these conclusions are not universal. For example, the USA study by Buryi and Gilbert uses suicide as their surrogate for wellbeing. They show how the probability of committing suicide rises when an individual acquires additional years of education beyond high school diploma, controlling for sex, race, marital status and age at death. They conclude that he or she will be 0.08 per cent less happy with each year and that a doctorate degree would result in decrease in happiness by 0.14 per cent (Buryi and Gilbert, 2014). Hu encountered similar results showing that in urban China there was a declining trend in the average enhancing effect of a college credential on subjective wellbeing between 2003 and 2010, a period of concerted state-drive higher education expansion (Hu, 2015).

H8. We learn that being male is associated with reduced wellbeing and age adopts its well-known U shape (Blanchflower and Oswald, 2008). Controlling for age (in its quadratic form) results in a slight flattening of the predicted margins, indicating an association between age and social contact. On the other hand, being born in the country of residence has no significant influence on average life satisfaction, although the sign is positive. Being married (+), hampered in daily activities through physical impairment (-) and feeling safe after dark (+) all assume their expected effect on average wellbeing.

After experimenting with successive entries of the demographic variables I found that it was not until I controlled for poor health that the negative effect of low social connection was reduced (from -2.31 to -2.12), confirming that the wellbeing of those experiencing low levels of social connection was worse for those whose daily activities are hampered by poor health. The negative effect of low social contact on wellbeing was also reduced once I controlled for the fear of personal safety, as one might expect. Importantly for the paradox thesis, the negative wellbeing effect of residence in the Big City held in the presence of demographic controls. As expected, the negative influence of living in Big Cities worsened when I controlled for social contact and fell further when I controlled for tertiary education. The net result on the wellbeing margins is depicted as the H8 (short dash) line in Figure 3.6.

Multicountry studies show that, when it comes to wellbeing, geography matters much more than psychology (Clark et al., 2005). In the case of the ESS6 survey, adding country controls almost doubles the proportion of the variance in wellbeing explained by the model. Controlling for the country of residence in model H9 raises the proportion of the variance explained from 13 to 21 per cent. In other words, there is almost as much variance in the wellbeing between countries as there is in the person-based arguments in the model.

Several other changes to the estimates in Table 3.2 occur once we recognise the effect of countries of residence in H9. As the predicted (dash.dot) H9 line in Figure 3.6 shows, controlling for country of residence flattens the estimated wellbeing function, alleviating some of the negative influence of low social contact but decreasing some of the positive effect of high levels of contact. This suggests that individuals whose wellbeing is reduced by their low level of social contact are more likely to be located in some countries than others.

The singular impact on wellbeing of holding a university degree is reduced only slightly when country membership is included in the model. However, country of residence has a greater influence on wellbeing if the respondent lives in a Big City. Although residence in a Big City has a negative effect, there is a marked variation by country in the degree to which this location decision reduces average wellbeing.[35]

In summary, the sequence of models in Table 3.2 and the plots of the corresponding predicted margins of selected models in Figure 3.6, confirm the positive influence of social contact and tertiary education and the negative effect of living in the Big City. While these results are only slightly conditioned by the presence of demographic controls, they are sensitive to country of residence. Against this background I now test the way the interaction between social contact, education and metropolitan residence affects average wellbeing.

## 3.7    INTERACTION EFFECTS

On the basis of the arguments advanced in Figure 3.4, I expected the relationship between wellbeing and social contact to be moderated by level of education and whether one is a graduate living in a metropolitan centre. The degree to which this stylised graphic holds empirically was tested by adding to Equation 1 the three-way interaction between social contact, tertiary education and residence in the Big City $\left( C . T . B \right)_{jk}$. Such an addition subsumes the three two-way interactions $\left( C . T \right)_{ijk}$, $\left( C . B \right)_{ijk}$ and $\left( T . B \right)_{ijk}$. The corresponding ANOVA table (with the demographic controls) is given in Table 3.3.

Of central interest in Table 3.3 is the statistical significance of the three-way effect (F= 8.71, p = 0.045). The predictive margins from the three-way model are plotted in Figure 3.7. The two panels describe the way in which average subjective wellbeing is enhanced by the positive relationship between the level of social interaction, education and residence outside and inside the Big City. While the average wellbeing of the tertiary educated (dashed line) sits above those without a degree (solid line) within the Big Cities (right panel), the difference in their wellbeing enhanced by their higher levels of social contact, as hypothesised.[36]

---

[35]   Residence in the Big City is associated with reduced wellbeing in 15 of the 20 countries in the sample, the five exceptions being Spain, Hungary, Lithuania, Poland and Slovenia. All are lower income countries positioned closer to phase A in Figure 3.1. At the same time, an inspection of the 20 separate country regressions shows that the negative effect of Big City residence weakens the higher the country's average level of wellbeing. It is those European countries with relatively lower levels of average wellbeing in which residence in the Big City has the most marked negative influence: Portugal, Ireland and France. As exceptions, Big City residents in Hungary and Lithuania return a positive effect on wellbeing relative to those living in smaller settlements within their country.

[36]   The smaller share of the tertiary educated in the sample is reflected in the wider confidence intervals (shaded) around the predicted life satisfactions. For visual clarity,

*Table 3.3*        *Three-way analysis of variance. Life satisfaction social*
*contact, Big City residence and tertiary education with*
*demographic controls – 20 countries in Europe, 2012*

| Source | Partial SS | df | MS | F | Prob>F |
|---|---|---|---|---|---|
| Model | 23,431.34 | 34 | 689.16 | 170.20 | 0.000 |
| Social contact | 2,428.15 | 6 | 404.69 | 99.95 | 0.000 |
| Big City | 39.82 | 1 | 39.82 | 9.84 | 0.002 |
| Tertiary | 415.78 | 1 | 415.78 | 415.78 | 0.000 |
| Social contact * Big City | 38.07 | 6 | 6.34 | 6.34 | 0.152 |
| Social contact * Tertiary | 24.28 | 6 | 4.05 | 4.05 | 0.424 |
| Big City * Tertiary | 0.70 | 1 | 0.70 | 0.70 | 0.678 |
| Social contact * Tertiary * Big City | 52.26 | 6 | 8.71 | 8.71 | 0.045 |
| Male | 54.71 | 1 | 54.71 | 54.71 | 0.000 |
| Age | 2427.40 | 1 | 2427.40 | 2427.39 | 0.000 |
| Age * age | 2542.37 | 1 | 2542.37 | 2542.36 | 0.000 |
| Born in country | 11.00 | 1 | 11.00 | 11.00 | 0.099 |
| Married | 2745.02 | 1 | 2745.02 | 2745.02 | 0.000 |
| Health hampered | 3868.24 | 1 | 3868.24 | 3868.24 | 0.000 |
| Unsafe after dark | 2401.01 | 1 | 2401.01 | 2401.01 | 0.000 |
| Residual | 149 730.61 | 36 979 | 4.05 | | |
| Total | 173 161.95 | 37 013 | 4.68 | | |
| Number of obs = | 37 014 | | Adj R-sq | 0.135 | |

*Source*:    European Social Survey, 2012.

In summary, while agglomeration is associated with higher rewards to skill, these rewards are less likely to accrue to those without formal qualifications, a higher proportion of whom work in the nontradeables sector offering face-to-face services, often far from affordable accommodation, which results in longer commutes and reduced opportunities for social contact with family and friends. It is primarily the lower wellbeing of this larger nontertiary population that reduces the average life satisfaction of those living in the large urban centres.

---

the estimates behind the predictions in Figure 3.7 are based on estimates without controlling for clustering within the countries. When clustering is recognised, the confidence bands widen, confining statistically significant differences to those with higher levels of social contact, primarily 12 contacts per month.

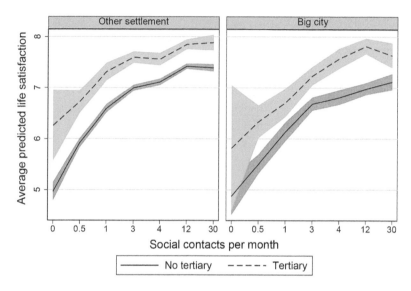

*Source*:    European Social Survey, 2012.

*Figure 3.7*       *Predicted average wellbeing of the tertiary and nontertiary*
                *educated at successive levels of social contact with*
                *demographic and country controls, inside and outside the Big*
                *City – 20 countries in Europe, 2012*

## 3.8    CONCLUSIONS

The urban wellbeing paradox refers to the fact that the average subjective
wellbeing of city dwellers in the largest agglomerations of developed, mainly
Western, countries is typically lower than the rest of the country in spite of the
fact that those same agglomerations are disproportionally responsible for economic growth. In this chapter I have argued that the lower average wellbeing
we witness in metropolitan Europe is largely a reflection of the heterogeneity
of these urban populations and that in order to resolve the urban wellbeing
paradox, it is necessary to drop reliance on the average and the implicit
assumption of a homogeneous population.

Six hypotheses were advanced on the basis of the conceptual framework
introduced in Figure 3.4. Most were supported empirically. My test of H1 confirmed, quite emphatically, that subjective wellbeing rises with social contact.
The ESS6 data also support the second hypothesis: that subjective wellbeing

rises with tertiary education, H2. My third hypothesis was also supported, namely that average wellbeing is lower in the metropolitan centres of Europe (H3).

My fourth hypothesis, H4, argued that the wellbeing of the tertiary educated would rise more rapidly with social contact compared to the nontertiary population, however, none of these tertiary social contact interactions in Table 3.3 were statistically significant. The fifth hypothesis, H5, that the relative wellbeing of the tertiary educated would be enhanced by residence in the Big City, was confirmed.

Of particular relevance to the urban wellbeing paradox was the hypothesis that wellbeing of the tertiary educated would rise more rapidly as a result of social interaction and residence in the Big City, H6. A formal test of the three way interaction was confirmed in Table 3.3 and the corresponding margins plots of Figure 3.7 showed that residence in metropolitan centres increased the wellbeing gap between the tertiary educated and much larger non-tertiary population, thereby lowering the average wellbeing of those in the metropolitan centres.

### 3.8.1 Contributions

This chapter makes three contributions to the literature. The first is to place the urban wellbeing paradox more firmly in a labour market context following the argument initiated by Easterlin et al. (2011). The second is to introduce the importance of social contact as a driver of wellbeing into the urban paradox literature. The third is to give tertiary education a more explicit role in explaining the urban wellbeing paradox by recognising the greater ability of graduates to exploit not only the infrastructural advantages of large urban size and density but its potential for generating greater social interaction by enhancing spatial clustering at work and in the community.

### 3.8.2 Limitations

In order to test the urban paradox argument linking education, social engagement and metropolitan residence I have defined each of the key variables in fairly simple terms: social engagement simply as social contact, education as the difference between holding and not holding a degree, and location as residence in a self-defined Big City. Each measure could stand extension, which would allow for more nuanced interpretations. On the social contact variable, for example, it is not simply the number and frequency of social contacts that influence wellbeing but also the warmth and quality of those connections. Similarly, it is quite likely that finer gradations of education and additional divisions in the urban hierarchy would have refined the empirical tests.

A remaining challenge posed is the marked differences countries exhibit when it comes to experiencing the urban wellbeing paradox. While the generalisations based on the European evidence are robust, there remain distinct differences between the countries themselves: differences in the degree to which social contact influences average wellbeing as well as in the nature and degree to which educational differences affect wellbeing and the marginal impact of metropolitan residence on life satisfaction. That the geographical differences persist is a challenge to future researchers.

Finally, despite its comprehensive nature, a single cross-sectional survey such as the ESS6 does not allow the dynamics behind the urban wellbeing paradox to be explored. This is another research frontier, given the fact that the wellbeing paradox arises out of an economic growth trajectory that transforms the labour market industrially and occupationally in ways that largely determine the relative wellbeing of the tertiary educated workers.

## ACKNOWLEDGEMENTS

An initial version of this chapter was presented at the 16th annual meeting of the International Society for Quality-of-Life Studies (ISQOLS), Hong Kong 14–16 June 2018. I wish to thank Peggy Schyns, (Netherlands Institute for Social Research, SCP) and Martijn Burger (the Erasmus Happiness Economics Research Organisation, EHERO) for their helpful comments. Originally prepared for the conference, Figure 3.1 was reproduced in two previous publications, the second edition of the *Handbook of Regional Science* (Morrison, 2020) and in Chapter 4 of the *World Happiness Report 2020* (Burger et al., 2020).

Declarations of interest: none. This research did not receive any specific grant from funding agencies in the public, commercial or not-for-profit sectors.

## REFERENCES

Abou-Zeid, M., and Ben-Akiva, M. (2011). The effect of social comparisons on commute well-being. *Transportation Research Part A: Policy and Practice*, *45*(4), 345–61.

Abou-Zeid, M., Witter, R. A., Bierlaire, M., Kaufmann, V., and Ben-Akiva, M. (2012). Happiness and travel mode switching: findings from a Swiss public transportation experiment. *Transport Policy*, *19*(1), 93–104.

Albouy, D. (2008). Are big cities really bad places to live? Improving quality-of-life estimates across cities *Working Paper* (vol. 14472). National Bureau of Economic Research.

Alonso, W. (1973). Urban zero population growth. *Daedalus*, *102*(4), 191–206.

Aslam, A., and Corrado, L. (2012). The geography of well-being. *Journal of Economic Geography*, *12*(3), 627–49.

Ballas, D. (2010). Geographical modelling of happiness and well-being. In J. Stillwell, P. Norman, C. Thomas and P. Surridge (Eds.), *Spatial and Social Disparities: Understanding Population Trends and Processes, Volume 2: Spatial and Social Disparities,* Vol. 2, 53–66.

Ballas, D., and Tranmer, M. (2012). Happy people or happy places? A multilevel modeling approach to the analysis of happiness and wellbeing. *International Regional Science Review, 35,* 70–102.

Bayer, P., and McMillan, R. (2012). Tiebout sorting and neighbourhood stratification. *Journal of Public Economics, 96*(11–12), 1129–43.

Becchetti, L, Pelloni, A., and Rossetti, F. (2008). Relationship goods, sociability, and happiness. *Kyklos, 61*(3), 343–63.

Behrens, K., and Robert-Nicoud, F. (2014). Survival of the fittest in cites: urbanisation and inequality. *The Economic Journal, 124*(581), 1371–400.

Berg, M., and Veenhoven, R. (2010). Income inequality and happiness in 119 nations. In B. Gerevew (Ed.), *Social Policy and Happiness in Europe* (pp. 174–94). Cheltenham: Edward Elgar.

Berry, B. J. L., and Okulicz-Kozaryn, A. (2009). Dissatisfaction with city life: a new look at some old questions. *Cities, 26,* 117–24.

Berry, B. J. L., and Okulicz-Kozaryn, A. (2011). An urban-rural happiness gradient. *Urban Geography, 32*(6), 871–83.

Berry, C., and Glaeser, E. L. (2005). The divergence of human capital levels across cities. *Papers in Regional Science, 84*(3), 407–44.

Betz, M. R., Partridge, M. D., and Fallah, B. (2015). Smart cities and attracting knowledge workers: which cities attract highly-educated workers in the 21st century? *Papers in Regional Science, 95*(4), 819–41.

Blanchflower, D. G., and Oswald, A. J. (2008). Is well-being U-shaped over the life cycle? *Social Science and Medicine, 66*(8), 1733–49.

Bolton, R. (1992). 'Place prosperity vs people prosperity' revisited: an old issue with a new angle. *Urban Studies, 29*(2), 185–203.

Botzen, K. (2016). Social capital and economic well-being in Germany's regions: an exploratory spatial data analysis. *Region, 3*(1), 1–24.

Bradburn, N. M. (1969). *The Structure of Psychological Well-Being.* Chicago, Il, Aldine.

Brereton, F., Clinch, P., and Ferreira, S. (2008). Happiness, geography and the environment. *Ecological Economics, 65,* 386–96.

Burger, M., Morrison, P. S., Hendricks, M., and Hoogerbrugge, M. (2020). Urban-rural happiness differentials across the world. In J. Helliwell (Ed.), *World Happiness Report 2020* (pp. 67–94). New York: Sustainable Development Solutions Network.

Burger, M. J., Meijers, E. J., Hoogerbrugge, M. M., and Masip Tresserra, J. (2015). Borrowed size, agglomeration shadows and cultural amenities in North-West Europe. *European Planning Studies, 23,* 1090–109.

Buryi, P., and Gilbert, S. (2014). Effects of college education on demonstrated happiness in the United States. *Applied Economics Letters, 21*(18), 1253–56.

Cacioppo, J. T., and Patrick, W. (2008). *Loneliness: Human Nature and the Need for Social Connection.* New York: W.W. Norton.

Campbell, A. (1981). *The Sense of Well-Being in America.* New York: McGraw Hill.

Campos, A. (2016). The cost of city life: the diseconomies of agglomeration. *Dossier: The Time of Cities* (Vol. June, pp. 36–7). CaixaBank Research.

Carlsen, F., and Leknes, S. (2021). Mobility and urban quality of life: a comparison of the hedonic pricing and subjective well-being methods. *Regional Studies, 55*(2), 245–55.

Carlsen, F., and Leknes, S. (2022a). For whom are cities good places to live? Regional Studies, 56(12), 2177–90.

Carlsen, F., and Leknes, S. (2022b). The paradox of the unhappy, growing city: reconciling evidence. *Cities, 126*(July): 103648.

Charalampi, A., Michalopoulou, C., and Richardson, C. (2020). Validation of the 2012 European Social Survey measurement of wellbeing in seventeen European countries. *Applied Research in Quality of Life, 15*, 73–105.

Chen, J., Davis, D. S., Wu, K., and Dai, H. (2015). Life satisfaction in urbanising China: the effect of city size and pathways to urban residency. *Cities, 49*, 88–97.

Chen, W. C. (2012). How education enhances happiness: comparison of mediating factors in four East Asian countries. *Social Indicators Research, 106*, 117–31.

Cheung, F., and Lucas, R. E. (2016). Income inequality is associated with stronger social comparison effects: the effect of relative income on life satisfaction. *Journal of Personality and Social Psychology, 110*(2), 332–41.

Chng, S., White, M., Abraham, C., and Skippon, S. (2016). Commuting and wellbeing in London: the roles of commute mode and local public transport connectivity. *Preventative Medicine, 88*, 182–8.

Clark, A., Etilé, F., Postel-Vinay, F., Senik, C., and Van der Straeten, K. (2005). Heterogeneity in reported well-being: evidence from twelve European countries. *The Economic Journal, 115*, C118–32.

Clark, A. E., Frijters, P., and Shields, M. A. (2006). Income and happiness: evidence, explanations and economic implications *Working Paper*: Paris-Jourdan Sciences economiques.

Clark, W., and Morrison, P. S. (2012). Socio-spatial mobility and residential sorting: evidence from a large scale survey. *Urban Studies, 49*(15), 3253–70.

Cummins, R. A., Davern, M., Okerstrom, E., Lo, S. K., and Eckersley, R. (2005). Report 12.1. Australian Unity Wellbeing Index. Special report on city and country living. Melbourne: The School of Psychology and Australian Centre on Quality of Life, Deakin University.

Dang, Y., Chen, L. J., Zheng, W., and Zhan, D. (2020). How does growing city size affect residents' happiness in urban China? A case study of Bohai rim area. *Habitat International, 97*, 102120.

Diener, E. (1984). Subjective wellbeing. *Psychological Bulletin, 95*, 542–75.

Diener, E., and Suh, E. (1997). Measuring quality of life: economic, social and subjective indicators. *Social Indicators Research, 40*, 189–216.

Diener, E., Eunkook, M. S., Lucas, R. E., and Smith, H. L. (1999). Subjective well-being: three decades of progress. *Psychological Bulletin, 125*(2), 276–303.

Diener, E., Oishi, S., and Lucas, R. E. (2002). Subjective well-being: the science of happiness and life satisfaction In C. R. Snyder and S. J. Lopez (Eds.), *Handbook of Positive Psychology*. Oxford and New York: Oxford University Press.

Dijkstra, L., and Papadimitriou, E. (2020). Using a new global urban-rural definition, called the degree of urbanisation, to assess happiness. In J. F. Helliwell, R. Layard, J. D. Sachs, and J.-E. De Neve (Eds.), *World Happiness Report 2020* (pp. 147–51). New York: Sustainable Development Solutions Network.

Dunlop. S., Davies, S., and Swales, K. (2016). Metropolitan misery: why do Scots live in 'bad places to live?'. *Regional Studies, Regional Science, 3*(1), 717–36.

Duranton, G. (2019). Agglomeration and jobs. In M. Fischer and P. Nijkamp (Eds.), *Handbook of Regional Science*. Berlin, Heidelberg: Springer.

Duranton, G., and Puga, D. (2004). Microfoundations of urban agglomeration economies. In J. V. Henderson and J. F. Thisse (Eds.), *Handbook of Regional and Urban Economics*. Amsterdam and New York: North-Holland.

Easterlin, R. A., Angelescu, L., and Zweig, J. S. (2011). The impact of modern economic growth on urban-rural differences in subjective wellbeing. *World Development*, *39*(12), 2187–98.

Escurra, R. (2007). Is income inequality harmful for regional growth? Evidence from the European Union. *Urban Studies*, *44*(10), 1953–71.

European Commission (2013). Quality of life in cities. *Flash Eurobarometer 366*. Luxembourg: Belgium: The European Union.

Feng, Z., Phillips, D. R., and Jones, K. (2018). A geographical multivariable multilevel analysis of social exclusion among older people in China: evidence from the China Longitudinal Aging Social Survey ageing study. *The Geographical Journal*, *184*, 413–28.

Ferrante, F. (2009). Education, aspirations and life satisfaction. *Kyklos*, *62*(4), 542–62.

Ferrer-i-Carbonell, A., and Frijters, P. (2004). How important is methodology for the estimates of the determinants of happiness? *The Economic Journal*, *114*(497), 641–59.

Fischer, C. S. (1973). Urban malaise. *Social Forces*, *52*, 221–35.

Fischer, C. S. (1982). *To Dwell among Friends: Personal Networks in Town and City*. Chicago: University of Chicago Press.

Fu, R., Noguchi, H., Tachikawa, H., et al. (2017). Relation between social network and psychological distress among middle-aged adults in Japan: evidence from a national longitudinal survey. *Social Science & Medicine*, *175*, 58–65.

Garcia-Lopez, M.-A., and Moreno-Monroy, A. I. (2018). Income segregation in monocentric and polycentric cities: does urban form really matter? *Regional Science and Urban Economics*, *71*, 62–79.

Geerling, D. M., and Diener, E. (2020). Effect size strengths in subjective well-being research. *Applied Research in Quality of Life*, *15*, 167–85.

Gesthuizen, M., van der Meer, T., and Scheepers, P. (2008). Education and dimensions of social capital: do educational effects differ due to educational expansion and social security expenditure? *European Sociological Review*, *24*(5), 617–32.

Glaeser, E. (2011). *Triumph of the City: How Our Greatest Invention Makes Us Richer, Smarter, Greener, Healthier, and Happier*. New York: Penguin Press.

Glaeser, E., Gottlieb, J. D., and Ziv, O. (2016). Unhappy cities. *Journal of Labor Economics*, *34*(2/2), S129–82.

Glaeser, E. L., and Maré, D. C. (2001). Cities and skills. *Journal of Labor Economics*, *19*, 316–42.

Glaeser, E. L., Resseger, M., and Tobio, K. (2009). Inequality in cities. *Journal of Regional Science*, *49*(4), 617–46.

Gordon, I. R., and Monastiriotis, V. (2006). Urban size, spatial segregation and inequality in educational outcomes. *Urban Studies*, *43*(1), 213–36.

Graham, C., and Pettinato, P. (2002). Frustrated achievers: winners, losers and subjective well-being in new market economies. *The Journal of Development Studies*, *38*(4), 100–40.

Han, C. (2012). Satisfaction with the standard of living in reform-era China. *The China Quarterly*, *212*, 919–40.

Helliwell, J., and Barrington-Leigh, C. P. (2010). Measuring and understanding subjective well-being. *Canadian Journal of Economics*, *43*(3), 729–53.

Helliwell, J., Huang, H., and Wang, S. (2016). *World Happiness Report 2016*. New York: Sustainable Development Solutions Network.

Helliwell, J., Layard, R., and Sachs, J. (Eds.) (2012). *World Happiness Report*. New York: The Earth Institute, Columbia University.

Helliwell, J., Layard, R., and Sachs, J. (Eds.) (2013). *World Happiness Report 2013*. New York: UN Sustainable Development Solutions Network.

Helliwell, J., Layard, R., and Sachs, J. (2015). *World Happiness Report 2015*. New York Sustainable Development Solutions Network (SDSN).

Helliwell, J., Layard, R., Sachs, J., and De Neve, J.-E. (2020). *World Happiness Report*. Vancouver: Sustainable Development Solutions Network.

Helliwell, J. F., and Putnam, R. D. (2004). The social context of well-being. *Philosophical Transactions of the Royal Society B*, *359*, 1435–46.

Helliwell, J. F., Shiplett, H., and Barrington-Leigh, C. P. (2019). How happy are your neighbours? Variation in life satisfaction among 1200 Canadian neighbourhoods and communities. *PLOS ONE*, *14*(1), 1–24.

Hoch, I. (1987). City size and U.S. urban policy. *Urban Studies*, *24*, 570–86.

Hu, A. (2015). The changing happiness-enhancing effect of a college degree under higher education expansion: evidence from China. *Journal of Happiness Studies*, *16*, 669–85.

Itaba, Y. (2016). Does city size affect happiness? In T. Tachibanaki (Ed.), *Advances in Happiness Research. A Comparative Perspective* (pp. 245–74). Tokyo: Springer.

Jabareen, Y., Eizenberg, E., and Zilberman, O. (2017). Conceptualising urban ontological security: 'being-in-the-city' and its social and spatial dimensions. *Cities*, *68*, 1–7.

Juster, F. T., and Stafford, F. P. (1991). The allocation of time: empirical findings, behavioural models, and problems of measurement. *Journal of Economic Literature*, *29*(2), 471–522.

Kasser, T., and Ryan, R. M. (1996). Further examining the American dream: differential correlates of intrinsic and extrinsic goals. *Personality and Social Psychology Bulletin*, *22*(3), 280–7.

Katic, I., and Ingram, P. (2017). Income inequality and subjective well-being: toward an understanding of the relationship and its mechanisms. *Business & Society*, *57*(6), 1010–44.

Kawachi, I. (2002). Income inequality and economic residential segregation. *Journal of Epidemiology and Community Health*, *56*, 165–6.

Kawachi, I., et al. (1997). Social capital, income inequality, and morality. *American Journal of Public Health*, *87*(1), 491–8.

Koslowsky, M., Kluger, A. M., and Reich, M. (1995). *Commuting Stress: Causes, Effects, and Methods of Coping*. New York: Plenum Press.

Kristoffersen, I. (2010). The metrics of subjective wellbeing: cardinal neutrality and additivity. *The Economic Record*, *86*(272), 98–123.

Lagas, P., van Dongen, F., van Rin, F., and Visser, H. (2015). Regional quality of living in Europe. *Region*, *2*(2), 1–26.

Layard, R. (1980). Human satisfactions and public policy. *Economic Journal*, *90*(363), 737–50.

Lee, S., Song, T., and Lim, U. (2022). How are happy and unhappy people differently affected by their local environments? The heterogeneous relationship between happiness and local environments in Seoul, Korea. *Cities*, *127* (online).

Lee, W. H., Ambrey, C., and Pojani, D. (2018). How do sprawl and inequality affect well-being in American cities? *Cities*, *76*, 70–7.

Lenzi, C., and Perucca, G. (2016a). Are urbanised areas source of life satisfaction? Evidence from EU regions. *Papers in Regional Science*, *97*(S1), S105-S122.

Lenzi, C., and Perucca, G. (2016b). Life satisfaction in Romanian cities on the road from post-communism transition to EU accession. *Region*, *3*(2), 1–22.

Lenzi, C., and Perucca, G. (2016c). Life satisfaction across cities: evidence from Romania. *The Journal of Development Studies*, *52*(7), 1062–77.

Lenzi, C., and Perucca, G. (2019). Subjective well-being over time and across space. *Scienze Regionali*, *18*(Special issue), 611–32.

Lenzi, C., and Perucca, G. (2022). No place for poor men: on the asymmetric effect of urbanisation on life satisfaction *Social Indicators Research* (online).

Leung, A., Kier, C., Fung, T. et al. (2011). Searching for happiness: the importance of social capital. *Journal of Happiness Studies*, *12*, 443–62.

Liang, O. (2016). *The Lonely City: Adventures in the Art of Being Alone*. Edinburgh: Canongate.

Loschiavo, D. (2019). Big-city life (dis)satisfaction? The effect of urban living on subjective well-being. *Banca D'Italia working paper (Temi di discussione)*. Italy: Bank of Italy.

Lu, C., Schellenberg, G., Hou, F., and Helliwell, J. F. (2015). How's life in the city? Life satisfaction across census metropolitan areas and economic regions in Canada. *Economic Insights* (pp. 11). Ottawa: Statistics Canada.

Luo, C. L. (2006). Urban-rural divide, employment, and subjective well-being. *China Economic Quarterly* (in Chinese), *5*(3), 817–40.

Maré, R. D., and Schwartz, C. R. (2006). Income inequality and educational assortative mating in the United States: accounting for trends from 1940–2003. Paper presented at the Annual Population Association of America, Los Angeles.

Martin, R., and Morrison, P. S. (2003). *Geographies of Labour Market Inequality*. London: Taylor Francis.

Migheli, M. (2016). Size of town, level of education and life satisfaction in Western Europe. *Tijdschrift voor Economische en Sociale Geografie*, *108*(2), 190–204.

Milne, G. (2017). *Uncivilised Genes: Human Evolution and the Urban Paradox*. Carmarthen, Wales, UK: Independent Thinking Press, Crown House Publishing.

Morris, E. A., Ettema, D., and Zhou, Y. (2020). Which activities do those with long commutes forego, and should we care? *Transport Research Interdisciplinary Perspectives*, *5* (online).

Morrison, P. S. (2005). Unemployment and urban labour markets. *Urban Studies*, *42*(12), 2261–88.

Morrison, P. S. (2007). Subjective wellbeing and the city. *Social Policy Journal of New Zealand*, *31*(July), 74–103.

Morrison, P. S. (2011). Local expressions of subjective well-being: the New Zealand experience. *Regional Studies*, *45*(8), 1039–58.

Morrison, P. S. (2015). The inequality debate, the neglected role of residential sorting. *The Policy Quarterly*, *11*(2), 72–9.

Morrison, P. S. (2020). Wellbeing and the region. In M. M. Fischer and P. Nijkamp (Eds.), *Handbook of Regional Science*. The Netherlands: Springer, Berlin.

Morrison, P. S. (2021). Whose happiness in which cities? A quantile approach. *Sustainability*, *13*(20), 11290–310.

Morrison, P. S., and Smith, R. A. (2018). Loneliness: an overview. In O. Sagan and E. Miller (Eds.), *Narratives of Loneliness: Multidisciplinary Perspectives from the 21st Century* (pp. 11–25). London: Routledge.

Ngamaba, K. H., Panagioti, M., and Armitage, C. J. (2018). Income inequality and subjective well-being: a systematic review and meta-analysis. *Quality of Life Research, 27*(3), 577–96.

Nikolaev, B., and Rusakov, P. (2016). Education and happiness: an alternative hypothesis. *Applied Economics Letters, 23*(12), 827–30.

NZIER (2018). *Distributional Aspects of New Zealand's Tradable and Non-Tradable Sectors.* NZIER: 1–34.

OECD (2010). *Trends in Urbanisation and Urban Policies in OECD Countries: What Lessons for China?* Paris: OECD.

OECD (2014). *How's Life in Your Region? Measuring Regional and Local Well-Being for Policy Making.* Paris: OECD Publishing.

OECD (2018). *Divided Cities: Understanding Intra-Urban Inequalities.* Paris: OECD Publishing.

Ogburn, W. F., and Duncan, O. D. (1964). City size as a sociological variable. In E. W. Burgess and D. J. Bogue (Eds.), *Urban Sociology* (pp. 58–76). Chicago: Phoenix Books. The University of Chicago Press.

Ormel, J., Lindenberg, S., Steverink, N., and Verbrugge, L. M. (1999). Subjective well-being and social production functions. *Social Indicators Research, 46*(1), 61–90.

Ory, D. T., Mokhtarian, P. l., Redmond, L. S., Salomon, I., Collantes, G. O., and Choo, S. (2004). When is commuting desirable to the individual? *Growth and Change, 35*(3), 334–59.

Oshi, S., and Kesebir, S. (2015). Income inequality explains why economic growth does not always translate into an increase in happiness. *Psychological Science, 26*(10), 1630–8.

Oshio, T., and Kan, M. (2019). Which is riskier for mental health, living alone or not participating in any social activity? Evidence from a population-based eleven year survey in Japan. *Social Science & Medicine, 233*, 57–63.

Ovaska, T., and Takashima, R. (2010). Does a rising tide lift all the boats? Explaining the national inequality of happiness. *Journal of Economic Issues, 44*(1), 205–24.

Pichler, F. (2006). Subjective quality of life of young Europeans. Feeling happy but who knows why? *Social Indicators Research, 75*, 419–44.

Pichler, F., and Wallace, C. (2009). Social capital and social class in Europe: the role of social networks in social stratification. *European Sociological Review, 25*(3), 319–32.

Piper, A. T. (2014). Europe's capital cities and the happiness penalty: an investigation using the European Social Survey. *Social Indicators Research, 123*(1), 103–26.

Pittau, M. G., Zelli, R., and Gelman, A. (2010). Economic disparities and life satisfaction in European regions. *Social Indicators Research, 96*, 339–61.

Powdthavee, N. (2008). Putting a price tag on friends, relatives, and neighbours: using surveys of life-satisfaction to value social relationships *Journal of Social Economics,* 37, 1459–80.

Reyes-Garcia, V., Angelsen, A., Shively, G. E., and Minkin, D. (2019). Does income inequality influence subjective wellbeing? Evidence from 21 developing countries. *Journal of Happiness Studies, 20*, 1197–215.

Richardson, H. W. (1973). *The Economics of Urban Size.* Westmead, England: Saxon House.

Rodriguez-Pose, A., and Maslauskaite, K. (2012). Can policy make us happier? Individual socioeconomic factors, and life satisfaction in Central and Eastern Europe. *Cambridge Journal of Regions, Economy and Society*, *5*, 77–96.

Ross, N. A., Nobrega, K., and Dunn, J. (2001). Income segregation, income inequality and mortality in North American metropolitan areas. *Geojournal*, *53*(2), 117–24.

Royuela, V., Veneri, P., and Ramos, R. (2014). *Income Inequality, Urban Size and Economic Growth in OECD Regions*. Paris: OECD, France.

Ruiu, G., and Ruiu, M. L. (2018). The complex relationship between education and happiness: the case of highly educated individuals in Italy. *Journal of Happiness Studies*, *20*(8), 2631–53.

Ryff, C. D., and Keyes, C. L. M. (1995). The structure of psychological well-being revisited. *Journal of Personality and Social Psychology*, *69*(4), 719–27.

Salim, S. (2008). Life satisfaction and happiness in Turkey. *Social Indicators Research*, *88*, 531–62.

Salinas-Jimenez, M., Artes, J., and Salinas-Jimenez, J. (2013). How do educational attainment and occupational and wage-earner statuses affect life satisfaction? A gender perspective study. *Journal of Happiness Studies*, *14*, 367–88.

Senik, C. (2009). Income distribution and subjective happiness: a survey. *OECD Social, Employment and Migration Working Papers*. Paris. Working Paper No. 96.

Shields, M., and Wooden, M. (2003). Investigating the role of neighbourhood characteristics in determining life satisfaction. Melbourne Institute Working Paper, no 24/03. Melbourne: Melbourne Institute of Applied Economic and Social Research.

Simmel, G. (1976). *The Metropolis and Mental Life*. New York: Free Press.

Smarts, E. (2012). Well-being in London: measurement and use. *GLA Economics Current Issues Note 35*. London: Mayor of London.

Studer, R., and Winkelmann, R. (2016). Econometric analysis of ratings – with an application to health and wellbeing. *SOEP Papers on Multidisciplinary Panel Data Research*. Berlin: SOEP – The German SocioEconomic Panel study at DW Berlin.

Sun, S. B., Huang, W. C., Hong, J. J., and Wang, J. H. (2014). City size, happiness and spatial optimization of migration. *Economic Research Journal* (in Chinese), *49*(1), 97–111.

Tabuchi, T. (2008). Separating urban agglomeration economies in consumption and production. *Journal of Urban Economics*, *48*, 70–84.

Tolly, G. S. (1974). The welfare economics of city bigness. *Journal of Urban Economics*, *1*(3), 324–45.

Uhlaner, C. J. (1989). 'Relational goods' and participation: incorporating sociability into a theory of rational action. *Public Choice*, *62*, 253–85.

United Nations (2016). *The World's Cities in 2016*. New York: United Nations.

Valdmanis, V. G. (2015). Factors affecting well-being at the state level in the United States. *Journal of Happiness Studies*, *16*, 985–97.

Veenhoven, R., and Choi, Y. (2012). Does intelligence boost happiness? Smartness of all pays more than being smarter than others. *International Journal of Happiness and Development*, *1*, 5–27.

Vives, C. (2017). Human capital and market size. *Papers in Regional Science*, *98*(1), 75–92.

Voydanoff, P., Donnelly, B. W., and Fine, M. A. (1988). Economic distress, social integration, and family satisfaction. *Journal of Family Issues*, *9*, 545–64.

Wellman, B. (1999). *Networks in the Global Village: Life in Contemporary Communities*. Boulder, Colorado: Westview Press.

Wilkinson, R. G., and Pickett, K. E. (2009). *The Spirit Level: Why More Equal Societies Almost Always Do Better*. London: Penguin.

Wirth, L. (1969). Urbanism as a way of life. In R. Sennett (Ed.), *Classic Essays on the Culture of Cities*. New York: Appleton-Century-Crofts.

World Bank (2009). World development report 2009. Reshaping economic geography. Washington DC: The International Bank for Reconstruction and Development/The World Bank.

Zagorski, K., Evans, M. D. R., Kelley, J., and Piotrowska, K. (2014). Does national income inequality affect individuals' quality of life in Europe? Inequality, happiness, finances and health. *Social Indicators Research*, *117*, 1089–110.

Zheng, L. (2016). What cities amenities matter in attracting smart people? *Papers in Regional Science*, *95*(2), 309–27.

# APPENDIX 3

The purpose of this appendix is to show that the results in the chapter '*Resolving the urban wellbeing paradox: the role of education and social contact*' are robust to the inclusion of paid work, household income and the subjective appraisal of income. Details of the three additional variables are discussed below and given in Table A.3.1.

The survey asks whether the respondent has been in paid work (F17c, CARD 53, p. 41): *Which of these descriptions best describes your situation (in the last seven days): in paid work (or away temporarily) (employee, self-employed, working for your family business).*

The ESS6 survey also asks the household's total net income from all sources (F41, CARD 58 p. 47): *Using this card, please tell me which letter describes your household's total income, after tax and compulsory deductions, from all sources? If you don't know the exact figure, please give an estimate. Use the part of the card you know best: weekly, monthly or annual income.* The card runs from 01 to 10, plus 'refused' and 'don't know'. As a result of this question, each household is allocated to an income decile based on their country's income distribution.

A second income question asks about the perceived standard of living experienced by the respondent as a result of occupying a given income decile (*F33 CARD p. 54*): *Which of the descriptions on this card comes closest to how you feel about your household's income nowadays? Living comfortably (1), coping (2), finding it difficult (3), finding it very difficult (4) on present income. DK.*

When it came to coping on present income, under five per cent of respondents to the ESS6 said they found living very difficult on their present (household) income, a further 16 per cent said they find it difficult, the majority (46.42 per cent) said they were coping and less than a third (32.5 per cent) said they were living comfortably. As expected, wellbeing increased as coping rose; average life satisfaction increased from 4.66 among those who were just copying to 5.82 among those who were finding it very difficult, to 7.07 who were finding it just difficult up to 8.05 for those who said they are living comfortably.

## Agglomeration and Paid Work

Agglomeration theory implicitly addresses those engaged in paid work, and hence those of working age. However, only half the ESS6 sample are in paid work and it is possible that by analysing the population as a whole in the main text I may have missed important differences between those inside and outside the paid work sector. In order to explore this possibility I reran the models reported in Table 3.2, effectively removing the three large nonworking sub-populations—students, 'homemakers' and the retired.

Based on the above definition, just over half the European sample were in paid work in the last seven days of the 2012 interview (52.1 per cent) and, as expected, they were more likely to hold a tertiary qualification – 30.87 per cent compared to the 13.03 per cent of those outside paid work.[1] As a group, paid workers were more satisfied with their life (7.28 > 6.85) even though they also reported lower levels of social contact (an average of 8.5 < 9.16 social contacts per month). Paid workers were also more likely to live in the Big City (20.23 > 18.2 per cent). Demographically, paid workers were more likely to be men, (50.7 > 43.2 per cent), younger, (43.7 < 55.6 years), married (54.3 > 44.5 per cent) and were considerably less likely to be hampered by poor health (16.79 < 38.5 per cent). They were also more likely to feel safe or very safe in their city (83.7 > 74.5 per cent) and to enjoy higher household incomes (see below).

*Table A.3.1     Supplementary variables – 20 countries in Europe, 2012*

| Variable | Number of Categories | Categories | Mean | S.D. |
|---|---|---|---|---|
| In paid work | 2 | (1) In paid work, (0) Other | 0.52 | 0.50 |
| Household income | 3 | (1) income deciles 1–3, (2) deciles 4–7, (3) deciles 8–10 | 1.96 | 0.75 |
| Coping on income | 4 | (1) Very difficult, (2) Difficult, (3) Coping, (4) Living comfortably | 3.06 | 0.82 |
| Settlement | 2 | | 0.31 | 0.47 |

*Source*:     European Social Survey, 2012.

The predicted average subjective wellbeing of those in and out of paid work both inside and outside the Big City were post-estimated from model 9 in Table 3.2 and are shown here in Table A3.2 together with their sample sizes.[2] Although mean wellbeing is lower in the Big City, this negative influence is less keenly felt by those in paid work, a difference of only 0.19 on the wellbeing scale, compared to the larger gap of 0.34 among unpaid workers, support-

---

[1]     Note in passing that over 72 per cent of those with tertiary education are in paid work compared to under 47 per cent of those without tertiary education. The proportion of females in paid work with a tertiary education was 34.4 per cent compared to only 27.4 per cent of males. However, similar proportions were in paid work: 71.68 per cent of women with a tertiary education were in paid work compared to 72.9 per cent of men.

[2]     Since they are differentially attracted to urban agglomerations, it is not surprising to learn that 43.5 per cent of those in paid work living in the Big City had a tertiary qualification compared to only 27.7 per cent of the paid workforce living outside Big Cities.

ing the claim that paid work acts a buffer against the negative externalities of the large city (Loschiavo, 2019).

*Table A.3.2*     *Post-estimated mean wellbeing of those with and without paid work, inside and outside the Big City – 20 countries in Europe, 2012*

| Employment\Residence | Other settlements | Big City |
|---|---|---|
| In the paid workforce | 7.32 | 7.13 |
| | (15 592) | (3949) |
| Outside the paid workforce | 6.91 | 6.57 |
| | (14 619) | (3245) |

*Source:*     European Social Survey, 2012.

I interrogate the data more fully by graphing the predicted wellbeing from model 9 (Table 3.2) for paid and unpaid members of the two education groups at different levels of social contact both inside and outside the Big City (Figure A.3.1). Two findings emerge from this construction. Firstly, in addition to tertiary education enhancing the wellbeing of the paid work force, the effect appears stronger in the Big City, where personal contacts at work likely to complement social contacts made outside (Kamerade et al., 2019).

Secondly, tertiary education buffers the negative wellbeing effects of low social contact when people are in paid work, especially when they live in the Big City. While the tertiary educated not in paid work still return a higher life satisfaction than the non-tertiary in paid work, if they are not in paid work they experience a lower wellbeing premium.

In summary, the difference between those inside and outside the paid work force supports the hypotheses advanced in the main text, albeit with subtle qualifications. While a higher education is consistently associated with higher wellbeing, the effect is moderated both by employment and residence. These differences are further moderated by the resident's level of social contact, and the effect of both education and the Big City is most marked when the level of social contact is very low.

So far, four of the five hypotheses outlined in the main text have attracted empirical support but two further questions remain: the effect of extending the definition of the Big City to include their suburbs, and the possible effect of household income.

**Big Cities and Suburbs**

The European Social Survey asks respondents to distinguish between living in the Big City and their suburbs, with sample sizes of 7223 and 4437, respec-

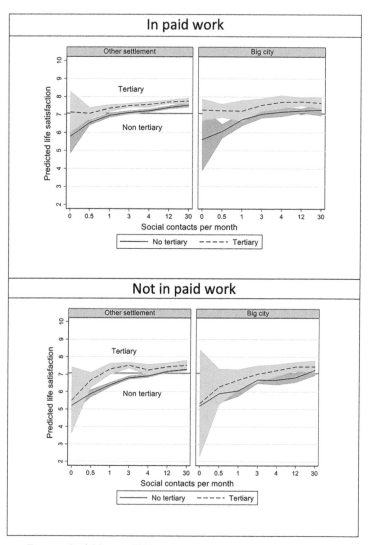

*Source*:    European Social Survey, 2012.

*Figure A.3.1    Wellbeing and social contact. Tertiary education and paid work inside and outside the Big City. Europe, 2012*

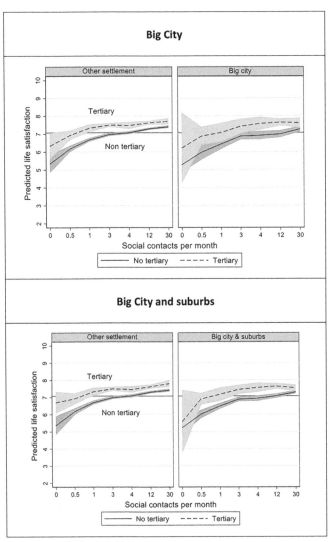

*Source*:    European Social Survey, 2012.

*Figure A.3.2    Wellbeing, social contact and tertiary education inside and
outside the Big City and Suburbs. Europe, 2012*

tively. Including the suburban population adds an additional 12 per cent to the 19 per cent who live in the Big City, reaching an average of nearly a third of the country's population (31 per cent). The issue at hand is whether the generalisations made on the basis of the strict Big City definition still hold if we also include their suburban population.

European suburban dwellers differ in a number of respects from those who live in the Big City. They are more social (9.17 > 8.80 social contacts per month), but fewer hold a tertiary degree (29.0 < 32.9 per cent). They are more likely to be male (48.4 > 46.5 per cent) and are slightly older on average (49.5 < 47.7 years). They have a higher marriage rate, (49.2> 43.1 per cent), and feel safer walking alone in their local area after dark (79.2 > 71.8 per cent). In other respects the two populations are very similar regarding being born in the country, hampered through physical or mental health, being in paid work and in terms of income.

When I rerun model 9 from Table 3.2 on those in the Big City and re-estimate the coefficients based on the larger, spatially more extensive concept of the Big City + Suburbs I find a remarkably similar relationship between wellbeing and residence. However, it is interesting to observe the reduced buffering tertiary education offers those with low social contact (<= 4) in the Big City compared to the Big City and Suburbs.

## Does Income Matter?

The foregoing models do not include income as an argument, either the income decile they belong to or how comfortable they are on their current income. There are two reasons for this. Firstly, my theoretical focus is on social contact, education and locational context and the way they interact in helping resolve the urban wellbeing paradox rather than income per se. The second reason is the high level of nonresponse to the income question. Over 20 per cent of respondents fail to report their income, either because they do not know (6 per cent), refuse (8.83 per cent), or simply because they are unable to answer the question (5.52 per cent).[3]

The relevant issue as far as household income is concerned is the degree to which it might moderate the key relationships already identified: the degree to which living in a high income household reduces the rate at which wellbeing falls with social contact substitutes for a higher degree or allows one to compensate for the negative externalities typically found in very large cities.

---

[3]   Also, past some adequate standard of living, individual income has a very low correlation with wellbeing, certainly much lower than the level of social support and the difference between countries (Geerling & Diener, 2020).

I found that wellbeing is higher for those holding a tertiary qualification, regardless of income or location, and that wellbeing in the Big City is lower for all six income × education categories. Therefore, income alone does not upset the two relationships of most interest in this study.

*Table A.3.3*  *Mean wellbeing by income, tertiary education and residence, inside (1ˢᵗ table) and outside (2ⁿᵈ table) the Big City – 20 countries in Europe, 2012*

| | No tertiary | Tertiary |
|---|---|---|
| Low income | 6.19 | 6.74 |
| Middle income | 6.8 | 7.36 |
| High income | 7.32 | 7.8 |
| | No tertiary | Tertiary |
| Low income | 6.5 | 6.87 |
| Middle income | 7.18 | 7.6 |
| High income | 7.65 | 7.96 |

*Source*:   European Social Survey, 2012.

A more sensitive measure of 'income' is the person's own perception of the standard of living their household income allows them to enjoy. This subjective measure captures differences in costs of living within countries as well as reflecting variations in people's consumption preferences. A further advantage of the subjective measure of income is that it is accompanied by an almost universal response rate.

I added 'felt income' to the fully controlled regression model in Table 3.2 while setting 'Very comfortable' as the variable's base. Adding the 'felt income' factor variable has the noticeable effect of reducing the wellbeing effect of social contact and, therefore, flattening the curve when predicted life satisfaction is plotted against social contact.

Including felt income in the regression also reduces the wellbeing effect of holding a tertiary degree simply because graduates are more likely to live comfortably on their income. I also found that including felt income in the regression greatly compresses the U shape in the wellbeing age relationship, softening the negative wellbeing effects of middle age. In addition, adding felt income halves the positive effect of marriage (suggesting that marriage and income interact to raise average life satisfaction) and reduces the fear of walking alone after dark (probably because higher income enables households to buy in safer areas). Adding felt income also raises the proportion of the variance explained by the model, from 13.4 to 24.6 per cent. At the end of the day, however, the inclusion of 'felt income' does not alter the role played by the three main predictors in the model – social contact, tertiary education and residence in metropolitan Europe, nor their three-way interactive effect on people's life satisfaction.

In summary, while recognising income (either in terms of the household's decile position or their subjective ability to cope) moderates the influence of social contact by lowering the rate at which wellbeing rises with social engagement, this neither proves the independent effect of income nor undermines the importance of social contact; it simply reminds us that the two are related and that causation can run in both directions.

## REFERENCES

Kamerade, D., Wang, S., Burchell, B., et al. (2019). A shorter working week for everyone: how much paid work is needed for mental health and wellbeing? *Social Science & Medicine, 241*, 112353.
Geerling, D. M., and Diener, E. (2020). Effect size strengths in subjective well-being research. *Applied Research in Quality of Life, 15*, 167–85.
Loschiavo, D. (2019). Big-city life (dis)satisfaction? The effect of urban living on subjective well-being. *Banca D'Italia working paper (Temi di discussione)*. Italy: Bank of Italy.

# 4. Housing and urban-rural differences in subjective wellbeing in the Netherlands

**Marloes Hoogerbrugge and Martijn J. Burger**

## 4.1 INTRODUCTION

Over recent years, there has been a burgeoning literature discussing the urban happiness paradox. In many Western nations, people living in larger cities report lower levels of subjective wellbeing (SWB) (Easterlin et al., 2011; Okulicz-Kozaryn, 2015; Lenzi and Perucca, 2018; Burger et al., 2020; Morrison, 2021) – also known as happiness or life satisfaction (Veenhoven, 2000) – despite urban places often being considered more attractive places to live and more and more people opting for an urban way of life. Studies have shown that lower levels of SWB in urban areas can be explained both by differences in the quality of the living environment and sociodemographic composition effects. On the one hand, lower levels of SWB in certain areas can be explained by the fact that urban, periurban and rural areas attract, and are home to, different sociodemographic groups of people, where cities typically host more single people, unemployed people, and immigrants. In this regard, Hoogerbrugge and Burger (2021) find for the United Kingdom that selective migration can partly explain higher SWB in rural areas, in that the average life satisfaction of people moving from the city to the countryside is higher than the average life satisfaction of people moving from the countryside to the city. At the same time, the authors did not find long-lasting SWB effects of migration either way. In a follow-up study for the Netherlands, Burger (2021) shows that selection and composition effects partly explain spatial differences in SWB in this country.

On the other hand, the existence of selection and composition effects does not mean that place effects do not play a role (Okulicz-Kozaryn, 2015). In this regard, lower SWB in cities could be attributed to the fact that the happiness benefits of living in cities do not outweigh the happiness costs. Although urban areas can offer access to amenities, facilities and public services (Glaeser et al., 2001), which tends to be positively correlated with SWB in cities (Leyden et al., 2011),[1] cities do also generate negative externalities. Where congestion and pollution are often mentioned as negative externalities of urbanisation, other (big) city characteristics that generally negatively affect people's SWB are a lack of green space, high crime rates, inequality, segregation, lower levels of social capital and more chance of social isolation and loneliness (Hoogerbrugge and Burger, 2021). As pointed out by Lenzi and Perucca (2022), these negative externalities of urbanisation disproportionately affect various segments of the population. Their study reveals that individuals with lower socioeconomic status primarily bear the costs of urbanisation, while more affluent individuals have a greater capacity to benefit from urbanisation's advantages. Overall, spatial differences in SWB are a complex phenomenon, which can be explained by both place-based and people-based effects.[2]

In this chapter, we focus on one of the factors that may drive spatial differences in SWB in the Western world. We examine whether housing explains (in part) lower SWB in Dutch large cities vis-à-vis other localities. As Florida, Mellander, and Rentfrow (2013) claimed, people might expect to be happier in places where housing is more available, less expensive and more affordable. Over the past decades, the Dutch housing market has been characterised by a housing shortage accompanied by high housing prices. Surging prices have made it particularly difficult for first-time homebuyers to enter the housing market, while the waiting lists for social housing (for lower income tenants) continue to grow and rental prices in the private sector have skyrocketed (Aalbers et al., 2021). The housing problems are the largest in urban areas of the Netherlands, where large cities like Amsterdam, Rotterdam, The Hague, and Utrecht are particularly struggling to house their inhabitants affordably. There are substantial differences in housing prices between urban and rural areas in the Netherlands. A study on regional spatial differences of housing prices illustrates that housing prices per square meter in the urban regions (Randstad provinces) is significantly higher compared to more rural regions in the Northern, Eastern and Southern parts of the Netherlands. Hence, the housing characteristics spatially differ in terms of quality. Where the average square meter living space per individual is around 65 m², living space is rather limited in the major Dutch cities ,with 49 m² in Amsterdam and 54 m² in Rotterdam and The Hague (CBS, 2018). In addition, urban dwellers often

---

[1]    At the same time, tourism can negatively affect the wellbeing of locals (Okulicz-Kozaryn and Strzelecka, 2017).
[2]    In addition, urban-rural differences in SWB can vary across groups. Typically, the SWB of younger and higher-educated people tends to be higher in cities (Morrison and Weckroth, 2018; Okulicz-Kozaryn and Valente, 2019; Burger et al., 2020; Hoogerbrugge and Burger, 2021; Carlsen and Leknes, 2022).

have to resort to rental housing in the private sector and generally experience a less socially cohesive, less safe and dirtier living environment compared to periurban and rural residents, despite have better access to amenities (Musterd, 2014; CBS, 2020).

In this chapter, we will discuss four possible pathways through which housing can affect urban-rural differences in SWB in the Netherlands: namely, housing tenure, housing affordability, housing and neighbourhood quality. We will use Dutch household data for the period 2008–19, whereby we distinguish between households living in urban versus periurban and rural areas. In order to unravel the spatial differences in SWB, we use Blinder–Oaxaca decomposition analysis to examine group differences. The remainder of this chapter is organised as follows. Section 2 discusses relevant literature on the relation between housing and SWB in general, and housing tenure, affordability and quality more specifically. Section 3 discusses the data and methodology while section 4 includes the empirical results. Section 5 offers some concluding remarks and suggestions for future research.

## 4.2    RELATED LITERATURE

### 4.2.1    Housing and SWB

Subjective wellbeing (SWB) refers to people's evaluation of their own lives – evaluations that are both affective and cognitive (Diener, 2000). Achieving high SWB is recognised as one of the main personal goals in life but is nowadays also considered as a major goal for public policy (OECD, 2013). The concept of SWB is relatively new in housing research (Clapham et al., 2018). Generally, studies focus on the relation between (mental and psychical) health and housing. Only recently has there been more attention paid to studying the impact of housing on SWB. Mouratidis (2020) analysed how commute satisfaction, neighbourhood satisfaction, and housing satisfaction can be used as indicators of urban quality of life and liveability due to their potential contribution to SWB. Housing satisfaction aims to capture the influence of one's dwelling characteristics on SWB. Although housing satisfaction intends to measure satisfaction with the dwelling itself, it is closely linked to the neighbourhood environment and neighbourhood satisfaction (Sirgy and Cornwell, 2002). Below, we discuss four pathways through which housing affects SWB: housing tenure, housing quality, neighbourhood quality and housing affordability.

### 4.2.2    Housing Tenure

A large number of studies have associated homeownership with SWB
(Clapham et al., 2018; Veenhoven et al., 2021), indicating that owners generally have higher SWB than renters (Rohe and Basolo, 1997; Elsinga and
Hoekstra, 2005). As homeownership is typically lower in cities, this could
explain part of the urban-rural gap in SWB in the Netherlands.

First, it has been argued that homeownership results in a higher level of
perceived control (i.e. internal locus of control). Perceived control means
an individual's belief that he or she is largely in command of important life
events rather than being subject to fate or to the will of others (Rohe and
Stegman, 1994). The rights and responsibilities that an individual has over
their living environment, typically categorised in terms of housing tenure, are
likely to affect SWB. Hence, homeownership serves to create wealth through
appreciation and decreasing mortgage liabilities. Wealth increasingly con-
centrates among long-term homeowners, typically middle-and higher income
households. The latter group sees the housing market as an attractive place to
store their assets (Aalbers et al., 2021). Second, it is believed that self-esteem
and social status mediates the relationship between housing tenure and SWB.
Indeed, self-esteem and social status are important factors in individual wellbeing and are largely determined by how a person believes others see him or
her (Rohe and Stegman, 1994). Given that homeowners are usually accorded
a higher social status, homeownership can promote self-esteem and SWB
accordingly.

There is mixed evidence of a causal effect of housing tenure on SWB.
Becoming a homeowner is positively associated with life satisfaction for
homeowners with a low financial burden, but negatively associated with life
satisfaction for homeowners with a high financial burden, implying that financial security moderates the effect of homeownership on SWB (Zumbro, 2014).

### 4.2.3    Housing Quality

Besides housing tenure, differences in housing quality may explain the spatial
gap in SWB. There is strong evidence supporting a link between physical
housing aspects and SWB, as several studies have shown the positive association between housing quality and SWB. In most studies, housing quality is
measured in terms of dwelling size. In this regard, Herbers and Mulder (2017)
find that house size is positively associated with the SWB of older Europeans.
Using the British Household Panel Survey, Foye (2017) finds a positive association between the increase in the number of rooms per person and life satisfaction, but only for men. They suggest that space signals wealth, which in turn

influences social status. It is proposed that wealth is a more important determinant of status for men than women and, therefore, the results are gendered.

Other studies also take other housing characteristics into account. Using European data, Hoekstra (2005) took the quality of the dwelling into account whereby two aspects were examined: the condition of the dwelling and the size of the dwelling (in terms of number of rooms). With regard to the condition of the dwelling, the following five variables were analysed: presence of light, presence of heating facilities, condition of the roof, presence of humidity problems and the presence of putrefaction. In all EU countries, Hoekstra (2005) found that residents in dwellings with a relatively large number of housing quality problems are generally less satisfied with their housing situation than residents in dwellings with relatively few housing quality problems; and that in all EU countries, the number of rooms is positively related with housing satisfaction. Hence, physical housing conditions can have an impact on SWB and, since housing conditions are typically worse in Dutch cities than in the countryside, housing quality may explain part of the urban-rural gap in SWB in the Netherlands.

At the same time, it should be mentioned that there are different incentives between homeowners and renters with respect to caring for property. Unlike homeowners, renters tend to over-utilise dwellings because they do not reap the economic benefits and because they are less attached to their dwellings. For the same reason, renters are less committed to maintaining and improving their homes. Although theory suggests that owner-occupied dwellings are on average in a qualitatively better condition than rented dwellings, not all owner-occupied dwellings are necessarily in good condition. Instead, some owner-occupied dwellings can be expected to be in poor condition, because the dwelling is very old, the owner lacks sufficient financial resources to undertake proper maintenance or the improvements are not expected to increase the dwelling's appraised value. Consequently, the positive effect of homeownership on life satisfaction could be dampened or even turns negative if the dwelling is in qualitatively poor condition (Zumbro, 2014).

### 4.2.4 Neighbourhood Quality

Another pathway through which housing can affect spatial differences in SWB is the quality of the neighbourhood. Sirgy and Cornwell (2002) examined how social, economic and physical neighbourhood features affect quality of life. They found that satisfaction with the social features of a neighbourhood (e.g. social interactions with people living in the neighbourhood) seem to affect life satisfaction through community satisfaction. These overall feelings about the community, in turn, play a significant role in life satisfaction. Satisfaction with the neighbourhood's physical features (such as crowding and noise level, quality of the environment, nearness of neighbourhood to facilities) affects life satisfaction through one's overall feelings about one's house and home. Likewise, satisfaction with neighbourhood economic features (such as home value in the neighbourhood, cost of living and socioeconomic status of the neighbourhood) affects life satisfaction in a similar manner.

Other subjective characteristics that are associated with neighbourhood satisfaction are perceived safety and fear of crime, place attachment, perceptions of accessibility, neighbourhood social cohesion and quietness (Mouratidis, 2020). The importance of neighbourhood-based social capital – both in terms of actual social contact with neighbours and the perceived social cohesion within a neighbourhood – are positively associated with residents' life satisfaction (Hoogerbrugge and Burger, 2018). Using European data, Sørensen (2014) found a higher level of social capital in rural areas that explained some – but far from all – of the rural-urban differences in life satisfaction. Okulicz-Kozaryn (2015) argues that particularly large cities have been associated with higher levels of crime, pollution and noise, which may reduce SWB in urban areas. Based on these findings, we would expect a lower neighbourhood quality in large cities compared to periurban and rural areas, explaining the urban-rural SWB differential in the Netherlands.

### 4.2.5    Housing Affordability

Housing is the single biggest cost factor for most individuals and households. It might be expected that happiness is higher in places where housing is more available, less expensive and more affordable (Florida et al., 2013). The urban economics and regional science literature found that housing costs are somewhat of a proxy for higher levels of amenities and a generally higher quality of life. Thus, housing costs may accompany other attributes that positively affect happiness and wellbeing (Glaeser et al., 2001; Florida et al., 2013).

Housing affordability has been linked to SWB (e.g. Florida et al., 2013; Burger et al., 2020) and mental health (e.g. Bentley et al., 2011; Reeves et al., 2016; Baker et al., 2020), especially for private renters (Pollack et al., 2010; Arundel et al., 2021). In particular, when housing expenses are high, fewer resources can be allocated to other wellbeing promoting activities such as healthcare, social networks and healthy nutrition (Pollack et al., 2010). In addition, financial stress due to high housing expenses (Rowley et al., 2015) can negatively impact SWB (Arampatzi et al., 2015; Tay et al., 2017).

The wage structure and high housing costs of cities favour well-educated people of working age (Morrison, 2021). Compared with low-skilled workers, high-skilled workers have relatively higher purchasing power in cities. Retired people do not benefit from a high wage level, and consequently this group may prefer to settle in areas with lower costs of living. The high urban housing costs per square meter favour single persons with low space requirements. Couples, and especially families with children, demand more space, which creates an incentive to move towards towns and rural areas with moderate costs of living. Indeed, since rural areas are, on average, more affordable that urban areas, housing affordability may explain part of the urban-rural gap in SWB in the Netherlands.

## 4.3     DATA AND METHODOLOGY

In this chapter, we make use of data of the LISS (Longitudinal Internet Studies for the Social Sciences) panel administered by Centerdata (Tilburg University, the Netherlands) to examine whether housing explains spatial differences in SWB in the Netherlands, specifically focusing on the gap between urban areas and periurban and rural areas. In the LISS survey, individuals report on several aspects of their life, including their housing situation, income and SWB. The personality (containing the SWB variable) and housing modules of the LISS are not filled out by every respondent every year. Consequently, in this study, we use the most recent available wave for each respondent, where we utilise the between-person variation in housing characteristics and SWB. Overall, our sample included 4446 adult respondents who answered the personality and housing modules in the same wave at least once.

### 4.3.1     Variables

#### 4.3.1.1     Subjective wellbeing
To measure SWB, we use a life satisfaction question asking: *How satisfied are you with the life you lead at the moment? 0 being equal to 'not satisfied at all' and 10 being equal to 'completely satisfied'*, which has been commonly utilised in the economics of SWB literature (Veenhoven, 2000). As a robustness check, we use a more emotional assessment of SWB using a 11-point scale of happiness: *On the whole, how happy would you say you are? 0 being equal to 'totally unhappy' and 10 being equal to 'totally happy'*.

#### 4.3.1.2     Urbanisation
The LISS data do not contain the place of residence of a respondent, but include information on the degree of urbanisation of the locality in which a respondent lives. In particular the data makes it possible to distinguish between respondents living in localities that are extremely urban (more than 2500 addresses per square kilometre), very urban (1500–2500 addresses per square kilometre), moderately urban (1000–1500 addresses per square kilometre), slightly urban (500–1000 addresses per kilometre) and not urban at all (less than 500 addresses per square kilometre). Where the largest and

medium-sized cities in the Netherlands are typically classified as very or extremely urban, localities that are considered periurban or rural are typically moderately to not urban at all. In this study, we are interested in comparing the SWB of larger city dwellers with that of people living in other types of localities. Hence, we compare the SWB of people living in extremely and very urban localities (which we label urban areas) with the SWB of people living in moderately urban, slightly urban, and nonurban localities (which we label periurban and rural areas). Our urban variable takes the value 1 if a respondent lives in an urban area, 0 otherwise.

### 4.3.1.3  Housing tenure

Housing tenure is measured based on the question: *Are you a tenant or (co-) owner of your current dwelling?* Please note that we excluded a small residual group of 'other' tenures, including subtenants as well as rent-free arrangements such as 'anti-squatting (antikraak)'.

The Dutch homeownership rate was around 45 per cent in 1990, and has in recent years stabilised at around 57 per cent, despite prior policy ambitions to increase homeownership rates to 65 per cent (Aalbers et al., 2021). In the four largest cities, however, homeownership is less common; in Amsterdam this percentage is only 29 per cent, in Rotterdam and in The-Hague 35 per cent and 54 per cent in Utrecht (CBS, 2021a). Given that homeownership is less common in those cities, this may explain part of the gap in SWB in the Netherlands between urban residents and periurban and rural residents.

### 4.3.1.4  Housing quality

We measure housing quality by using an index on dwelling problems based on the following seven questions: *Does your dwelling have one or more of the following problems? (a) the dwelling is too small, (b) the dwelling is too dark, (c) the dwelling has inadequate heating, (d) the dwelling has a leaking roof, (e) the dwelling has damp walls or floors, (f) the dwelling has rotten window frames or floors, (g) the dwelling is too noisy.* On all questions, the respondents had to answer Yes (0) or No (1); the composite housing quality index takes the value 0 to 7, where 7 indicates a high (perceived) housing quality.

### 4.3.1.5  Neighbourhood quality

We measure neighbourhood quality using an index on home environment problems based on the following four questions: *Are you ever confronted with the problems listed below in your home environment? (a) noise annoyance caused by neighbours, (b) noise annoyance caused by factories, traffic or other street sounds, (c) stench, dust or dirt, caused by traffic or industry, (d) vandalism or crime.* On all questions, respondents had to answer Yes (0) or No (1);

the composite housing quality index takes the value 0 to 4, where 4 indicates a high (perceived) neighbourhood quality.

### 4.3.1.6 Housing affordability

Regarding housing affordability, we largely follow the method applied by Arundel et al. (2021) and look at mortgage capital repayments and interest costs for homeowners and monthly rent for rental sector. These costs can be considered as base house costs only, but due to inconsistencies in the data collection over time, we were not able to include other costs. To measure affordability stress, we look at households that spend more than 30 per cent of gross income on housing and which belong to the lower half of the income distribution. Hence, our housing affordability stress variable is a dummy variable that takes the value 1 if the household spends more than 30 per cent of gross income on housing and their gross household income is below the median household income. In this fashion, we avoid the situation that a lot of higher income households may spend a large part of their income on housing but retain a lot of disposable income to cover all the other living costs (see also Nepal et al., 2010; Arundel et al., 2021).

### 4.3.1.7 Control variables

We include several control variables that may confound the relationship between place of living, housing and SWB, such as gender, age, education level, employment status and civil status. An overview of all variables included in the analysis can be found in Table A.4.1 in the Appendix to this chapter.

### 4.3.2 Empirical Strategy

To examine factors associated with urban-rural differences in SWB in the Netherlands, we apply Blinder–Oaxaca decomposition analysis (Blinder, 1973; Oaxaca, 1974). The Blinder–Oaxaca decomposition divides the SWB differential into two components: the first component shows the explained differences in SWB scores between urban and rural areas, while the second one refers to the unexplained part:

$$\Delta SWB = [E(XU) - E(XPR)]'\beta^* + [E(XU)'(\beta U - \beta^*) - E(XPR)'(\beta PR - \beta^*)] \quad (4.1)$$

where $\Delta SWB$ is the difference in SWB between urban areas and periurban and rural areas, subscript U refers to urban areas and subscript PR to periurban and rural areas, $\beta_U$ and $\beta_{PR}$ are vectors of coefficients, and $\beta^*$ is a nondiscriminatory vector of coefficients, estimated with a pooled regression and used to determine the deviation in the relative importance of each factor in the model between urban and rural areas. The explained part $(E(X_U) - E(X_{PR})]'\beta^*)$—or the 'endowment effect'—shows how much of the overall differential in the average SWB can be attributed to differences in the level of the explanatory variables (X) between the two types of areas. Hence, this 'endowment effect' reflects the differences in housing characteristics and control variables between urban and rural areas. The unexplained part $(E(X_U)'\ (\beta_U-\beta^*) - E(X_P)'\ (\beta_{PR}-\beta^*)])$ captures omitted variables as well as differences in the estimated coefficients between urban areas and periurban and rural areas, accounting for the fact that there can be spatial differences in the relative importance of the factors driving SWB.

## 4.4    EMPIRICAL RESULTS

### 4.4.1    Descriptive Statistics

In line with the previous literature on urban-rural differences of SWB in the Western world in general (e.g. Easterlin et al., 2011; Okulicz-Kozaryn, 2015; Lenzi and Perucca, 2018; Burger et al., 2020; Morrison, 2021) and the Netherlands in specific (Burger, 2021), we find that inhabitants of extremely to very urban areas are generally less satisfied with their lives than inhabitants of areas that are periurban and rural.

Table 4.1 shows that all spatial differences between urban areas and periurban and rural areas are statistically significant. With regard to the housing characteristics, we see that homeownership is less prevalent in urban areas compared to periurban and rural areas. Where almost 64 per cent of the respondents in rural areas own their home, this percentage is 20 per cent lower in urban areas. In addition, housing quality and neighbourhood quality are, in all respects, worse in the larger cities. In particular, deficiencies given as 'dwelling is noisy' and 'dwelling is too small' report substantial differences between both types of areas, while noise annoyance (both by neighbours and factories and/or traffic) explains a lower neighbourhood quality in urban areas compared to periurban and rural areas. At the same time, housing affordability stress is also higher in urban areas. Where 22 per cent of the below-median income respondents in urban areas are above the 30 per cent housing costs threshold level, this is only the case for 14 per cent of the periurban and rural residents in the sample. There are also some striking differences between urban and rural areas in terms of sociodemographic characteristics. Urban areas generally have more singles and fewer families compared to rural areas; whereas, there is a higher percentage of people with a tertiary education in urban areas, which are most likely students and young urban professionals who are attracted to larger cities due to the presence of jobs and education facilities.

*Table 4.1*       *Spatial differences of included variables and comparison of means*

|  | Urban | Periurban and rural | T-test difference |
|---|---|---|---|
| Life satisfaction | 7.22 | 7.35 | 3.06** |
| Happiness | 7.34 | 7.43 | 2.23* |
| Housing characteristics |  |  |  |
| Homeownership (%) | 44.4% | 63.6% | 13.03** |
| Housing quality (index) |  |  |  |
| Too small (%) | 12.4% | 6.0% | 7.50** |
| Too dark (%) | 3.7% | 1.9% | 3.56** |
| Inadequate heating (%) | 5.6% | 2.4% | 5.54** |
| Leaking roof (%) | 2.3% | 1.0% | 3.53** |
| Damp wall or floors (%) | 6.0% | 4.4% | 2.43** |
| Rotten window frames or doors (%) | 4.4% | 2.7% | 3.07** |
| Dwelling is noisy (%) | 19.6% | 10.1% | 9.00** |
| Neighbourhood quality (index) |  |  |  |
| Noise annoyance neighbours (%) | 28.6% | 18.9% | 7.64** |
| Noise annoyance factories/traffic (%) | 16.5% | 8.7% | 7.95** |
| Stench, dust, or dirt (%) | 7.3% | 4.0% | 4.70** |
| Vandalism/crime (%) | 9.4% | 4.6% | 6.26** |
| Housing affordability stress (%) | 22.3% | 14.2% | 7.05** |
| Sociodemographic characteristics |  |  |  |
| Age | 51.9 | 55.3 | 6.54** |
| Gender: male (%) | 46.3% | 46.2% | 0.08 |
| Having a partner (%) | 47.5% | 61.8% | 9.57** |
| Having child(ren) (%) | 22.1% | 31.3% | 6.93** |
| Tertiary education (%) | 44.8% | 35.7% | 6.24** |
| Income (ln) | 7.20 | 7.04 | 3.61** |
| Unemployed/disabled (%) | 9.0% | 7.2% | 2.08* |
| Out of work (%) | 38.2% | 41.8% | 2.45** |

*Notes*:    **p<0.01, *p<0.05. Estimations based on two-sample t-test with equal variances. N=4,446 (N=4,389 for the happiness variable).

### 4.4.2    Blinder–Oaxaca Decomposition

Table 4.2 shows that difference in the levels of the independent and control variables explain the life satisfaction and happiness differentials between urban areas and periurban and rural areas. Most of the differences are explained by

*Table 4.2        Blinder–Oaxaca decomposition of the spatial SWB
              differential*

|                                               | Life satisfaction | Happiness |
|-----------------------------------------------|-------------------|-----------|
| Differential                                  |                   |           |
| Predicted average urban areas                 | 7.22              | 7.34      |
| Predicted average periurban and rural areas   | 7.35              | 7.43      |
| Difference                                    |                   |           |
| Total difference                              | -0.135            | -0.091    |
| Explained                                     | -0.174            | -0.147    |
| Unexplained                                   | 0.039             | 0.056     |
| Observations                                  | 4,446             | 4,389     |

*Note*:     The decomposition uses robust clustered standard errors.

differences in housing conditions and the sociodemographic composition of the population and not by differences in the relative importance of predictors between urban areas and periurban and rural areas and/or excluded variables. In both the Blinder–Oaxaca estimations for life satisfaction and happiness, we did not find strong evidence that the predictors for life satisfaction and happiness are different in urban areas compared to periurban and rural areas; only having children is more negatively correlated to both life satisfaction and happiness in urban areas.[3] Hence, the positive value in the unexplained part might be explained by urban SWB advantages that are not included in our model because of data availability that are most likely related to access to amenities, jobs and (public) services.

Figures 4.1 and 4.2 show that the spatial SWB differential is associated with differences in both sociodemographic composition and housing characteristics between urban areas and periurban areas, where we can draw rather similar conclusions for the life satisfaction and happiness estimations. On the one hand, urban areas have relatively more single and unemployed people, which suppresses the average SWB in cities, despite having relatively fewer middle-aged people (who are typically less happy than younger and older people) and more people with a tertiary education (who are typically happier than people without tertiary education). On the other hand, lower levels of homeownership and housing affordability stress explain lower levels of SWB in urban areas compared to periurban and rural areas. This also holds true for housing and neighbourhood quality, which are measured according to different types of problems. Please note that, for these problems, we look at the joint significance of the individual dummy variables included in the analyses. For

---

[3]     See Tables A.4.2 and A.4.3 in the Appendix to this chapter.

life satisfaction estimations (Figure 4.1) neighbourhood quality seems to be the strongest explanator for the urban-rural SWB differential, while for the happiness estimations (Figure 4.2), the different housing characteristics are closer to each other.

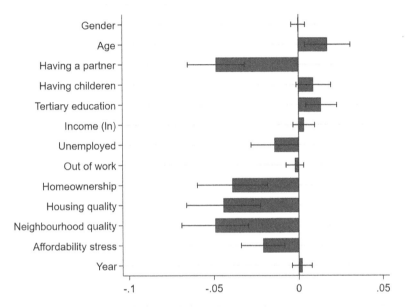

*Notes:*     Horizontal lines show 95 per cent confidence range. Some findings are not significant or only significant at the 10 per cent level (see Table A.4.3 in Appendix).

*Figure 4.1*     *Blinder–Oaxaca decomposition for spatial SWB differential: life satisfaction*

Table A.4.2 in the Appendix specifies the housing and neighbourhood quality index for the different types of problems and deficiencies. The individual components of housing quality report slightly significant coefficients for inadequate heating, dwelling is too dark and leaking roof. This indicates that these three problems mainly contribute to the explained part of the SWB urban-rural differential. Interestingly, we do not find a significant result for perceived housing size, since the coefficient for 'dwelling is too small' is negative but insignificant. This may suggest that urban residents accept less living space – as the average square meter living space is substantially lower in urban areas compared to periurban and rural areas (CBS, 2018) – in return for the proximity of urban amenities and facilities. The explained part of the decomposition

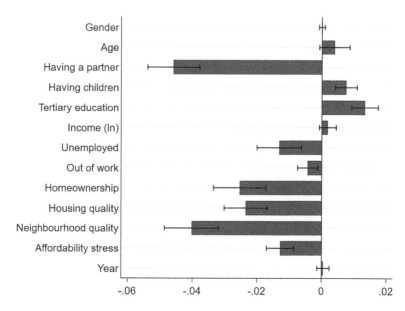

*Notes:* Horizontal lines show 95 per cent confidence range. Some findings are not significant or only significant at the 10 per cent level (see Table A.4.3 in Appendix).

*Figure 4.2*     *Blinder–Oaxaca decomposition for spatial SWB differential: happiness*

of neighbourhood quality is mainly driven by noise annoyance by neighbours and noise annoyance by factories, traffic or other street sounds, as both problems report highly significant results. This may suggest that high urban densities – in combination with older and less isolated dwellings – explains part of the urban-rural SWB differential between urban and periurban and rural areas.

## 4.5 CONCLUDING REMARKS

This chapter aims to unravel the spatial differences in SWB in the Netherlands by taking a closer look at housing. As previous studies indicate that urban-rural differences can be explained by both place-based and people-based factors (Burger et al., 2020), this chapter examines whether urban-rural SWB differences are driven by differences in the quality and affordability of housing. Using a Dutch household database, linking housing characteristics to SWB, we found that differences in housing tenure, housing and neighbourhood quality and affordability partly explain the urban-rural SWB differential in the

Netherlands. An on average lower quality of housing (measured by housing deficiencies), higher percentage of rental housing and higher affordability stress seem to contribute to relatively lower SWB levels in the Dutch cities. However, housing characteristics explain only a part of the spatial SWB differential as people-based factors and other place-based factors are also important. In particular, the Blinder–Oaxaca decompositions show that the sociodemographic composition of the population explains a part of the spatial SWB differential, as there are more single and unemployed people in the Dutch large cities, and those groups generally report lower levels of SWB.

Although this study takes some aspects of the Dutch housing market into account, several aspects are left out of our analysis due to data limitations. Specifically, housing characteristics included in this study mainly focus on deficiencies and problems as perceived by the residents, while more (objective) housing indicators are not included. Likewise, the neighbourhood characteristics in this study are limited to problems such as (perceived) noise, crime and vandalism. To gain more insight into the quality of the neighbourhood it would benefit the analysis to take more social aspects (e.g. social cohesion and social contacts) and physical aspects (e.g. presence of, and accessibility of, facilities and green spaces) into account.

Despite the limitations of this study, the insights give some directions for (Dutch) housing policies. For example, stimulating increasing homeownership rates in the larger cities, which are dominated by high percentages of rental housing. This would benefit first-time buyers especially, for whom it is nowadays difficult to become a homeowner. The affordability of housing remains an issue in the largest Dutch cities due to high pressure on the housing market in the more urbanised part of the Netherlands. Currently, the Dutch government pursue sustainability policies in order to improve housing conditions. One can think of subsidising insulation measures such as new – more insulated – windows, floors, or walls and/or more sustainable heating systems. Along these lines, Dutch housing corporations could be encouraged to make their housing stock more sustainable. Since this study suggests that, in particular, inadequate heating and noise annoyances are important drivers for SWB in general and the urban-rural SWB differential specifically, these policies might be beneficial to close the gap, as better insulated dwellings are more sound-proof and energy-saving.

For future research, it would be interesting to study the (long-term) effects of the COVID-19 pandemic. During the pandemic, high housing prices – in combination with the possibilities of remote working – resulted in an increasing number of households (both with and without children) moving from the more urbanised part of the Netherlands (Randstad) to the less urbanised parts of the country (CBS, 2021b). Since it is too early to conclude whether the housing preferences of households permanently changed or whether this is only temporary, triggered by the COVID-19 pandemic, future research on the effects of the COVID-19 pandemic is welcomed. A recent study on metropolitan areas in the United States found that the COVID-19 pandemic brought house price and rent declines in city centres and thereby flattening the bid-rent curve (Gupta et al., 2021). It would be interesting to find out whether a similar trend is prevalent in European metropolitan areas. The extension of this analysis to more recent years can capture the effects of the widespread diffusion of remote working practices for higher-educated people, pushed by the COVID-19 pandemic. Another study on the effect of the COVID-19 pandemic on the US housing market found a reduced housing demand in dense neighbourhoods, as there was less need for living in these neighbourhoods due to remote working, and due to the declining value of access to amenities, as there was a drop in visits to consumption amenities during the pandemic (Liu and Su, 2021).

To examine the external validity of this study, it would be interesting to examine whether housing characteristics also drive urban-rural SWB differences in other (Western) countries. On the one hand, the Dutch housing market might be rather specific, as it is traditionally strongly regulated by the government and characterised by a high percentage of social housing in the largest cities. Hence, housing may not play a big role in explaining the urban-rural SWB divide in other Western nations. On the other hand, the housing market situation in urban vis-à-vis rural areas might be rather similar for most (Western) countries as in many countries there is high pressure on housing prices in the larger cities. This should be addressed in future research.

## REFERENCES

Aalbers, M., Hochstenbach, C., Bosma, J., and Fernandez, R. (2021). The death and life of private landlordism: how financialized homeownership gave birth to the buy-to-let market. *Housing, Theory and Society*, 38(5), 541–63.

Arampatzi, E., Burger, M. J., and Veenhoven, R. (2015). Financial distress and happiness of employees in times of economic crisis. *Applied Economics Letters*, 22(3), 173–9.

Arundel, R., Li, A., Baker, E., and Bentley, R. (2021). Linking housing affordability stress and mental health across tenure and age cohorts: the case of the Netherlands. Working Paper.

Baker, E., Pham, N. T. A., Daniel, L., and Bentley, R. (2020). New evidence on mental health and housing affordability in cities: a quantile regression approach. *Cities*, 96, 102455.

Bentley, R., Baker, E., Mason, K., Subramanian, S. V., and Kavanagh, A. M. (2011). Association between housing affordability and mental health: a longitudinal analysis of a nationally representative household survey in Australia. *American Journal of Epidemiology*, 174(7), 753–60.

Blinder, A. S. (1973). Wage discrimination: reduced form and structural estimates. *Journal of Human Resources*, 436–55.

Burger, M. J. (2021). Urban-rural happiness differentials in the Netherlands. In *The Pope of Happiness* (pp. 49–58). Springer, Cham.

Burger, M. J., Morrison, P. S., Hendriks, M., and Hoogerbrugge, M. M. (2020). Urban-rural happiness differentials across the world. *World Happiness Report 2020*, 66–93.

Carlsen, F., and Leknes, S. (2022). For whom are cities good places to live? *Regional Studies*, 1–14.

CBS (2018). Woonoppervlakte in Nederland [Living space in the Netherlands] https://www.cbs.nl/nl-nl/achtergrond/2018/22/woonoppervlakte-in-nederland. Statistics Netherlands (CBS).

CBS (2020). Regionale Monitor Brede Welvaart toont grote verschillen stad en platteland [Regional Monitor Broad Welfare shows major differences between city and countryside]. https://www.cbs.nl/nl-nl/nieuws/2020/49/regionale-monitor-brede-welvaart-toont-grote-verschillen-stad-en-platteland. Statistics Netherlands (CBS).

CBS (2021a). Regional data on housing stock and division in homeownership (1 January 2020) https://opendata.cbs.nl/statline/#/CBS/nl/dataset/70072ned/table?dl=41DA7. Statistics Netherlands (CBS).

CBS (2021b). Meer verhuizingen naar regio's buiten de Randstad [More movements to regions outside the Randstad] https://www.cbs.nl/nl-nl/nieuws/2021/08/meer-verhuizingen-naar-regio-s-buiten-de-randstad. Statistics Netherlands (CBS).

Clapham, D., Foye, C., and Christian, J. (2018). The concept of subjective well-being in housing research. *Housing, Theory and Society*, 35(3), 261–80.

Diener, E. (2000). Subjective well-being: The science of happiness and a proposal for a national index. *American Psychologist*, 55(1), 34–43.

Easterlin, R. A., Angelescu, L., and Zweig, J. S. (2011). The impact of modern economic growth on urban–rural differences in subjective well-being. *World Development*, 39(12), 2187–98.

Elsinga, M., and Hoekstra, J. (2005). Homeownership and housing satisfaction. *Journal of Housing and the Built Environment*, 20(4), 401–24.

Florida, R., Mellander, C., and Rentfrow, P. J. (2013). The happiness of cities. *Regional Studies*, 47(4), 613–27.

Foye, C. (2017). The relationship between size and living space and subjective well-being. *Journal of Happiness Studies*, 18, 427–61.

Glaeser, E. L., Kolko, J., and Saiz, A. (2001). Consumer city. *Journal of Economic Geography*, 1(1), 27–50.

Gupta, A., Mittal, V., Peeters, J., and Van Nieuwerburgh, S. (2021). Flattening the curve: pandemic-induced revaluation of urban real estate. *Journal of Financial Economics*, doi.org/10.1016/j.jfineco.2021.10.008.

Herbers, D. J., and Mulder, C. H. (2017). Housing and subjective well-being of older adults in Europe. *Journal of Housing and the Built Environment*, 32(3), 533–58.

Hoekstra, J. (2005). Is there a connection between welfare state regime and dwelling type? An exploratory statistical analysis. *Housing Studies*, 20(3), 475–95.

Hoogerbrugge, M. M., and Burger, M. J. (2018). Neighborhood-based social capital and life satisfaction: the case of Rotterdam, the Netherlands. *Urban Geography*, 39(10), 1484–509.

Hoogerbrugge, M., and Burger, M. (2021). Selective migration and urban–rural differences in subjective well-being: evidence from the United Kingdom. *Urban Studies*, 00420980211023052.

Lenzi, C., and Perucca, G. (2018). Are urbanized areas source of life satisfaction? Evidence from EU regions. *Papers in Regional Science*, 97, S105–22.

Lenzi, C., and Perucca, G. (2022). No place for poor men: on the asymmetric effect of urbanization on life satisfaction. *Social Indicators Research*, doi.org/10.1007/ s11205-022-02946-1.

Leyden, K. M., Goldberg, A., and Michelbach, P. (2011). Understanding the pursuit of happiness in ten major cities. *Urban Affairs Review*, 47(6), 861–88.

Liu, S., and Su, Y. (2021). The impact of the COVID-19 pandemic on the demand for density: evidence from the U.S. housing market. *Economics Letters*, 207, doi.org/10 .1016/j.econlet.2021.110010.

Morrison, P. S. (2021). Whose happiness in which cities? A quantile approach. *Sustainability*, 13(20), 11290.

Morrison, P. S., and Weckroth, M. (2018). Human values, subjective well-being and the metropolitan region. *Regional Studies*, 52(3), 325–37.

Mouratidis, K. (2020). Commute satisfaction, neighborhood satisfaction, and housing satisfaction as predictors of subjective well-being and indicators of urban livability. *Travel Behaviour and Society*, 21, 265–78.

Musterd, S. (2014). Public housing for whom? Experiences in an era of mature neo-liberalism: the Netherlands and Amsterdam. *Housing Studies*, 29(4), 467–84.

Nepal, B., Tanton, R., and Harding, A. (2010). Measuring housing stress: how much do definitions matter? *Urban Policy and Research*, 28(2), 211–24.

Oaxaca, R. L. (1974). Another look at tests of equality between sets of coefficients in two linear regressions. *The American Economist*, 18(1), 23–32.

OECD (2013). *OECD Guidelines on Measuring Subjective Well-Being*. OECD Publishing https://doi.org/10.1787/9789264191655-en.

Okulicz-Kozaryn, A. (2015). *Happiness and Place: Why Life is Better outside of the City*. Springer.

Okulicz-Kozaryn, A., and Strzelecka, M. (2017). Happy tourists, unhappy locals. *Social Indicators Research*, 134(2), 789–804.

Okulicz-Kozaryn, A., and Valente, R. R. (2019). No urban malaise for Millennials. *Regional Studies*, 53(2), 195–205.

Pollack, C. E., Griffin, B. A., and Lynch, J. (2010). Housing affordability and health among homeowners and renters. *American Journal of Preventive Medicine*, 39(6), 515–21.

Reeves, A., Clair, A., McKee, M., and Stuckler, D. (2016). Reductions in the United Kingdom's government housing benefit and symptoms of depression in low-income households. *American Journal of Epidemiology*, 184(6), 421–9.

Rohe, W. M. and Basolo, V. (1997). Long-term effects of homeownership on the self-perceptions and social interaction of low-income persons. *Environment and Behavior*, 29(6), 793–819.

Rohe, W. M., and Stegman, M. A. (1994). The effects of homeownership on the self-esteem, perceived control and life satisfaction of low-income people. *Journal of the American Planning Association*, 60(2), 173–84.

Rowley, S., Ong, R., and Haffner, M. (2015). Bridging the gap between housing stress and financial stress: the case of Australia. *Housing Studies*, 30(3), 473–90.

Sirgy, M. J., and Cornwell, T. (2002). How neighborhood features affect quality of life. *Social Indicators Research*, 59, 79–114.

Sørensen, J. F. L. (2014). Rural-urban differences in life satisfaction. Evidence from the European Union. *Regional Studies*, 48(9), 1451–66.

Tay, L., Batz, C., Parrigon, S., and Kuykendall, L. (2017). Debt and subjective well-being: the other side of the income-happiness coin. *Journal of Happiness Studies*, 18(3), 903–37.

Veenhoven, R. (2000). The four qualities of life. *Journal of Happiness Studies*, 1(1), 1–39.

Veenhoven, R., Chiperi, F., Kang, X., and Burger, M. (2021). Happiness and consumption: a research synthesis using an online finding archive. *SAGE Open*, 11(1), 2158244020986239.

Zumbro, T. (2014). The relationship between homeownership and life satisfaction in Germany. *Housing Studies*, 29(3), 319–38.

# APPENDIX 4

*Table A.4.1     Descriptive statistics*

|                                  | Mean | SD   | Min | Max   |
|----------------------------------|------|------|-----|-------|
| Life satisfaction                | 7.29 | 1.47 | 0   | 10    |
| Happiness                        | 7.39 | 1.35 | 0   | 10    |
| Urban                            | 0.46 | 0.50 | 0   | 1     |
| Housing characteristics          |      |      |     |       |
| Homeownership                    | 0.55 | 0.50 | 0   | 1     |
| Housing quality                  | 0.40 | 0.80 | 0   | 7     |
| Neighbourhood quality            | 0.48 | 0.76 | 0   | 4     |
| Housing affordability stress     | 0.18 | 0.38 | 0   | 1     |
| Sociodemographic characteristics |      |      |     |       |
| Age                              | 53.7 | 17.1 | 17  | 97    |
| Gender                           | 0.54 | 0.50 | 0   | 1     |
| Having a partner                 | 0.55 | 0.50 | 0   | 1     |
| Having child(ren)                | 0.27 | 0.44 | 0   | 1     |
| Tertiary education               | 0.40 | 0.49 | 0   | 1     |
| Income (ln)                      | 7.11 | 1.47 | 0   | 11.80 |
| Unemployed/disabled              | 0.09 | 0.28 | 0   | 1     |
| Out of work                      | 0.40 | 0.49 | 0   | 1     |

*Note:*     N = 4,446 (N = 4,389 for happiness variable).

*Table A.4.2    Blinder–Oaxaca decomposition for spatial SWB differential: life satisfaction*

| | Explained Part | Unexplained Part |
|---|---|---|
| Housing characteristics | | |
| Homeownership | -0.039 (0.011)** | -0.020 (0.057) |
| Housing quality (index)[a] | -0.044 (0.011)** | 0.045 (0.030) |
| Too small | -0.008 (0.006) | 0.011 (0.015) |
| Too dark | -0.008 (0.004)* | -0.014 (0.008)# |
| Inadequate heating | -0.012 (0.005)* | -0.001 (0.011) |
| Leaking roof | -0.007 (0.004)* | 0.011 (0.007)# |
| Damp wall or floors | -0.002 (0.002) | 0.009 (0.011) |
| Rotten window frames or doors | -0.000 (0.002) | 0.017 (0.010)# |
| Dwelling is noisy | -0.006 (0.007) | 0.011 (0.023) |
| Neighbourhood quality (index)[a] | -0.049 (0.010)** | 0.022 (0.035) |
| Noise annoyance neighbours | -0.028 (0.007)** | 0.001 (0.029) |
| Noise annoyance factories/traffic | -0.018 (0.006)** | -0.005 (0.018) |
| Stench, dust or dirt | -0.002 (0.003) | 0.023 (0.012)# |
| Vandalism/crime | -0.001 (0.005) | 0.004 (0.014) |
| Housing affordability stress | -0.021 (0.007)** | -0.001 (0.026) |
| Sociodemographic characteristics | | |
| Gender | -0.000 (0.002) | 0.053 (0.137) |
| Age | 0.017 (0.007)* | -0.491 (0.426) |
| Having a partner | -0.048 (0.009)** | 0.080 (0.053) |
| Having child(ren) | 0.008 (0.005) | -0.060 (0.025)* |
| Tertiary education | 0.013 (0.005)** | 0.026 (0.036) |
| Income (ln) | 0.003 (0.003) | 0.063 (0.307) |
| Unemployed/disabled | -0.014 (0.007)* | 0.011 (0.018) |
| Out of work | -0.002 (0.003) | -0.066 (0.055) |
| Intercept | | 0.428 (0.590) |
| Total | -0.174 (0.021)*** | 0.039 (0.044) |

*Notes:*    \*\*p<0.01, \*p<0.05, #p<0.10. Robust standard errors in parentheses. N=4,446; [a] Joined effects of variables that constitute the index. Please note that we run two separate regressions: one with composite indicators and one in which the composite indicators were replaced by the subindicators.

*Table A.4.3*    *Blinder–Oaxaca decomposition for spatial SWB differential: happiness*

|                                          | Explained Part       | Unexplained Part   |
|------------------------------------------|----------------------|--------------------|
| Housing characteristics                  |                      |                    |
| Homeownership                            | -0.037 (0.010)**     | 0.003 (0.052)      |
| Housing quality (index)[a]               | -0.039 (0.010)**     | 0.040 (0.028)      |
| Too small                                | -0.007 (0.005)       | 0.012 (0.014)      |
| Too dark                                 | -0.006 (0.003)*      | -0.006 (0.007)     |
| Inadequate heating                       | -0.011 (0.005)*      | -0.006 (0.010)     |
| Leaking roof                             | -0.005 (0.003)       | 0.010 (0.006)      |
| Damp wall or floors                      | -0.003 (0.002)       | 0.018 (0.010)#     |
| Rotten window frames or doors            | -0.001 (0.002)       | 0.012 (0.009)      |
| Dwelling is noisy                        | -0.007 (0.007)       | -0.001 (0.021)     |
| Neighbourhood quality (index)[a]         | -0.037 (0.009)**     | 0.029 (0.032)      |
| Noise annoyance neighbours               | -0.024 (0.006)**     | 0.007 (0.026)      |
| Noise annoyance factories/traffic        | -0.015 (0.006)*      | -0.017 (0.016)     |
| Stench, dust or dirt                     | -0.003 (0.003)       | 0.028 (0.011)*     |
| Vandalism/crime                          | -0.004 (0.004)       | 0.012 (0.011)      |
| Housing affordability stress             | -0.022 (0.006)**     | -0.013 (0.023)     |
| Sociodemographic characteristics         |                      |                    |
| Gender                                   | -0.000 (0.002)       | -0.133(0.128)      |
| Age                                      | 0.023 (0.006)**      | -0.501 (0.382)     |
| Having a partner                         | -0.046 (0.008)**     | 0.078 (0.049)      |
| Having child(ren)                        | 0.007 (0.005)        | -0.064 (0.027)*    |
| Tertiary education                       | 0.011 (0.004)**      | 0.007 (0.033)      |
| Income (ln)                              | 0.001 (0.003)        | -0.157 (0.291)     |
| Unemployed/disabled                      | -0.012 (0.006)#      | 0.014 (0.016)      |
| Out of work                              | -0.001 (0.002)       | -0.062 (0.051)     |
| Intercept                                |                      | 0.840 (0.546)      |
| Total                                    | -0.147 (0.019)**     | 0.056 (0.041)      |

*Notes:*    **p<0.01, *p<0.05, #p<0.10. Robust standard errors in parentheses. N=4,389; [a] Joined effects of variables that constitute the index.

# 5. Urbanization and the geography of societal discontent

**Camilla Lenzi and Giovanni Perucca**

## 5.1 INTRODUCTION

The generalized increase of economic inequalities and their spatial polarization in specific regions is more and more at the core of the debate on the societal wellbeing of Europe (European Union, 2020). This debate approached inequalities from two different perspectives.

The first one (Iammarino et al., 2019) concerns the highly unequal economic trajectories of regions, and the consequent slowdown (if not reversal) of economic convergence within the European Union (EU). This has led to a rise of interregional inequalities, where lagging-behind areas are increasingly distant from the living standards of the richest and best performing regions.

The second perspective refers to the insurgence of an unequal distribution of wealth within regions and communities. Stemming from the influential work by Piketty (2018), several studies have shown how intraregional inequalities persist and even increased in Europe over recent decades (Castells-Quintana et al., 2015). Importantly, the spatial dimension of this phenomenon matters, in that urbanized areas are those where intraregional inequalities are more intense (Florida, 2017).

The attention on inequalities is justified by the increasing recognition of their impact on societal wellbeing. While there is ample evidence on their detrimental effect on economic growth (Royuela et al., 2019), recent studies suggested that inequalities also influence other domains of wellbeing. The works on the so-called 'geography of discontent', for instance, have pointed to the association between inequalities and the rise of populism in Europe (Dijkstra et al., 2020; McCann, 2020). Despite these first attempts, however, we are still far from a full understanding of the relationship between inequalities and societal wellbeing.

This lack of knowledge is also due to the poor availability of empirical measures of wellbeing, alternative to the traditional, strictly economic indicators. Surprisingly, only recently economists have started to pay attention to the definition and systematic assessment of such measures (Stiglitz et al., 2018). Consequently, the general agreement on the multifaceted nature of societal wellbeing (encompassing economic, health, educational and other domains) is still not matched with adequate measurements.

Among these measurements, subjective wellbeing, i.e. individual self-reported life satisfaction, has emerged as a satisfactory indicator of the overall quality of one's own existence. The use of such an indicator was validated by a long stream of research (Helliwell, 2003) showing the strong empirical association between subjective wellbeing and indicators of material prosperity of a different nature, related to both individual economic prospects (e.g. income, occupation) and other characteristics (e.g. education, social relationships, health, etc.). Based on these findings, statistical institutes operationalized subjective wellbeing, developing guidelines for its measurement and using it as an indicator of human progress at both national and regional levels (OECD, 2013a).

Importantly, space is not at all neutral in the variation of subjective wellbeing across regions. In fact, one of the most recurrent results within the literature identifies the lowest levels of subjective wellbeing as belonging to the largest cities, at least in developed countries (Lenzi and Perucca, 2018; Burger et al., 2020). The explanation of this empirical regularity is still an open question, and scholars agree that it should be sought in the compensation mechanisms between urbanization advantages and disadvantages on the wellbeing of different social categories of individuals (Morrison and Weckroth, 2018; Lenzi and Perucca, 2021a, 2021b).

This assumption strongly suggests that intraregional inequalities, i.e. the extent to which the wealth generated by an economic system is more or less equally distributed within the society, represent a promising research direction in order to disentangle the urban puzzle of subjective wellbeing.

This study is aimed at exploring this conjecture. More precisely, its goal is to shed light on the relationship between intraregional inequalities and subjective wellbeing, and the mediating effect of urbanization. This mediating effect could manifest itself in two opposite ways. On the one hand, cities are historically places characterized by higher social mobility, due to the availability of better job opportunities and educational facilities (Connor and Storper, 2020). This may suggest a mitigating role of urbanization on the negative effect of intraregional inequalities on subjective wellbeing. On the other hand, intense urbanization often leads to processes of social segregation, thus preventing people left behind from climbing the social ladder (Tammaru et al., 2014), which could support the hypothesis of a worsening effect of urbanization on the relationship between intraregional inequalities and subjective wellbeing. These two conjectures are tested here, thanks to a measure of agglomeration able to capture different forms of urbanization.

The discussion is organized as follows. The next section discusses the literature on subjective wellbeing, inequalities and urbanization and the research question addressed by the present study. The third section presents the data used in the empirical analysis and the methodology applied. Section 4 discusses our results, and is followed by a final section on conclusions and policy implications.

## 5.2  SUBJECTIVE WELLBEING AND INEQUALITIES: WHAT ROLE FOR URBANIZATION?

The systematic study of subjective wellbeing within the economic literature originates from the seminal work by Easterlin (1974). Since the beginning, the interest of researchers focused around the so-called Easterlin paradox, i.e. the evidence on the nil association between economic growth (typically measured in terms of increases in gross domestic product – GDP) and subjective wellbeing. While many studies provided further verifications of this paradox with mixed results (Stevenson and Wolfers, 2008), some scholars postulated theoretical explanations for this puzzling evidence.

In particular, Clark et al. (2008) suggested that individuals evaluate their wellbeing not just over time, i.e. through comparison with the past, but also in relative terms, i.e. comparing themselves with the other members of the society. Put differently, what matters is not just the performance of the economic system in which people are living (i.e. aggregate GDP growth), but also the way in which the benefits from this overall performance are distributed within the society.

The possibility of empirically testing this hypothesis was constrained by the limited availability of time-series data on the evolution of intraregional inequalities. If, at both the country and regional level, GDP growth has been systematically measured over the last six decades, indicators of economic inequality are much more scarce.[1]

This limitation has been partially overcome in recent years. The recent stream of research on inequalities has underlined how the distribution of wealth within developed economies became more and more unequal in the last 60 years – a fact of which a large share of the social scientists' and policy makers' communities seemed largely unaware (Piketty and Saez, 2014). The debate stemming from these studies stimulated the interest of statistical

---

[1]  As an example, the World Bank provides data on national GDP growth for almost all western EU countries from 1961 on (https://data.worldbank.org/indicator/ NY.GDP.MKTP.KD.ZG). For the same sample of countries, the annual variation of the Gini index (a traditional measurement of income inequality) is available only from 2003 on (https://data.worldbank.org/indicator/SI.POV.GINI).

institute for systematically providing a measurement, for the first time also at the subnational level (Boulant et al., 2016). This represents an important improvement, as the distribution of inequalities within countries is not at all uniform. Many works have demonstrated that the largest cities are the places in which intraregional inequalities are higher (Florida and Mellander, 2016; Castells-Quintana, 2018).

The availability of new data on intraregional inequalities allowed for studying their relationship with subjective wellbeing, thus testing the conjecture by Clark et al. (2008) mentioned above. All the studies devoted to this issue pointed to a negative and statistically significant effect of economic inequalities on life satisfaction (Pittau et al., 2010; Ravazzini and Chávez-Juárez, 2018; Bernini and Tampieri, 2019; Lenzi and Perucca, 2021b). What is left unexplored by this literature, however, is the role of cities in this framework.

This issue deserves attention, since the relationship between subjective wellbeing and urbanization is indeed another puzzling and recurrent finding of the literature. Many studies find that, other things constant, living in the largest cities is associated with lower levels of subjective wellbeing with respect to less urbanized settings (Morrison 2007; Lenzi and Perucca 2019; Hanell, 2022). The reasons explaining what was labelled as the 'urban paradox' (Morrison, 2021) are still not fully understood.

The most popular conjecture assumes that, above a certain threshold in terms of city size, urbanization diseconomies, in the form of congestion, pollution, cost of living, etc., overcome the agglomeration advantages related to the availability of amenities, better job opportunities, etc. (Okulicz-Kozaryn, 2015). In the largest cities, the net effect on subjective wellbeing is, therefore, expected to be negative. Several works have tested this conjecture by analyzing the occurrence of urbanization economies (as in the case of innovation, see Lenzi and Perucca, 2020) and diseconomies (like the lack of green spaces and pollution, see Menz, 2011; Ambrey and Fleming, 2014) on subjective wellbeing.

Adopting a similar perspective, intraregional inequalities are another aspect in which urbanization may manifest its effects. On the one hand, urbanization economies, like occupational opportunities and easier access to schools and public services, may mitigate the negative effect of intraregional inequalities on subjective wellbeing, making cities the most favorable setting for social mobility to take place (Connor and Storper, 2020). On the other hand, urbanization diseconomies, like urban land rent and cost of living, may induce mechanisms of spatial segregation, in which disadvantaged individuals have a very limited access to the benefits of urbanization. Access to schooling is a typical example (Bernelius and Vilkama, 2019). When the effect of diseconomies prevails on the one generated by the advantages of urbanization, the urban environment is expected to reinforce, rather than mitigate, the negative effect of intraregional inequalities on subjective wellbeing.

The present study is aimed at empirically testing this conjecture. Our hypothesis is that, in correspondence to the highest levels of urbanization, diseconomies prevail over urbanization economies, thus leading to a worsening of the effect of intraregional inequalities on subjective wellbeing. Urbanization is instead expected to mitigate the negative effect of intraregional inequalities in contexts with an intermediate level of urbanization, where the disadvantages are still more than compensated for by the advantages of cities. Finally, in non-urbanized settings, we expect the relationship between intraregional inequalities and subjective wellbeing to be similar with that of the largest cities; this is because a peripheral location, with no access to urbanization economies, also leads to forms of socioeconomic segregation, hence hampering social mobility (Binder and Matern, 2020).

The next section presents the method and data used to empirically test these hypotheses. Importantly, it presents our measurement for urbanization, fundamental to disentangling the different typologies of settings, discussed above.

## 5.3    DATA AND METHODS

The aim of this work is to study the association between subjective wellbeing and intraregional inequalities, shedding light on the mediating effect of urbanization. Therefore, we have three key variables to be measured.

Subjective wellbeing is typically measured in the literature using data on individuals' life satisfaction from survey studies. We follow the same approach, using Eurobarometer (EB) data collected in 2018. Eurobarometer survey studies have been conducted on behalf of the European Commission since 1973. Among the numerous questions, a recurrent one concerns the level of life satisfaction experienced by the interviewee, who is asked to rate it on a four-point scale.[2] It is worth mentioning that all the surveys include information on the NUTS2 region of residence of the respondents.[3]

Compared with previous literature, which relies mostly on individual observations, we build an aggregated indicator of societal discontent (i.e. poor sub-

---

[2]    More precisely, the question wording is the following one: 'On the whole, are you very satisfied, fairly satisfied, not very satisfied or not at all satisfied with the life you lead?'.

[3]    NUTS is the official nomenclature of territorial units for statistics adopted by the EU. For Germany and the United Kingdom, survey studies report only the NUTS1 region of residence.

jective wellbeing) at the regional (NUTS2) level.[4] The reason for this choice is that using an aggregated indicator at the regional level allows for a direct comparison of wellbeing among different areas. This indicator is defined as the ratio, for each region, between the number of people who declared to be either 'not very satisfied' or 'not at all satisfied' and the total number of respondents:

$$Societal\ discontent_r = \frac{No.\ of\ respondents\ either\ not\ very\ satisfied\ or\ not\ at\ all\ satisfied_r}{Number\ of\ respondents_r} \qquad (5.1)$$

Figure 5.1 shows a map of the indicator of societal discontent. The figure reports the quintiles of the continuous variable defined in Equation [5.1]. The lowest quintiles (light gray) are therefore associated with lower discontent, while the opposite holds for the highest quintiles (dark gray). In general, the highest levels of societal discontent are in southern and eastern Europe, while northern countries are characterized by the lowest number of individuals unsatisfied with their life. Societal discontent is certainly influenced by country-specific factors, but the map shows how in large countries strong differences in discontent among regions do exist, in some cases mirroring gaps in socioeconomic development, as, for instance, when comparing northern vs southern Italy or western vs eastern Germany.

Intraregional inequalities are measured by the Gini index of disposable income, after taxes and transfers, provided by the OECD database on regional wellbeing indicators (OECD, 2013b). This indicator measures the extent to which the distribution of income among individuals within a region deviates from a perfectly equal distribution; its value ranges from 0 (perfectly equal distribution) to 1 (perfectly unequal distribution).

Urbanization is, among the three key variables, the most difficult to empirically measure. The literature pointing to the 'urban paradox' in subjective wellbeing, discussed above, generally adopts categorical classifications of regions, based on the size of the largest city (Hand, 2020). The idea is that, in every administrative unit, the urbanization externalities generated by the main city propagate to the whole region, thus influencing the wellbeing of all its inhabitants. As pointed out by some recent works, however, such an empirical measurement of urbanization overlooks the (potentially) highly differentiated variety of settings within each region. For instance, rural communities may be embedded within regions characterized by the presence of a large city; also,

---

[4]   EB surveys do not provide poststratification weights at the regional level. Therefore, the aggregated values are not weighted. However, the pooling of survey data of 2018 leads to a sample size of more than 171 000 observations, thus mitigating the issue of statistical representativeness of regional populations.

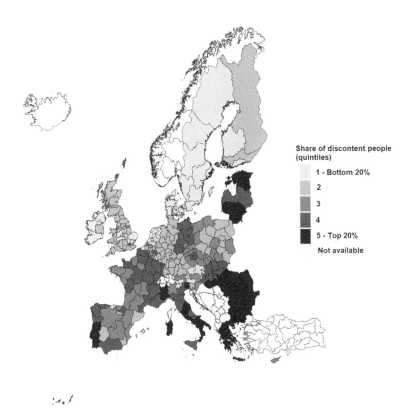

Share of discontent people (quintiles)

1 - Bottom 20%
2
3
4
5 - Top 20%
Not available

*Figure 5.1     Societal discontent in EU regions (2018)*

multiple cities of different size may be co-present within the same region (Lenzi and Perucca, 2021a; Hoogerbrugge et al., 2022).

Based on this reasoning, we adopt two empirical measurements of urbanization. The first one is consistent with the mainstream approach in the literature and is represented by a dummy equal to 1 if the main city of the region has more than 1 million inhabitants. The second variable is instead aimed at capturing the intensity of urbanization within the region, i.e. the share of regional population living in an urban area, as defined according to EUROSTAT classification.[5]

---

[5]     https://ec.europa.eu/eurostat/web/metropolitan-regions/background, last visited 31/01/2022.

*Spatial inequalities and wellbeing*

*Table 5.1*        *Definition and source of the empirical variables*

| Name | Description | Source |
|---|---|---|
| Societal discontent | Ratio between the number of people who declared to be either 'not very satisfied' or 'not at all satisfied' and the number of respondents who consider themselves either 'fairly satisfied' or 'highly satisfied' (year: 2018). | Authors' own elaboration on Eurobarometer data |
| Intraregional inequalities | Gini index of disposable income, after taxes and transfers (year: 2014) | OECD |
| Urbanization (rank) | Dummy equal to 1 if the main city of the region has more than 1 million inhabitants (year: 2018) | Eurostat |
| Urbanization (diffusion) | Share of regional population living in an urban area, i.e. a city with more than 1 million inhabitants (year: 2018) | Eurostat |
| Interregional inequalities | Average yearly per capita GDP growth rate (2008–18) | Eurostat |
| GDP per capita | Per capita GDP (year: 2017) | Eurostat |
| Activity rate | Share of the active persons relative to the regional population (year: 2017) | Eurostat |
| Tertiary education | Share of the regional population with tertiary education (year: 2017) | Eurostat |

Summing up, we expect our measurement of societal discontent to be negatively associated with intraregional inequalities, with a varying intensity, based on the degree of urbanization. More formally, the relationship to be studied takes the following form:

$$\begin{aligned} &Societal\ discontent_r \\ &= intraregional\ ineq._r + urbanization\ (rank)_r + urbanization\ (diffusion)_r + \\ &Societal\ discontent_r + interregional\ ineq._r + other\ controls_r \end{aligned} \tag{5.2}$$

where $r$ stands for the region. Subjective wellbeing is, therefore, considered as dependent on some regional characteristics, among which intraregional inequalities and urbanization are the focus of our analysis. The way in which urbanization affects the association between intraregional inequalities and societal wellbeing is empirically tested by interacting inequalities with the two variables of urbanization in Equation [1]. The other controls include further regional characteristics that are expected to influence subjective wellbeing. A list of these variables is reported in Table 5.1. Among them, the inclusion of an indicator of interregional inequalities (i.e. the variation of the regional economic performance over time) is important, since it allows testing of the simultaneous effect of interregional and intraregional inequalities on subjective wellbeing.

Equation (5.2) is estimated by the means of ordinary least squares (OLS) regression; results are robust to estimations based on random effects multilevel models, which are more and more common in the literature on subjective wellbeing.

## 5.4 INTRAREGIONAL INEQUALITIES AND SUBJECTIVE WELLBEING: THE ROLE OF URBANIZATION

The results of the empirical analysis are shown in Table 5.2. Column [1] reports the coefficients of the independent variables in a model without any control for urbanization. Consistently with previous research, growing intraregional inequalities are associated with higher levels of societal discontent. The same reasoning applies to interregional inequalities. Those regions with a higher per capita GDP growth rate in the previous 10 years are characterized, on average, by a lower share of discontent inhabitants. Interestingly, this finding is matched with the statistically insignificant coefficient of GDP per capita. This implies that regional differences in societal discontent within the EU do not relate on the differences in the level of wealth but, rather, on the different economic performance occurring in the preceding decades. Compared with previous literature, this result, therefore, is at odds with the Easterlin paradox, but it is consistent with some recent findings (Lenzi and Perucca, 2021b). The sign and significance of the other two variables is the expected one. A higher activity rate, which mirrors a demographic structure of the population more oriented towards young cohorts, is associated with lower levels of societal discontent. The same occurs when increasing the share of population with higher education.

The estimates reported in columns [2] and [3] adds the measurements of urbanization, respectively in terms of rank and diffusion. The sign of both coefficients is negative, but only the one associated with the spreading of urbanization within the region is slightly statistically significant. Moreover, when the two variables are simultaneously included in the model specification (column [4]) their effect on societal discontent vanishes.

This result seems inconsistent with the evidence on the urban paradox on subjective wellbeing, which associates urbanization with higher discontent. As discussed in the previous sections, however, this paradox arises only in correspondence with the highest levels of urbanization. Based on this reasoning, we try to isolate the regions characterized by the most intense urbanization, in order to check whether, in these kinds of settings, societal discontent is significantly higher than elsewhere. Empirically, we do this by introducing the interaction between the two variables of urbanization (column [5]). Results confirm our hypothesis. The negative and statistically significant coefficient of the presence of cities over 1 million inhabitants implies that, when the share of people living in metropolitan areas is low, the presence of large cities is associated with lower societal discontent. Similarly, the negative and statistically significant coefficient of the urbanization diffusion suggests that, when the region has no city over 1 million inhabitants (i.e. in regions without top-rank cities), increasing the people living in metropolitan settings is associated with lower societal discontent. The positive coefficient of the interaction between the two variables, however, shows that when the two conditions coexist (i.e. in situations of extreme and diffused urbanization) the beneficial effect of urbanization on discontent vanishes.

Taken together, these results indicate that urbanization reduces discontent, but only until it reaches a certain threshold in terms of city size and diffusion. This is, therefore, consistent with previous studies on life satisfaction in cities of different rank (Lenzi and Perucca, 2016), but also with recent evidence on the higher level of subjective wellbeing occurring in polycentric regions compared with monocentric ones (Hoogerbrugge et al., 2022).

The last column in Table 5.2 is aimed at investigating the mediating role of urbanization on the association between intraregional inequalities and subjective wellbeing (column [6]). This issue is addressed by adding to the model specification a triple interaction between the two indicators of urbanization and the variable of intraregional inequalities. The joint effects of the regressors are rather difficult to interpret from Table 2, as they are equal to the sum of the different coefficients. For an easier reading of our findings, they are graphically represented in Figures 5.2 and 5.3.

Figure 5.2 shows, for regions without a city of more than 1 million inhabitants, the marginal effects of a change in intraregional inequalities on societal discontent at low (10th percentile) and high (90th percentile) levels of urbanization diffusion. Therefore, the straight line represents the marginal effect of an increase of intraregional inequalities in those regions characterized by the highest levels of rurality, since they do not host any top-rank city and their share of metropolitan population falls within the lowest 10 per cent of the EU. The slope of the line indicates the strongly positive association between the variables represented on the horizontal and vertical axes: when intraregional inequalities increase from the minimum to the maximum value, the predicted share of discontented people triples, moving from 12 to 38 per cent. The dashed line reports the same relationship, but for those regions that do not host any city with more than 1 million inhabitants and have a share of metropolitan population falling within the highest 10 per cent of the EU. Compared with the other group, these areas are characterized by a higher level of urbanization, not concentrated in one single top-rank city, but rather diffused over space. When intraregional inequalities are at their minimum, the figure shows that the predicted level of social discontent is basically the same in the two groups

*Table 5.2*          *Societal discontent as a function of intraregional inequalities and urbanization: regression results*

| Dependent variable: Societal discontent | [1] | [2] | [3] | [4] | [5] | [6] |
|---|---|---|---|---|---|---|
| Intraregional inequalities | 1.3589*** | 1.4677*** | 1.4518*** | 1.4959*** | 1.4348*** | 2.2924*** |
|  | (0.386) | (0.371) | (0.371) | (0.367) | (0.349) | (0.443) |
| Interregional inequalities | -4.4713** | -4.3643** | -4.3292** | -4.2942** | -4.0963** | -4.2556** |
|  | (1.757) | (1.690) | (1.616) | (1.605) | (1.526) | (1.522) |
| GDP per capita | -0.1493 | -0.0353 | 0.1553 | 0.1676 | -0.1679 | 0.0159 |
|  | (0.569) | (0.635) | (0.627) | (0.671) | (0.649) | (0.612) |
| Activity rate (%) | -0.0070** | -0.0068** | -0.0065** | -0.0065** | -0.0067** | -0.0062** |
|  | (0.003) | (0.003) | (0.003) | (0.003) | (0.003) | (0.002) |
| Tertiary education (%) | -0.0018** | -0.0017** | -0.0016* | -0.0016* | -0.0017** | -0.0014* |
|  | (0.001) | (0.001) | (0.001) | (0.001) | (0.001) | (0.001) |
| Urbanization (rank) |  | -0.0256 |  | -0.0139 | -0.1223*** | 0.7567* |
|  |  | (0.015) |  | (0.013) | (0.036) | (0.383) |
| Urbanization (diffusion) |  |  | -0.0498* | -0.0417 | -0.0608* | 0.4832** |
|  |  |  | (0.027) | (0.026) | (0.031) | (0.203) |
| Urbanization (rank) × Urbanization (diffusion) |  |  |  |  | 0.1638*** | -0.9592* |
|  |  |  |  |  | (0.048) | (0.486) |
| Intraregional ineq. × Urbanization (diffusion) |  |  |  |  |  | -1.8992** |
|  |  |  |  |  |  | (0.745) |
| Intraregional ineq. × Urbanization (rank) |  |  |  |  |  | -2.8703** |
|  |  |  |  |  |  | (1.254) |
| Intraregional ineq. × Urbanization (diffusion) × Urbanization (rank) |  |  |  |  |  | 3.7171** |
|  |  |  |  |  |  | (1.612) |
| Constant | 0.1383 | 0.1421 | 0.0938 | 0.1253 | 0.1737 | -0.1134 |
|  | (0.172) | (0.165) | (0.171) | (0.166) | (0.161) | (0.192) |
| $R^2$ | 0.6563 | 0.6613 | 0.6654 | 0.6667 | 0.6779 | 0.7007 |

*Notes:*     N = 199. Standard errors in parentheses. * $p < 0.10$, ** $p < 0.05$, *** $p < 0.01$. Country group dummies included. East = Bulgaria, Czech Republic, Hungary, Latvia, Lithuania, Poland, Romania, Slovakia, Slovenia; South = Italy, Greece, Spain, Portugal, Cyprus; Centre = France, Belgium, Netherlands, Luxembourg, Germany, Austria; North = Denmark, Ireland, Finland, Sweden, UK.

of regions. Nevertheless, when intraregional inequalities increase, the slope of the dashed line is much lower than the solid one: moving from the minimum to the maximum level of intraregional inequalities less than doubles the predicted value of societal discontent (from 13 to 22 per cent).

Summing up the evidence from Figure 5.2, we can conclude that in the absence of top-rank cities, a diffused urbanization mitigates the effect of intraregional inequalities on societal discontent. The next step of the analysis consists of testing whether similar conclusions hold for regions hosting a top-rank city. These results are reported in Figure 5.3.

The interpretation of Figure 5.3 is analogous to the one of Figure 5.2, and, therefore, shows, for regions with a city of more than 1 million inhabitants, the marginal effects of a change in intraregional inequalities on societal discontent at low (10th percentile) and high (90th percentile) levels of urbanization diffusion.

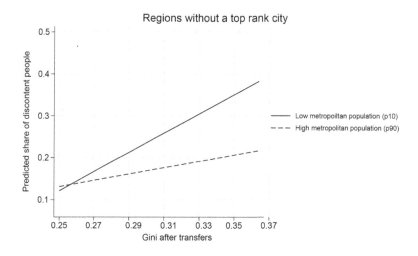

*Figure 5.2*        *Marginal effects of a change in intraregional inequalities on societal discontent at low (10th percentile) and high (90th percentile) levels of urbanization diffusion: regions without a top-rank city*

The straight line in the figure represents the marginal effect of an increase of intraregional inequalities in those regions characterized by a high level of urbanization, spatially concentrated and not diffused over space. In fact, they host a top-rank city surrounded by more rural settings, as mirrored by the low share of metropolitan population, falling within the lowest 10 per cent of the EU. The slope of the line is weakly positive, and if we move from the minimum to the maximum level of intraregional inequalities, the increase in the predicted level of societal discontent is negligible (from 12 to 14 per cent). The dashed line conveys the same message, but considering those regions hosting a top-rank city and with a share of metropolitan population within the highest 10 per cent of the EU. These regions are, therefore, those at the top of the urban hierarchy, in terms of both rank and diffusion. The slope of the line reported in Figure 5.3 is positive, and it shows that increasing intraregional inequalities over the horizontal axis leads to an increase in predicted societal discontent from 13 to 23 per cent. Hence, if we compare the two lines in Figure 5.3, in this case, higher urbanization exacerbates the effect of intraregional inequalities on societal discontent.

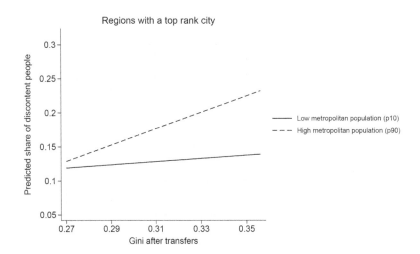

*Figure 5.3*      *Marginal effects of a change in intraregional inequalities on societal discontent at low (10th percentile) and high (90th percentile) levels of urbanization diffusion: regions with a top-rank city*

The joint analysis of Figures 5.2 and 5.3 conveys some further interesting results. First, urbanization is neutral when inequalities are at their lowest levels. In the two graphs, when inequalities are equal to their minimum, the differences of predicted societal discontent among the four different kinds of setting are negligible. Second, when inequalities grow, the role of urbanization in mediating their effect becomes significant. The worst scenario is the one characterized by lack of urbanization (Figure 5.2, straight line). Based on the assumptions discussed in section 5.2, this may be explained by the lack of those advantages typical of cities, like professional and educational opportunities, making rural communities stratified, crystallized societies, where the possibility of climbing the social ladder is extremely limited. In such a context, high inequalities are expected to significantly influence societal discontent. The opposite situation is the one characterized by high levels of urbanization, concentrated in a single large city, surrounded by more rural settings (Figure 5.3, straight line). In this case urbanization mitigates the effect of intraregional inequalities on societal discontent, and this could be explained by the urbanization economies supplied by the top-rank city, which also spread (within the same region) to the surrounding communities, which do not face the costs typical of large towns, like high costs of living and congestion. This finding is in line with the studies that identified in rural communities embedded in highly urbanized regions the places with the highest levels of subjective wellbeing (Lenzi and Perucca, 2021a). Avoiding these urbanization costs is instead not possible when the presence of a top-rank city is matched with a metropolitan population spread over the whole region. This case (Figure 5.3, dashed line) is, compared with the previous two, an intermediate scenario where increasing inequalities raise discontent, without, however, the intensity of the rural communities. This situation is basically analogous to the one of diffused urbanization without the presence of a top-rank city (Figure 5.2, dashed line).

## 5.5    CONCLUSIONS

This study analysed the role of different forms of urbanization in mediating the negative effect of intraregional inequalities on societal discontent. The empirical analysis presented here conveys two main messages.

The first one is that urbanization has a highly diversified effect on subjective wellbeing, based on both its intensity and diffusion. This suggests, once more, that an urban vs rural dichotomy is not a satisfactory instrument for understanding the complex association between cities and subjective wellbeing. The narrative of a bucolic paradise, opposed to the miserable urban life, goes against both almost all theories of agglomeration and the empirical evidence on subjective wellbeing. Similarly, the celebration of the city and urban life as the unique path to happiness totally overlooks the costs of agglomeration, and their unequal impact on the wellbeing of different categories of people.

The second message is that an important channel through which urbanization manifests its effect on subjective wellbeing consists of the mediating role of the negative impact of intraregional inequalities. We know very little about these mechanisms, and the present study is a first piece of evidence towards the understanding of a very relevant issue. While we have highlighted the mediating role of cities in different kinds of settings, future research should focus on the way in which these mechanisms work for different categories of individuals, i.e. disadvantaged vs non-disadvantaged people. Put differently, it would be extremely interesting to know whether the moderating effects of urbanization on societal discontent found here (see, for instance, Figures 5.2 and 5.3) affect in the same way the subjective wellbeing of those who suffer the most from intraregional inequalities (i.e. poor and uneducated individuals, temporary workers, etc.) and the others.

## REFERENCES

Ambrey, C., and Fleming, C. (2014). Public greenspace and life satisfaction in urban Australia. Urban Studies, 51(6), 1290–321.

Bernelius, V., and Vilkama, K. (2019). Pupils on the move: school catchment area segregation and residential mobility of urban families. Urban Studies, 56(15), 3095–116.

Bernini, C., and Tampieri, A. (2019). Happiness in Italian cities. Regional Studies, 53(11), 1614–24.

Binder, J., and Matern, A. (2020). Mobility and social exclusion in peripheral regions. European Planning Studies, 28(6), 1049–67.

Boulant, J., Brezzi, M., and Veneri, P. (2016). Income levels and inequality in OECD metropolitan areas. A Comparative Approach in OECD Countries. OECD Regional Development Working Papers, 2016/06, OECD Publishing, Paris.

Burger, M. J., Morrison, P. S., Hendriks, M., and Hoogerbrugge, M. M. (2020). Urban-rural happiness differentials across the world. World Happiness Report, 2020, 66–93.

Castells-Quintana, D. (2018). Beyond Kuznets: Inequality and the size and distribution of cities. Journal of Regional Science, 58(3), 564–80.

Castells-Quintana, D., Ramos, R., and Royuela, V. (2015). Income inequality in European Regions: recent trends and determinants. Review of Regional Research, 35(2), 123–46.

Clark, A. E., Frijters, P., and Shields, M. A. (2008). Relative income, happiness, and utility: an explanation for the Easterlin paradox and other puzzles. Journal of Economic literature, 46(1), 95–144.

Connor, D. S., and Storper, M. (2020). The changing geography of social mobility in the United States. Proceedings of the National Academy of Sciences, 117(48), 30309–17.

Dijkstra, L., Poelman, H., and Rodríguez-Pose, A. (2020). The geography of EU discontent. Regional Studies, 54(6), 737–53.

Easterlin, R. A. (1974). Does economic growth improve the human lot? Some empirical evidence. In Nations and households in economic growth (pp. 89–125). Academic Press.

European Union (2020). Territorial Agenda 2030: a future for all places, document of the informal meeting of Ministers responsible for spatial planning, territorial development and/or social cohesion, 1 December 2020, Germany.

Florida, R. (2017). The new urban crisis: how our cities are increasing inequality, deepening segregation, and failing the middle class – and what we can do about it. Hachette UK.

Florida, R., and Mellander, C. (2016). The geography of inequality: difference and determinants of wage and income inequality across US metros. Regional Studies, 50(1), 79–92.

Hand, C. (2020). Spatial influences on domains of life satisfaction in the UK. Regional Studies, 54(6), 802–13.

Hanell, T. (2022). Unmet aspirations and urban malaise. Social Indicators Research, 1–21. DOI: 10.1007/s11205-021-02864-8.

Helliwell, J. F. (2003). How's life? Combining individual and national variables to explain subjective well-being. Economic modelling, 20(2), 331–60.

Hoogerbrugge, M. M., Burger, M. J., and Van Oort, F. G. (2022). Spatial structure and subjective well-being in North-West Europe. Regional Studies, 56(1), 75–86.

Iammarino, S., Rodríguez-Pose, A., and Storper, M. (2019). Regional inequality in Europe: evidence, theory and policy implications. Journal of Economic Geography, 19(2), 273–98.

Lenzi, C., and Perucca, G. (2016). Life satisfaction across cities: evidence from Romania. The Journal of Development Studies, 52(7), 1062–77.

Lenzi, C., and Perucca, G. (2018). Are urbanized areas source of life satisfaction? Evidence from EU regions. Papers in Regional Science, 97, S105–22.

Lenzi, C., and Perucca, G. (2019). Subjective well-being over time and across space. Thirty years of evidence from Italian regions. Scienze Regionali, 18(Speciale), 611–32.

Lenzi, C., and Perucca, G. (2020). The nexus between innovation and wellbeing across the EU space: what role for urbanisation?. Urban Studies, 57(2), 323–49.

Lenzi, C., and Perucca, G. (2021a). Not too close, not too far: urbanisation and life satisfaction along the urban hierarchy. Urban Studies, 58(13), 2742–57.

Lenzi, C., and Perucca, G. (2021b). People or places that don't matter? Individual and contextual determinants of the geography of discontent. Economic Geography, 97(5), 415–45.

McCann, P. (2020). Perceptions of regional inequality and the geography of discontent: insights from the UK. Regional Studies, 54(2), 256–67.

Menz, T. (2011). Do people habituate to air pollution? Evidence from international life satisfaction data. Ecological Economics, 71, 211–19.

Morrison, P. S. (2007). Subjective wellbeing and the city. Social Policy Journal of New Zealand, 31, 74.

Morrison, P. S. (2021). Wellbeing and the region. In: Fischer, M. M., and Nijkamp, P. (eds), Handbook of Regional Science. Berlin and Heidelberg: Springer, pp. 779–98.

Morrison, P. S., and Weckroth, M. (2018). Human values, subjective well-being and the metropolitan region. Regional Studies, 52(3), 325–37.

OECD (2013a). OECD Guidelines on Measuring Subjective Well-Being. OECD Publishing.

OECD (2013b). How's Life? 2013: Measuring Well-Being. OECD Publishing.

Okulicz-Kozaryn, A. (2015). Happiness and Place: Why Life is Better outside of the City. Springer.

Piketty, T. (2018). Capital in the Twenty-First Century. Harvard University Press.

Piketty, T., and Saez, E. (2014). Inequality in the long run. Science, 344(6186), 838–43.

Pittau, M. G., Zelli, R., and Gelman, A. (2010). Economic disparities and life satisfaction in European regions. Social indicators research, 96(2), 339–61.

Ravazzini, L., and Chávez-Juárez, F. (2018). Which inequality makes people dissatisfied with their lives? Evidence of the link between life satisfaction and inequalities. Social Indicators Research, 137(3), 1119–43.

Royuela, V., Veneri, P., and Ramos, R. (2019). The short-run relationship between inequality and growth: evidence from OECD regions during the Great Recession. Regional Studies, 53(4), 574–86.

Stevenson, B., and Wolfers, J. (2008). Economic growth and subjective well-being: reassessing the Easterlin paradox. Brookings Papers on Economic Activity, 39(1), 1–102.

Stiglitz, J., Fitoussi, J., and Durand, M. (2018). Beyond GDP: Measuring What Counts for Economic and Social Performance. OECD Publishing.

Tammaru, T., Marcińczak, S., Van Ham, M., and Musterd, S. (2014). Socio-Economic Segregation in European Capital Cities. Abingdon: Routledge.

# 6. Regional disparities in the sensitivity of wellbeing to poverty measures

**Cristina Bernini, Silvia Emili and Maria Rosaria Ferrante**

## 6.1 INTRODUCTION

For national and international agencies and governments, the measurement and investigation of poverty[1] levels and quality of life, at the country and regional level, are key topics. The complexity of the phenomena and the difficulties in comparing poverty and wellbeing measures between areas has a significant effect on policies, which are usually developed without accounting for within-countries differences.

These limits to evaluating people's living conditions are stressed by researchers, who have generally shown that regional and contextual characteristics play a substantial role in the definition of poverty and wellbeing (Ayala and Jurado, 2011; Ballas et al., 2017; Bramley, Lancaster and Gordon, 2000). The standard approach to measuring poverty at the country level might provide a biased picture of the degree and distribution of poverty over the population and across territories, due to the lack of attention to differences in regional prices or the needs of those people (Ayala, Jurado and Pérez-Mayo, 2014; Mogstad, Langørgen and Aaberge, 2007; Chauhan, Mohanty and Subramanian, 2016). The regional dimension also affects subjective wellbeing (SWB), where the cultural dimension, social context, religion, traditions and lifestyle are recognized as fundamental predictors of SWB variability across territories. Lawless and Lucas (2011) stressed that 'studies of cross-national well-being cannot address within-nation variance, which may exist despite the cultural and economic homogeneity of a nation. Importantly, this within-nation variance will be most relevant in the use of well-being to determine policy decisions'. Based on this evidence, we expect the magnitude of the relationship

---

[1]    In this study the word 'poverty' is used meaning exclusively (objective) economic poverty.

between poverty and SWB to be strongly affected by contextual, cultural, as well as regional aspects; and, if ignored, an analysis of the nexus between these aspects may provide unreliable results (Clark 2017, Giarda and Moroni, 2018).

The purpose of this study is to investigate whether the sensitivity of SWB to poverty conditions changes across areas, reflecting regional disparities. The rationale is that SWB and poverty follow different distributions if they refer to heterogeneous populations at the regional level; thus, to obtain unbiased estimates, it becomes fundamental to analyse the relationships between SWB and poverty in different macroareas, separately modelling this nexus across the territory. To provide deeper insights on this relationship, we also exploit the multidimensionality in the concepts of both satisfaction and poverty (Van Praag and Ferrer-i-Carbonell, 2004; Foster, Greer and Thorbecke, 2010). Therefore, the following research questions are posed: To what extent are regional disparities present in the SWB-poverty relationship? What are the main territorial aspects affecting this nexus? What aspects of poverty primarily affect the SWB? Are there different responses at the regional level? Since SWB is a multidimensional concept, which dimensions of SWB are generally impacted by poverty conditions? Are regional disparities detected in these nexuses?

To investigate these aspects, Italy represents an interesting case-study, due to its well-documented regional disparities. The North and South are marked by a historically significant socioeconomic gap (Capello, 2016; Giarda and Moroni, 2018; Patacchini, 2008; Tubadji et al., 2022); the economic aspects in the South are vulnerable, including weakened labour markets, industrial productivity, employment level, and GDP, and social features are lacking (e.g. social security and participation rates).

There is no single survey in Italy that allows for an exhaustive analysis of poverty and the SWB of Italian households, other than resorting to the statistical matching of two separate Italian surveys: the Multipurpose Survey on Households: Aspects of Daily Life (ADL) and the Household Budget Survey (HBS). This combined dataset creates a basis allowing different poverty aspects and SWB to be investigated simultaneously for overall quality of life and other macrodomains, which can then be analysed to tease out the sensitivity of this relationship to territorial characteristics.

Our analysis contributes to the growing literature in several ways. First, it extends earlier empirical studies, which only depicted the impact of poverty on individuals at the country level, by providing evidence of differences at the macroarea level. Second, in addition to considering the impact of being poor on individual life satisfaction, different aspects of poverty are considered, such as the intensity and severity of poverty. Finally, an overall measure of life satisfaction is accompanied by macrodomains of economic and social satisfaction, creating a more complete picture of the role poverty plays in the lives of individuals.

## 6.2 POVERTY, LIFE SATISFACTION AND REGIONAL DISPARITIES

This study intertwines three strands of literature: the regional characteristics of the poverty-SWB nexus, the multidimensional concept of SWB and poverty measurements.

In the economics of happiness literature, studies using different methodological approaches have highlighted the role of territorial characteristics in mediating the impact of poverty on SWB. Among others, Giarda and Moroni (2018) considered a dynamic random effects probit model for the UK, Italy and France separately, including regional (NUTS-1) dummies in the specification. The authors showed that, when regional effects within countries are disregarded, the poverty persistence is highest in Italy compared to other European countries, while if regional disparity is considered, the degree of poverty persistence in Italy approaches that of some other countries. Similar approaches have been considered by Ravallion and Lokshin (2001), Shams (2014; 2016), Simona-Moussa (2020) and Strotmann and Volkert (2018). Luttmer (2005) and Ferrer-i-Carbonell (2005) included regional determinants as measures of regional material wellbeing. In the literature, the most utilized macroeconomic variables included in the SWB function are regional income, regional unemployment rate, population density, level of prices and ageing. In this group of studies we include, among others, Welsch and Biermann (2019), Okulicz-Kozaryn (2012), Lawless and Lucas (2011) and Carver and Grimes (2019). Finally, a spatial effect in the relationship across geographic territories is investigated by Lin, Lahiri and Hsu (2014). The authors, moving from a regional to a cross-country perspective, not only investigate the role of country-specific variables on the national level of subjective wellbeing, but also consider possible spatial 'spillover effects of one country's well-being on the well-being of the neighboring countries'. The findings do not confirm the existence of spatial phenomena but suggest the need to group territories in clusters with respect to the economic conditions of the spatial units. Aiming to jointly model the contextual and the individual dimension of SWB as a function of poverty conditions are Buhmann et al. (1988), Morrison, Tay and Diener (2011) and Reyes-García et al. (2019).

Differently from these studies, we control for territorial characteristics, taking into account the diverse distributions of the variables (i.e. SWB and poverty) across households living in different areas of Italy; thus, we suggest the SWB–poverty relationship for the main macroareas should be modelled separately.

The literature regarding the concept of SWB has focused primarily on overall life satisfaction as a proxy of people's wellbeing; however, it is used in reference to wellbeing as a multidimensional phenomenon (Cummins, 1996; Van Praag and Ferrer-i-Carbonell 2004). Among the studies improving the understanding of the role of poverty on different life domains, Hsieh (2002) and Ng and Diener (2014) focused on satisfaction with financial conditions, Clark and Oswald (1994) investigated job satisfaction, Biwas-Diener and Diener (2001) analysed the relationship between poverty and satisfaction with leisure activities, Helmert et al. (1997) considered the health domain and Galinha et al. (2016) focused on family, friendships and the affective sphere of life in countries with extreme poverty. Van Praag and Ferrer-i-Carbonell (2008) combined different aspects of wellbeing (measured through a question-naire on satisfaction) to provide a measure of subjective poverty. The authors approach economic and subjective poverty as complementary aspects of an individual's wellbeing. In a similar manner, Rojas (2008) investigated the impact of poverty on the satisfaction level of life domains, finding income has a greater impact on those aspects of life that would be expected to be strongly related to income. Mysíková et al. (2019) separated the economic and noneconomic aspects of life into two main macro classes of domains, then, they focused only on the economic domain, suggesting that 'the more general happiness/satisfaction approach can include numerous non-economic domains reflecting individuals' perceptions of health, productivity, intimacy, safety, community, and emotional well-being', which renders an analysis of objective and perceived economic conditions less clear.

Following the distinction between economic and noneconomic domains, we enrich our analysis with an investigation of the effect poverty conditions have, not only on life as a whole (i.e. measured as a factor extracted from different life domains), but also considering economic and social macrodomains sepa-rately. The aim is to depict possible differences in the sensitivity to poverty in people's satisfaction with other aspects of their lives.

The last branch of literature involved in this study relates to the assessment of poverty conditions. The idea that poverty embodies different aspects of indi-viduals' lives is widely accepted by researchers, leading to the aggregation of various attributes of people's lives into a single index (Alkire and Foster, 2011; Muñoz, Àlvarez-Verdejo and García-Fernández, 2018). Despite attempts to account for the various life domains in the literature reporting on poverty measures, when the definition of poverty is related to a monetary perspective, the FGT class of decomposable poverty measures is still the main tool used in empirical investigations. The Foster, Greer and Thorbecke (1984) poverty metric $FGT(\alpha)$ (from the names of its creators) has been the focus of atten-tion in empirical, methodological and policy literature (for a comprehensive review see Foster, Greer and Thorbecke (2010)). The simplicity, the axiomatic properties and the ability to capture the complex structure of the phenomenon makes this class of poverty measures strongly appealing. Operatively, the class is formalized as powers (i.e. $\alpha$ poverty aversion parameter) of normalized shortfalls from a specific reference point, the poverty line. In particular, when the parameter $\alpha$ is set to zero, the FGT(0) allows researchers to account for the spread of poverty; when $\alpha$ is equal to one (i.e. FGT(1)), it measures how far poor individuals are from the not-poverty condition; and when the aversion is assumed to equal two, the FGT(2), known as poverty severity, accounts for the inequality among the poor. Clark (2017) provided a comprehensive review of the large number of empirical studies handling poverty with FGT(0) and FGT(1), while use of FGT(2) is limited in the literature (e.g. Muñoz, Àlvarez-Verdejo and García-Fernández, 2018).

In this study, we utilize FGTs to fully exploit the different measures of poverty in order to capture the relevance of the different aspects of being poor, on wellbeing and to investigate whether regional disparities exhibit a role in mediating this nexus.

## 6.3    MODELLING THE POVERTY AND LIFE SATISFACTION NEXUS

This analysis aims to investigate to what extent different aspects of poverty affect the individual satisfaction for the macrodomains of life, and the existence of regional disparities in these relationships. In line with literature about poverty and SWB, we estimate microeconometric satisfaction models in which the subjective wellbeing of individual $i$, $SWB_i$, depends on different individual poverty measures, a set of individual-level controls and some macroeconomic contextual variables. The baseline model is given by:

$$SWB_i = \alpha_0 + \beta'poverty_i + \gamma'Ind_i + \zeta'Eco_i + \psi'Terr_i + \varepsilon_i, \; \varepsilon_i \sim iid(0,\Sigma) \qquad (6.1)$$

where $poverty_i$, $i = 1,\dots, n$, represents the vector of alternative combinations of poverty metrics and the vector $Ind_i$ includes demographic variables of each statistical unit. The model is further enhanced to account for several macroeconomic variables, $Eco_i$, to evaluate the impact of contextual characteristics (Luttmer, 2005; Welsch and Biermann, 2019). Finally, in line with Lenzi and Perucca's (2018, 2021) findings about the high level of unexplained regional-level variability, the specification is enriched by the set of dummy variables ($Terr_i$) related to both the well-known divide across Italian macroareas and the degree[2] of urbanization characterizing individuals' living environment in their area of residence.

The first step in the empirical specification and estimation of the model in Equation 6.1, is the measurement of subjective wellbeing. We started by considering all the life satisfaction scores, collected at the individual level. Six domains are measured on a 1–4 scale referring to the level of satisfaction with: relationship with friends (Friends) and relatives (Family), economic condition (EconomicC), health status (Health), living environment (Environment), leisure time (FreeTime). Alongside the six domains are two questions about: the available household income in relation to their needs (AvailableInc, collected on a scale from 1 to 4), and the current economic condition of the family compared to the previous year (PreviousInc, measured on a 1–5 scale, unlike the other variables).

Based on this information, we extracted three SWB measures through a factor analysis on the polychoric covariance matrix for the considered satisfaction scores (further methodological details on factor analysis are available on request). The first SWB measure (hereinafter, TotWB), is obtained by extracting one factor from the analysis, without distinguishing among macro-domains, which is then interpretable as a proxy for overall life satisfaction. The analysis of the eigenvalues (2.3 and 0.98) and the portion of explained variability (88%), show that it would be possible to distinguish between two separate factors: a first, strongly associated with economic aspects, and a second, not directly related to economic aspects of life (i.e. Health, FreeTime, Friends, Family, Environment). Then, focusing on the two separated sets of satisfaction domains, we repeat the factor analysis, first on EconomicC, PreviousInc and AvailableInc, extracting the factor identified hereinafter as EcoWB, and then on Health, FreeTime, Friends, Family and Environment, building a measure of social satisfaction, henceforth called SocWB.

The next step concerns the definition of the variables measuring relative individual poverty. In order to account for the scale of economies, we follow the official Italian Statistical Institute (ISTAT) practice, by transforming total household consumption into an equivalent individual consumption through the Carbonaro equivalence scale (ISTAT, 2016). Then, the definition of relative individual poverty is based on a poverty line equal to the mean per capita consumption expenditure at the national level. To capture different dimensions of poverty we consider the Foster-Greer-Thorbecke (FGT) class of decomposable

---

[2]    Following ISTAT classification of territories, we identify municipalities with less than 50 000 residents as rural areas, and those with more than 50 000 inhabitants as urbanized territories. The 12 Metropolitan areas of Bari, Bologna, Cagliari, Catania, Firenze, Genova, Milano, Napoli, Palermo, Roma, Torino and Venezia are included as the largest Italian cities with specific administrative and territorial characteristics.

poverty measures. The FGT indexes are among the most well-known metrics used to measure this economic phenomenon, given their ability to go beyond the most common poverty status, and are defined as:

$$FGT\left(\alpha\right) = \frac{1}{N}\sum_{i=1}^{q} \left(\frac{z - x_i}{z}\right)^{\alpha} \alpha \geq 0 \tag{6.2}$$

where $z$ is the poverty line, $x_i$ is the equivalent expenditure of the $i$-th individual, $N$ is the total population size, $q$ is the number of persons who are poor (that is with $x_i \leq z$), and $\alpha \geq 0$ is a 'poverty aversion' parameter. In particular, the higher the value of the aversion parameter, the higher the relevance accounted for in the lower tail of the consumption distribution and the use of this parameter links the analysis of poverty conditions to the inequality among the sample of poor individuals. In the literature, when the poverty aversion parameter $\alpha$ is set to zero, the so-called incidence of poverty is obtained, which is also identified as headcount ratio, while poverty intensity (or poverty gap index) and poverty severity (or severe poverty gap index) are obtained with $\alpha=1$ and $\alpha=2$, respectively. In general, when $\alpha$ goes to infinity, the index relates only to the lowest incomes.

As individual measures of poverty incidence, intensity and severity, we adopt the individual scaled gap

$$P_{\alpha,i} = \left(\frac{z - x_i}{z}\right)^{\alpha} 1_{x_i \leq z} \quad i = 1,\dots,n, \; \alpha = 0,1,2 \tag{6.3}$$

where $1_{x_i \leq z}$ is an indicator function that assumes a value equal to one is the equivalent expenditure for the i-th individual, $x_i$, is lower than the poverty line $z$ (poor individual), zero otherwise.

Then we consider the $P_{\alpha,i}$ variables as poverty covariates by naming them, for sake of simplicity, as the correspondent poverty indexes, that is incidence, intensity and severity, respectively, for $\alpha = 0,1,2$. We specify the models by considering two different combinations of these variables: incidence and intensity with $P_{0,i}$, $P_{1,i}$ and incidence and severity with $P_{0,i}$, $P_{2,i}$, by means of the following specifications:

$$SWB_i = \alpha_0 + \beta_1 P_{0,i} + \beta_2 P_{1,i} + \theta X_i + \varepsilon_i \tag{6.4}$$

$$SWB_i = \alpha_0 + \beta_1 P_{0,i} + \beta_2 P_{2,i} + \theta X_i + \varepsilon_i \tag{6.5}$$

where $SWB = \{ TotWB, EcoWB, SocWB \}$, in other words, life satisfaction, satisfaction with the economic macrodomain and satisfaction with social macrodomain. $X$ includes the different sets of controls (**Ind**, **Eco**, **Terr**) previously introduced. Following the literature (Clark, 2017), we control for individual sociodemographic determinants by means of: *Gender*, a dummy variable equal to one for female; *Age*, built as the midpoints of the 13 classes harmonized from the two surveys; a dummy variable represented by *LowEducation*, a dummy variable taking the value of one for people with no education or primary school education; two dummies, *Unemployed*, *Retired*, representing two labour-force statuses of being unemployed or being retired; the set of dummy variables *Married*, *Divorced*, *Widower*, introduced to account for the three classes of marital statuses; *nComp*, the number of components in the household.

The determinants collected in **Eco** are observed at regional NUTS-2 level, including the logarithm: of the unemployment rate (*lnUnempl*), regional per capita gross domestic product (*lnGDP*), and the consumer price index (*lnCPI*), aiming to account for price divides across Italy.

The remaining set of variables, **Terr**, is composed of two dummies *North* and *South*, referring to the regions located in the Centre as reference group, and *South* also including the two islands, Sicily and Sardinia, and the dummies *Metropolis* and *Urban* (i.e. *Rural* as the reference group), to account for the degree of urbanization in the living environment. In the following section we provide an accurate description of the variables.

Finally, with the aim of measuring regional disparities in the SWB-poverty relationship, the models in Equations (6.4) and (6.5) are estimated for the whole Italian territory and compared to results obtained from the three specific macroareas (i.e. North, Centre and South).

## 6.4    THE DATA

In Italy, detailed information on poverty and SWB is provided in two separate surveys, both conducted by the Italian Office of Statistics (ISTAT), the Multipurpose Survey on Households: Aspects of Daily Life (ADL) and the Household Budget Survey (HBS). Using appropriate statistical procedures, we matched the two surveys, obtaining a complete database at the individual level, allowing us to apply it to our research hypotheses.

The ADL survey is developed to collect information on the habits, living conditions and satisfaction scores of Italian residents. Specifically, in the ADL, information on life domains satisfaction (i.e. economic conditions, relationship with relatives and with friends, health status, living environment and leisure time and activities) are collected as well as information on own economic conditions. The HBS survey represents a detailed collection of expenditure data and spending habits of Italians, as it is the reference survey to calculate poverty measures for Italian public agencies and organizations.

Following the ISTAT approach, in our analysis, household expenditures has been transformed into individual spending by applying the Carbonaro equivalence scale (Carbonaro, 1985, 1990). By moving from the household to an individual level, we aim to preserve the individuality and reliability of the SWB scores. Moreover, this transformation preserves the relevance, in monetary terms, of several spending categories, such as food, dwelling expenses and services. These aggregates involve the whole household equivalently and impact on the whole household budget. In this sense, the poverty line for a one-component household in 2016 is given by 636.81 euros (monthly expenditure).

The matched dataset is obtained by using micro nonparametric statistical matching techniques (D'Orazio et al., 2006). The idea behind statistical matching techniques (also known as data fusion) is to fuse two independent samples, where observations are considered independent and identically generated from appropriate models. A set of variables is observed only in one of the two surveys. The objective is then to use common information in the two samples to obtain a final comprehensive collection of data. Without making assumptions on the joint unobservable distribution of the matched variables (D'Orazio et al., 2006), distance hot deck procedure (one of the most commonly used micro approaches in empirical applications) appears to be a natural solution. Operatively, the satisfaction scores of ADL (the donor-largest-survey) are imputed to the HBS records. In addition to being intuitive, this approach is a good solution for properties such as those shown by Marella et al. (2008), when they find that when distance hot deck procedures are used, the matching noise due to imputation decreases as the sample size of the donor sample increases. To evaluate the final results obtained, we use a set of statistical measures on the dataset representativeness (see D'Orazio et al., 2006 for a review). For the detailed description of the matching procedure used in this analysis, see Bernini et al. (2021).

Table 6.1 presents some descriptive statistics on the main variables used in the analysis at the country and macroareas levels.

The average overall level of life satisfaction in Italian residents is equal to 3.98 (on the range 1.41 and 5.66, corresponding to 60 per cent of the maximum) and it decreases when we move from North to South, while the variability increases slightly (Figure 6.1). A similar pattern is detected for the economic macrodomain, which has an average of 2.54 (i.e. 47 per cent of its maximum value) but reduces in the South of Italy. The mean of the social macrodomain is 3.47 (67 per cent of the maximum value); for this macrodomain we detect a lower variability across areas.

Poor people represent 10 per cent of the Italian population, 20 per cent of which reside in the North, 14 per cent in the Centre and 66 per cent in the South (Table 6.1). The poverty indicators show further substantial difference across the territory; 17 per cent of individuals residing in the South are below the poverty line, while this percentage reduces to 5 per cent and 8 per cent

*Table 6.1*    *Descriptive statistics*

|  | Italy | | North | | Centre | | S&I | |
|---|---|---|---|---|---|---|---|---|
|  | Mean | sd | Mean | sd | Mean | sd | Mean | Sd |
| Life satisfaction | | | | | | | | |
| TotWB | 3.98 | 0.58 | 4.10 | 0.56 | 4.00 | 0.56 | 3.85 | 0.59 |
| EcoWB | 2.54 | 0.54 | 2.63 | 0.51 | 2.58 | 0.51 | 2.43 | 0.57 |
| SocWB | 3.47 | 0.57 | 3.55 | 0.56 | 3.46 | 0.56 | 3.38 | 0.57 |
| Poverty measures | 3.98 | 0.58 | 4.10 | 0.56 | 4.00 | 0.56 | 3.85 | 0.59 |
| $P_0$(Incidence) | 0.10 | 0.30 | 0.05 | 0.21 | 0.08 | 0.27 | 0.17 | 0.38 |
| $P_1$(Intensity) | 0.02 | 0.09 | 0.01 | 0.06 | 0.01 | 0.07 | 0.04 | 0.12 |
| $P_2$(Severity) | 0.01 | 0.04 | 0.00 | 0.03 | 0.00 | 0.03 | 0.02 | 0.06 |
| Individual characteristics | | | | | | | | |
| Gender (Female=1) | 0.64 | 0.48 | 0.63 | 0.48 | 0.66 | 0.47 | 0.64 | 0.48 |
| Ncomp | 2.44 | 1.13 | 2.34 | 1.06 | 2.40 | 1.15 | 2.56 | 1.18 |
| Age | 49.41 | 22.18 | 49.56 | 21.76 | 51.23 | 22.42 | 48.41 | 22.46 |
| LowEducation | 0.16 | 0.37 | 0.15 | 0.36 | 0.17 | 0.37 | 0.18 | 0.38 |
| Unemployed | 0.13 | 0.34 | 0.09 | 0.29 | 0.10 | 0.30 | 0.18 | 0.39 |
| Retired | 0.23 | 0.42 | 0.26 | 0.44 | 0.26 | 0.44 | 0.19 | 0.39 |
| Married | 0.32 | 0.47 | 0.33 | 0.47 | 0.33 | 0.47 | 0.30 | 0.46 |
| Divorced | 0.07 | 0.25 | 0.08 | 0.27 | 0.08 | 0.28 | 0.05 | 0.22 |
| Widower | 0.11 | 0.32 | 0.10 | 0.30 | 0.13 | 0.34 | 0.12 | 0.32 |
| Economic aspects | | | | | | | | |
| lnGDP | 10.19 | 0.28 | 10.45 | 0.09 | 10.30 | 0.11 | 9.87 | 0.12 |
| lnCPI | 4.60 | 0.04 | 4.61 | 0.00 | 4.60 | 0.00 | 4.59 | 0.06 |
| lnUnempl | 2.42 | 0.42 | 2.04 | 0.16 | 2.33 | 0.07 | 2.88 | 0.24 |
| Territorial aspects | | | | | | | | |
| Metropolis | 0.12 | 0.33 | 0.12 | 0.32 | 0.18 | 0.38 | 0.10 | 0.30 |
| Urban | 0.27 | 0.44 | 0.25 | 0.43 | 0.29 | 0.45 | 0.28 | 0.45 |
| Rural | 0.61 | 0.49 | 0.64 | 0.48 | 0.53 | 0.50 | 0.62 | 0.48 |
| North | 0.43 | 0.49 | | | | | | |
| Centre | 0.18 | 0.38 | | | | | | |
| South | 0.39 | 0.49 | | | | | | |

in the North and Centre, respectively. Intensity and severity,[3] indicated with $FGT(1)$ and $FGT(2)$, show similar results, with the highest poverty gaps observed in the South. Even if the remaining territories show similar distributions of the two indicators, the intensity of poverty in the North is lower than in the Centre.

Referring to the set of individual characteristics, Table 6.1 depicts notable differences across the regions, especially for the number of components in a household (largest in the Southern regions), the percentage of population with a low level of education (from 15 per cent in the North, to 17 per cent in the Centre, to 18 per cent in the South of Italy) and the unemployment rate (doubling from 0.09 in the North to 0.18 in the South). A similar pattern can be seen with the macroeconomic variables, showing that, also at a regional level, the well-known economic divide is seen (Capello, 2016): the Northern areas are the richest parts of Italy, with higher levels of both GDP per capita and CPI, and the lowest unemployment rates.

All these data confirm significant differences in SWB and poverty across the country, supporting our modelling strategy to estimate Equations (6.4) and (6.5) separately for the three macroareas.

## 6.5    RESULTS

### 6.5.1    Domains Satisfaction and Poverty Measures at Country Level

The starting point of this analysis is the estimates carried out over the whole Italian territory, for life satisfaction (*TotWB*) and for the two macrodomains of satisfaction (*EcoWB* and *SocWB*), considering poverty incidence and intensity. Testing a set of nested models on *TotWB*, obtained from different sets of controls and reported in Table 6.2, we empirically assessed the evidence in favour of the unrestricted specification (M1_Tot) by LR tests (i.e. including all individual, territorial and macroeconomic variables previously described). This result is confirmed by the application of the same selection procedure for the model specification of two macrodomain factors. For brevity, in Table 6.2 we show only the estimates of the unrestricted models M1_Eco and M1_Soc, however, the whole set of estimates is available on request.

With the overall life satisfaction-poverty nexus described by the model M1_Tot, we find negative and statistically significant associations both for

---

[3]    This distribution of poverty across the Italian territory is confirmed by the Poverty Intensity and Severity Indexes, calculated by the ISTAT as averages of poverty gaps and poverty squared gaps only on the subsample of poor people (not the whole population as with the FGTs).

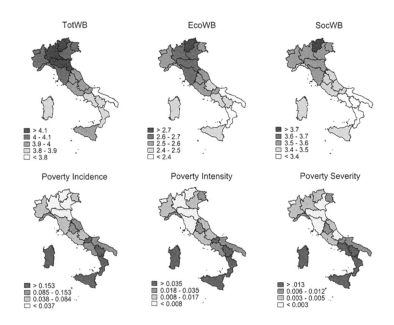

*Figure 6.1    The Italian map of life satisfaction and poverty measures*

*Source*:    Authors' computations.

incidence and intensity of poverty, in line with previous literature (Deeming, 2013; Clark, 2018). Poverty incidence shows a strong association with life satisfaction; individuals below the poverty line have an overall satisfaction with life that is 0.150 points lower than non-poor individuals. The effect of poverty on life satisfaction dramatically increases with its intensity: with relative poverty line gap growths of one unit, the overall life satisfaction significantly reduces of 0.439 points.

The complexity of the phenomenon and its strong association with individual factors such as behaviour, genetics and contextual features, requires a deeper analysis of the results related to demographic variables (Huppert, 2009; Diener, 2012; Dolan et al., 2008). First, we show negative effects on wellbeing due to low education levels and not living with a partner (divorced and widowed) (e.g. Felton and Graham, 2006); the negative effects of being widowed or divorced reinforce the social relevance of subjective wellbeing. Second, we show that the labour-force condition has a substantial effect on individual wellbeing. Employment is one of the main contributors to life satisfaction, representing a source of and structure to facilitate access to social

*Table 6.2*    *Model estimates for overall, social and economic SWB: poverty incidence and intensity*

|  | M5_Tot | M4_Tot | M3_Tot | M2_Tot | M1_Tot | M1_Eco | M1_Soc |
|---|---|---|---|---|---|---|---|
| $P_0$ (Incidence) | -0.215*** | -0.200*** | -0.148*** | -0.159*** | -0.150*** | -0.211*** | -0.054*** |
| $P_1$ (Intensity) | -0.515*** | -0.470*** | -0.441*** | -0.442*** | -0.439*** | -0.730*** | -0.085 |
| Gender |  | 0.011 | 0.015* | 0.015* | 0.015* | 0.020** | 0.006 |
| Ncomp |  | -0.004 | 0.000 | 0.000 | -0.001 | 0.014*** | -0.009** |
| Age |  | -0.003*** | -0.003*** | -0.003*** | -0.003*** | -0.001*** | -0.005*** |
| LowEducation |  | -0.104*** | -0.103*** | -0.101*** | -0.103*** | -0.131*** | -0.042*** |
| Unemployed |  | -0.159*** | -0.130*** | -0.134*** | -0.130*** | -0.208*** | -0.028** |
| Retired |  | 0.088*** | 0.062*** | 0.063*** | 0.061*** | 0.038*** | 0.051*** |
| Married |  | 0.016 | 0.019 | 0.018 | 0.020 | 0.014 | 0.015 |
| Divorced |  | -0.152*** | -0.161*** | -0.162*** | -0.160*** | -0.176*** | -0.087*** |
| Widower |  | -0.137*** | -0.117*** | -0.119*** | -0.114*** | -0.098*** | -0.083*** |
| lnGDP |  |  | 0.056 |  | -0.014 | -0.022 | -0.012 |
| lnIPC |  |  | -0.287*** |  | -0.357*** | -0.505*** | -0.129 |
| lnUnempl |  |  | -0.192*** |  | -0.171*** | -0.110*** | -0.142*** |
| Metropolis |  |  |  | -0.011 | 0.014 | 0.039*** | -0.008 |
| Urban |  |  |  | -0.021** | -0.012 | -0.019** | -0.001 |
| North |  |  |  | 0.080*** | 0.034*** | 0.005 | 0.034*** |
| South |  |  |  | -0.118*** | -0.035* | -0.050*** | -0.014 |
| const | 4.018*** | 4.217*** | 5.400*** | 4.205*** | 6.394*** | 5.358*** | 4.796*** |
| Model | AIC | BIC | ll(model) | df | LR | LR | LR |
| M1 | 37742 | 37 894.6 | -18 852.0 | - |  |  |  |
| M2 | 37 829.7 | 37 958.2 | -18 898.9 | 3 | 93.7 | 75.0 | 52.0 |
| M3 | 37 795.5 | 37916 | -18 882.7 | 4 | 61.5 | 55.3 | 49.6 |
| M4 | 38 427.9 | 38 524.3 | -19 202.0 | 7 | 700.0 | 395.1 | 454.7 |
| M5 | 39 272.5 | 39 296.6 | -19 633.3 | 16 | 1562.6 | 1308.5 | 1421.9 |

networks (Huppert and Whittington, 2003; Stansfeld et al., 2013), and is one of the main determinants of human distress (Clark and Oswald, 1994). The results indicate that both age and retirement are significant predictors of life satisfaction (Pinquart and Sörensen, 2000), however, they present opposite signs: the distribution of satisfaction scores for retired individuals is a concave function depicting a descending pattern of satisfaction scores for people over age 65.

As far as the contextual characteristics included in the model are concerned, the effect of the consumer price index, inserted in the model at NUTS-2 level to account for price differentials on goods across the regions, shows a negative effect on individual SWB, when, as expected, prices increase. Similarly, the negative sign associated with the unemployment rate is a milestone in the literature: when individuals experience an increase in the unemployment level, regardless of whether they are employed or not, two different mechanisms can be detected: the first channel relates to the loss of one's own occupation, and the second is defined by feelings of fear and uncertainty for those who are searching for a job, of their relatives and friends, but also by those who are employed, but in temporary employment and precarious economic conditions (Di Tella et al., 2003). Finally, aiming to account for the part of regional variability in the data not explained by NUTS-2 economic variables, macroareas dummies confirm the expected divergence between North, Central and Southern territories (with a significant positive coefficient estimated for the richest Italian regions, i.e. Northern areas, with respect to the Centre of Italy). The aspect of living in metropolitan areas compared to urban territories and the *lnGDP* are not statistically significant.

When the analysis moves to the two macrodomains, the role of poverty conditions becomes meaningful in only one: if both measures of poverty appear to be significant on the economic aspects of life for individuals, in *SocWB* the effect of poverty intensity is not statistically different from zero, while the impact of incidence, even if significant, substantially decreases (from -0.211 for *EcoWB*, to -0.054 for *SocWB*).

The relationship between poverty and economic conditions is well known in the literature: economic position is one of the main dimensions of the multidimensional concept of subjective poverty (Chen and Lin, 2014 Zhou et al., 2021), representing basic needs in the individual's life; on the other hand, the relevance of poverty on aspects of life that are not directly related to economic conditions either decreases or it is not particularly clear (Rojas, 2008; Mysíková et al., 2019). Even if being poor has a significant effect on dimensions such as leisure time (Rojas, 2008) and living environment, the idea of supporting potential links between poverty intensity and social conditions is not supported by the empirical evidence.

Focusing on the combination of poverty incidence $P_0$ and severity $P_2$, we find that the condition of being poor has a higher impact in magnitude when we account for severity compared to intensity (Table 6.3). As noted earlier, the higher the parameter $\alpha$ of the poverty metrics, the higher the relevance associated to the tail of distribution of poor individuals, and therefore, the poverty aversion (Foster et al., 2010). Subjective wellbeing turns out to be highly sensitive to the severity of the poor condition; thus, increasing inequality among poor people is related to a larger reduction in satisfaction (-0.711) with respect to reduction of satisfaction related to poverty intensity (-0.439). The increase in magnitude of both measures of poverty conditions observed in Table 6.2 for *EcoWB* and the decrease in the relevance of the same measures for *SocWB*, are still observed for the combination $P_0$-$P_2$. However, in this case the changes in

*Table 6.3*     *Model estimates for overall, social and economic SWB:*
                *poverty incidence and severity*

| | M5_Tot | M4_Tot | M3_Tot | M2_Tot | M1_Tot | M1_Eco | M1_Soc |
|---|---|---|---|---|---|---|---|
| $P_0$ (Incidence) | -0.264*** | -0.244*** | -0.190*** | -0.200*** | -0.192*** | -0.274*** | -0.065*** |
| $P_2$ (Severity) | -0.822*** | -0.758*** | -0.714*** | -0.721*** | -0.711*** | -1.245*** | -0.094 |
| Gender | | 0.011 | 0.015* | 0.015* | 0.015* | 0.019** | 0.006 |
| Ncomp | | -0.004 | 0.000 | 0.000 | -0.001 | 0.014*** | -0.010** |
| Age | | -0.003*** | -0.003*** | -0.003*** | -0.003*** | -0.001*** | -0.005*** |
| LowEducation | | -0.104*** | -0.102*** | -0.101*** | -0.102*** | -0.131*** | -0.042*** |
| Unemployed | | -0.159*** | -0.130*** | -0.134*** | -0.130*** | -0.207*** | -0.028** |
| Retired | | 0.088*** | 0.062*** | 0.063*** | 0.061*** | 0.038*** | 0.051*** |
| Married | | 0.017 | 0.019 | 0.018 | 0.021* | 0.015 | 0.015 |
| Divorced | | -0.151*** | -0.160*** | -0.162*** | -0.160*** | -0.175*** | -0.087*** |
| Widower | | -0.136*** | -0.116*** | -0.118*** | -0.113*** | -0.096*** | -0.083*** |
| lnGDP | | | 0.057 | | -0.014 | -0.022 | -0.012 |
| lnIPC | | | -0.286*** | | -0.357*** | -0.504*** | -0.130 |
| lnUnempl | | | -0.192*** | | -0.171*** | -0.108*** | -0.142*** |
| Metropolis | | | | -0.011 | 0.014 | 0.038*** | -0.008 |
| Urban | | | | -0.021** | -0.012 | -0.019** | -0.001 |
| North | | | | 0.080*** | 0.034*** | 0.006 | 0.034*** |
| South | | | | -0.118*** | -0.036* | -0.050*** | -0.014 |
| const | 4.018*** | 4.218*** | 5.387*** | 4.206*** | 6.391*** | 5.352*** | 4.796*** |
| Model | AIC | BIC | ll(model) | df | LR | LR | LR |
| M1 | 37 739.5 | 37 892.5 | -18 850.8 | - | | - | - |
| M2 | 37 826.5 | 37 955.1 | -18 897.3 | 3 | 93.0 | 73.9 | 51.9 |
| M3 | 37 793.1 | 37 913.7 | -18 881.6 | 4 | 61.6 | 55.2 | 49.6 |
| M4 | 38 425.6 | 38 522.1 | -19 200.8 | 7 | 700.1 | 394.8 | 455.1 |
| M5 | 39 271.0 | 39 295.1 | -19 632.5 | 16 | 1563.5 | 1303.7 | 1422.1 |

both magnitude and significance appear even more evident. As for the effects of macroeconomic variables on SWBs, results are in line with those observed in Table 6.2.

### 6.5.2   The Sensitivity Across the Macroareas of Italy

Aiming to measure regional disparities in the life satisfaction–poverty relationships, the models in Equations. (6.4) and (6.5) are also estimated for the three Italian macroareas (North, Centre and South including the Islands). Table 6.4 shows the results of the different measures of wellbeing and poverty.

To assess the statistical reliability of the estimates among the three macroareas, we performed a set of LR tests. In particular, the LR tests (Table 6.4) are used to compare the M1_Tot, M1_Eco and M1_Soc estimates for the full sample (constrained models) with the estimates obtained by the subsampling estimation approach (unconstrained models) for the null hypothesis of homogeneous effects of poverty measures on SWB for the whole population. The tests aim to evaluate the strength of the degree of heterogeneity with the individuals' SWB-poverty relationship in the three territories. As shown in Table 6.4, the results of the LR tests for all the models reveal the appropriateness of the subsampling approach.

Focusing on model estimates, the satisfaction of citizens living in the Northern regions is the most sensitive to poverty, reporting a greater aversion to this condition with respect to the other territories. In this macroarea, overall life satisfaction is very responsive to poverty intensity, reducing to 0.573 points for people becoming poorer. Overall, poverty measures have a strong impact on the subjective wellbeing of people living in the North, with a higher level for intensity than those observed at the national level. Similarly, in the South, both incidence and intensity of poverty have a significant impact on people's overall satisfaction, even if the magnitudes are markedly lower than the ones observed in the North. In the Centre, the impact of being poor is negligible, while the satisfaction level of poor people significantly reduces to 0.607 points as they become poorer.

The analysis of the poverty severity shows a higher sensitivity of SWB but of different magnitudes across regions. People living in the Centre of Italy exhibit the highest sensitivity to poverty severity, followed by citizens in the North. In particular, the effect of the squared gap is three times that of the incidence parameter in the North, underscoring that increasing inequality among poor people living in this area causes a very large reduction in satisfaction. The South is characterized by the lowest response of satisfaction to the poverty severity, but also, in this case, we see a relevant sensitivity with respect to the condition of being poor.

All these findings highlight a large variability in the response of SWB to poverty. The difference in the response of SWB to poverty varies across territories due to economic and social diversities, confirming the divergence in the disparities and disequilibrium between Northern and Southern areas (Giarda and Moroni, 2018). Italy shows relevant regional disparities in employment, education and social protection between macroareas, where the South is the most penalized. The negative social consequences of low employment rates are exacerbated in the South by problems such as the disproportionately low rate of youth employment, increasing duration of unemployment and the low level of education. All these issues increase the risk of poverty. Conversely, the higher education level combined with a higher level of employment, as

*Table 6.4*        *Comparing incidence-intensity, incidence-severity impacts*
                   *over macroareas*

| | | Italy | North | Centre | South |
|---|---|---|---|---|---|
| TotWB | | | | | |
| | $P_0$ (Incidence) | -0.150*** | -0.252*** | 0.011 | -0.149*** |
| | $P_1$ (Intensity) | -0.439*** | -0.573*** | -0.607*** | -0.377*** |
| LR test: | Italy vs North, Centre, South | | | | 264.89*** |
| | $P_0$ (Incidence) | -0.192*** | -0.304*** | -0.035 | -0.185*** |
| | $P_2$ (Severity) | -0.711*** | -0.941*** | -1.176*** | -0.612*** |
| LR test: | Italy vs North, Centre, South | | | | 266.46*** |
| EcoWB | | | | | |
| | $P_0$ (Incidence) | -0.211*** | -0.348*** | -0.060 | -0.197*** |
| | $P_1$ (Intensity) | -0.730*** | -0.844*** | -0.824*** | -0.692*** |
| LR test: | Italy vs North, Centre, South | | | | 461.81*** |
| | $P_0$ (Incidence) | -0.274*** | -0.417*** | -0.118*** | -0.261*** |
| | $P_2$ (Severity) | -1.245*** | -1.462*** | -1.664*** | -1.151*** |
| LR test: | Italy vs North, Centre, South | | | | 461.46*** |
| SocialWB | | | | | |
| | $P_0$ (Incidence) | -0.054*** | -0.094** | 0.048 | -0.060** |
| | $P_1$ (Intensity) | -0.085 | -0.143 | -0.209 | -0.047 |
| LR test: | Italy vs North, Centre, South | | | | 222.06*** |
| | $P_0$ (Incidence) | -0.065*** | -0.110*** | 0.029 | -0.067*** |
| | $P_2$ (Severity) | -0.094 | -0.194 | -0.334 | -0.052 |
| LR test: | Italy vs North, Centre, South | | | | 222.21*** |

well as the government social protection benefits, contribute to the low level of poverty in the North; indeed, such transfers have an important redistributive effect that helps to reduce the number of people living in poverty conditions. In sum, our results show that where the risk of poverty is high, as in the South, the condition of being poor has a negative impact on individual satisfaction, but the intensity of this impact is not particularly high. Conversely, in richer areas where poverty affects only a minor percentage of all the residents, the condition of poverty becomes more effective in influencing individual wellbeing. A possible explanation is that people tend to compare their own conditions to others living in the neighbourhood: where poverty is a limited phenomenon, the impact on the poor is much higher and the magnitude of this effect augments as the intensity and the severity of poverty increases.

Finally, we focus on the SWB domains-poverty nexus at the macroarea level, finding a substantial difference in the impact of poverty on the economic and social domains. Results confirm the relevance of the poverty measures only for the economic sphere, while satisfaction associated with social satisfaction appears not to be significantly affected by the different poverty aspects (Mysíková et al., 2019). Specifically, for the *EcoWB*, our results confirm the greater impact of poverty conditions for people living in the Northern regions with respect to the other territories; and this evidence is confirmed for both the intensity and the severity of poverty. Moreover, when satisfaction concerns only economic-related aspects of people's lives, the incidence of poverty also becomes statistically different from zero for the Centre, thus affecting individual wellbeing. Conversely, results for the social macrodomain *SocWB* reveal a negligible effect of poverty on satisfaction in all regions. In particular, as with Italy as a whole, the North and South confirm that the only aspect of poverty showing a significant effect on satisfaction is $P_0$, i.e. living below the poverty line. None of the measures of poverty play a role on satisfaction levels related to social aspects for people living in the Centre of Italy.

## 6.6     CONCLUSIONS AND FURTHER DEVELOPMENTS

In the economics of happiness literature, poverty and people's life satisfaction are an interrelated phenomenon largely affected by contextual and territorial characteristics, leading to issues when developing appropriate country level policies. Positioned in this stream of research, this study investigated the regional dimension of the SWB-poverty nexus to provide a comprehensive portrait of the two intertwined phenomena. Specifically, the territorial disparity of this nexus is tested by combining different measures of both SWB and poverty measures, aiming to provide a description of the sensitivity of the SWB-poverty nexus across regions.

Our results confirm that the response of people's satisfaction to poverty varies across territories due to economic and social diversities, confirming the divergence in the disparities and disequilibrium between Northern and Southern of Italy (Giarda and Moroni, 2018). The diffusion of poverty and the comparison with one's peers may have a role in explaining the magnitude of the difference in the impact of poverty on individual wellbeing. As expected, the highest level of sensitivity to this nexus is mainly related to the economic macrodomain. This effect is particularly evident in the Northern regions, where people's level of satisfaction appears to be strongly affected by the fact of living below the poverty line. The social macrodomain is, in general, less affected by poverty conditions; people appear to be unable to differentiate between the degrees of poverty, but their satisfaction is influenced only by living below the poverty line. The differences in the magnitude of the nexus between Northern and Southern areas are still observed, while people living in the Centre appear not to be influenced by poverty.

Findings highlight possible implications of the study and suggest policy recommendations. First, poverty conditions have different impacts at a regional level on the subjective wellbeing of residents, confirming the need for place-based policies aiming at reducing poverty, which could also foster life satisfaction. Second, the incidence, intensity and severity of economic poverty are more related to economic wellbeing, and this is expected. What is not necessarily expected is that economic poverty is much less related to social wellbeing even though economic aspects (i.e. health and leisure time) are included in the social wellbeing index. Finally, the severity of poverty has a major role in influencing the satisfaction of citizens, making it clear that policies need to be proposed that aim at reducing the largest disparities among poor people.

Results also suggest some further development of this research. First, one of the possible motivations behind the disparities in the effects observed across the three regions can be associated to the choice of using a country poverty line that is equal for all the regions. The country poverty line may be too low for richer areas, leading to finding people living in very hard poverty conditions; on the other hand, this sufferance in terms of impact of poverty on satisfaction is less evident if the poverty line is too high with respect to the actual economic conditions and the actual level of economic inequalities perceived by people. Second, it could be interesting to directly control for the impact of peers in the SWB-poverty models, allowing us to measure to what extent a comparison with the mean as well as the diffusion of poverty may affect the perceptions and the wellbeing of people living below the poverty line.

## REFERENCES

Alkire S., Foster J. (2011) Understandings and Misunderstandings of Multidimensional Poverty Measurement. Journal of Economic Inequality, 9, 289–314.

Ayala L., Jurado A. (2011) Pro-Poor Economic Growth, Inequality and Fiscal Policy: The Case of Spanish Regions. Regional Studies, 45(1), 103–21.

Ayala L., Jurado A., Pérez-Mayo J. (2014) Drawing the Poverty Line: Do Regional Thresholds and Prices Make a Difference? Applied Economic Perspectives and Policy, 36(2), 309–32.

Ballas D., Dorling D., Hennig B. (2017) Analysing the Regional Geography of Poverty, Austerity and Inequality in Europe: A Human Cartographic Perspective. Regional Studies, 51(1), 174–85.

Bernini C., Emili S., Galli F. (2021) Does Urbanization Matter in the Expenditure-Happiness Nexus? Papers in Regional Science, 100(6), 1403–28.

Biwas-Diener R., Diener E. (2001) Making the Best of a Bad Situation: Satisfaction in the Slums of Calcutta. Social Indicator Research, 55, 329–52.

Bramley G., Lancaster S., Gordon D. (2000) Benefit Take-up and the Geography of Poverty in Scotland. Regional Studies, 34(6), 507–19.

Buhmann B., Rainwater L., Schmaus G., Smeeding T.M. (1988) Equivalence Scales, Well-Being, Inequality, and Poverty: Sensitivity Estimates across Ten Countries Using the Luxembourg Income Study (Lis) Database. Review of Income and Wealth, 34(2), 115–42.

Capello R. (2016) What Makes Southern Italy Still Lagging Behind? A Diachronic Perspective of Theories and Approaches. European Planning Studies, 24(4), 668–86.

Carbonaro G. (1985) Nota Sulla Scale di Equivalenza. In La Povertà in Italia, Presidenza del Consiglio dei Ministri, Istituto Poligrafico dello Stato, Rome.

Carbonaro G. (1990) Global Indicators of Poverty. In: Dagum C., Zenga M. (eds) Income and Wealth Distribution, Inequality and Poverty. Studies in Contemporary Economics. Springer, Berlin, Heidelberg. https://doi.org/10.1007/978-3-642-84250-4_17.

Carver T., Grimes A. (2019) Income or Consumption: Which Better Predicts Subjective Well-Being? International Review of Economics, 65(S1), 256–80. doi: 10.1111/roiw.12414.

Chauhan R.K., Mohanty S.K., Subramanian S., et al. (2016) Regional Estimates of Poverty and Inequality in India, 1993–2012. Social Indicator Research, 127, 1249–96.

Chen S.-K., Lin S.S.J. (2014) The Latent Profiles of Life Domain Importance and Satisfaction in a Quality of Life Scale. Social Indicators Research, 116, 429–45.

Clark A.E. (2017) Happiness, Income and Poverty. International Review of Economics, 64, 145–58.

Clark A.E. (2018) Four Decades of the Economics of Happiness: Where Next? Review of Income and Wealth, 64(2), 245–69.

Clark A.E., Oswald A.J. (1994) Unhappiness and Unemployment. Economic Journal, 104, 424, 648–59.

Cummins R.A. (1996) The Domains of Life Satisfaction: An Attempt to Order Chaos. Social Indicators Research, 38, 303–32.

Deeming C. (2013) Addressing the Social Determinants of Subjective Well-Being: The Latest Challenge for Social Policy. Journal of Social Policy, 42, 541–65.

Di Tella R., MacCulloch R. J., Oswald A. J. (2003) The Macroeconomics of Happiness. Review of Economics and Statistics, 85(4), 809–827.

Diener E. (2012) New Findings and Future Directions for Subjective Well-Being Research. American Psychologist, 67, 590–7.

Dolan P., Peasgood T., White M. (2008) Do We Really Know What Makes Us Happy? A Review of the Economic Literature on the Factors Associated with Subjective Wellbeing. Journal of Economic Psychology, 29, 94–122.

D'Orazio M., Di Zio M., Scanu M. (2006) Statistical Matching, Theory and Practice. Wiley, New York.

Felton A., Graham C.L. (2006) Inequality and Happiness: Insights from Latin America. Journal of Economic Inequality, 4(1), 107–22.

Ferrer-i-Carbonell A. (2005) Income and Well-Being: An Empirical Analysis of the Comparison Income Effect. Journal of Public Economics, 89, 997–1019.

Foster J., Greer J., Thorbecke E. (1984) A Class of Decomposable Poverty Measures. Econometrica, 52(3), 761–5.

Foster J., Greer J., Thorbecke E. (2010) The Foster-Greer-Thorbecke (FGT) Poverty Measures: 25 Years Later. Journal of Economic Inequality, 8(4), 491–524.

Galinha I.C., Garcia-Martín M.A., Gomes C., Oishi S. (2016) Criteria for Happiness among People Living in Extreme Poverty in Maputo, Mozambique. International Perspectives in Psychology, 5, 67–90.
Giarda E., Moroni G. (2018) The Degree of Poverty Persistence and the Role of Regional Disparities in Italy in Comparison with France, Spain and the UK. Social Indicators Research, 136(1), 163–202.
Helmert U., Mielck A., Shea S. (1997) Poverty, Health, and Nutrition in Germany. Reviews on Environmental Health, 12(3), 159–70.
Hsieh C.M. (2002) Trends in Financial Satisfaction: Does Poverty Make a Difference? International Journal of Aging and Human Development, 54, 15–30.
Huppert F. (2009) Psychological Well-Being: Evidence Regarding Its Causes and Consequences. Applied Psychology: Health and Well-Being, 1, 137–64.
Huppert F.A., Whittington J.E. (2003) Evidence for the Independence of Positive and Negative Well-Being: Implications for Quality of Life Assessment. British Journal of Health Psychology, 8, 107–22.
ISTAT (2016) La povertà in Italia – Anno 2016, Statistiche Report.
Lawless N.M., Lucas R.E. (2011) Predictors of Regional Well-Being: A County Level Analysis. Social Indicators Research, 101, 341–57.
Lenzi C., Perucca G. (2018) Are Urbanized Areas Source of Life Satisfaction? Evidence from EU Regions. Papers in Regional Science, 97(S1), S105–22.
Lenzi C., Perucca G. (2021) Not Too Close, Not Too Far: Urbanisation and Life Satisfaction along the Urban Hierarchy. Urban Studies, 58(13), 2742–57.
Lin C.-H., Lahiri S., Hsu C.P. (2014) Happiness and Regional Segmentation: Does Space Matter? Journal of Happiness Studies, 15(1), 57–83.
Luttmer E.P.F. (2005) Neighbours as Negatives: Relative Earnings and Well-Being. Quarterly Journal of Economics, 120, 963–1002.
Marella D., Scanu M., Conti P.L. (2008) On the Matching Noise of Some Nonparametric Imputation Procedures. Statistics and Probability Letters, 78, 1593–600.
Mogstad M., Langørgen A., Aaberge R. (2007) Region-Specific versus Country-Specific Poverty Lines in Analysis of Poverty. Journal of Economic Inequality, 5, 115–22.
Morrison M., Tay L., Diener E. (2011) Subjective Well-Being and National Satisfaction: Findings from a Worldwide Survey. Psychological Science, 22(2), 166–71.
Muñoz J.F., Àlvarez-Verdejo E., García-Fernández R.M. (2018) On Estimating the Poverty Gap and the Poverty Severity Indices with Auxiliary Information. Sociological Methods and Research, 47(3) 598–625.
Mysíková M., Želinský T., Garner T.I., et al. (2019) Subjective Perceptions of Poverty and Objective Economic Conditions: Czechia and Slovakia a Quarter Century after the Dissolution of Czechoslovakia. Social Indicators Research, 145, 523–50.
Ng W., Diener E. (2014) What Matters to the Rich and the Poor? Subjective Well-Being, Financial Satisfaction, and Postmaterialist Needs across the World. Journal of Personality and Social Psychology, 107(2), 326–38.
Okulicz-Kozaryn A. (2012) Income and Well-being across European Provinces. Social Indicators Research, 106(2), 371–92.
Patacchini E. (2008) Local Analysis of Economic Disparities in Italy: A Spatial Statistics Approach. Statistical Methods and Applications, 17, 85–112.
Pinquart M., Sörensen S. (2000) Influences of Socioeconomic Status, Social Network, and Competence on Subjective Well-Being in Later Life: A Meta-Analysis. Psychology and Aging 15, 187–224.
Ravallion M., Lokshin M. (2001) Identifying Welfare Effects Using Subjective Questions. Economica, 68, 335–57.

Reyes-García V., Angelsen A., Minkin D. (2019) Does Income Inequality Influence Subjective Wellbeing? Evidence from 21 Developing Countries. Journal of Happiness Studies, 20, 1197–215.

Rojas M. (2008) Experienced Poverty and Income Poverty in Mexico: A Subjective Well-Being Approach. World Development, 36(6), 1078–93.

Shams K. (2014) Determinants of Subjective Well-Being and Poverty in Rural Pakistan: A Micro-Level Study. Social Indicators Research, 119(3), 1755–73.

Shams K. (2016) Developments in the Measurement of Subjective Well-Being and Poverty: An Economic Perspective. Journal of Happiness Studies, 17, 2213–36.

Simona-Moussa J. (2020) The Subjective Well-Being of Those Vulnerable to Poverty in Switzerland. Journal of Happiness Studies, 21, 1561–80.

Stansfeld S.A., Shipley M.J., Head J., Fuhrer R., Kivimaki M. (2013) Work Characteristics and Personal Social Support as Determinants of Subjective Wellbeing. PLoS ONE 8(11). doi: 10.1371/journal.pone.0081115.

Strotmann H., Volkert J. (2018) Multidimensional Poverty Index and Happiness. Journal of Happiness Studies, 19, 167–89.

Tubadji A., Gheasi M., Crociata A., Odoardi I. (2022) Cultural Capital and Income Inequality across Italian Regions. Regional Studies, 56(3), 459–75.

van Praag B.M.S., Ferrer-i-Carbonell A. (2004) Happiness Quantified – A Satisfaction Calculus Approach. Oxford University Press, Oxford.

van Praag B.M.S., Ferrer-i-Carbonell A. (2008) A Multidimensional Approach to Subjective Poverty. In: Kakwani N., Silber J. (eds) Quantitative Approaches to Multidimensional Poverty Measurement. Palgrave Macmillan, London.

Welsch H., Biermann P. (2019) Poverty is a Public Bad: Panel Evidence from Subjective Well-Being Data. Review of Income and Wealth, 65(1), 187–200.

Zhou D., Cai K., Zhong S. (2021) A Statistical Measurement of Poverty Reduction Effectiveness: Using China as an Example. Social Indicators Research, 153, 39–64.

# 7. Spatial inequalities and international cooperation projects: a bottom-up wellbeing model for inclusion

**Daniela De Leo and Valentina Vittoria Calabrese**

## 7.1    INTRODUCTION

Urban planners who work in a different country from the one in which they live and were trained often assume different approaches, ranging from the tendency to impose their own (mostly Western) schemes on the host territory, which is very frequent indeed, to the rarer tendency to enter on tiptoe in order to listen, watch and understand, to then be better able to act in dealing with complex problems. In these less common but important situations, it is in fact possible to experiment with practices without ending up replicating 'alien models' that are difficult (if not impossible) to implement. A rule that has now been acquired in planning for development is to not neglect the most vulnerable groups in the participatory process, above all, including young people, who not only represent the future but are also the largest share of the population in areas with strong demographic growth trends. These forgotten groups also have the right to experience the city, and the link between planning and children's rights is often overlooked.

Such a vision is also considered to be useful in fostering transformation processes oriented toward the treatment of spatial inequalities and in favour of the wellbeing of the most vulnerable populations, which are too often excluded from international development cooperation processes. In particular, the youngest age groups are the most neglected, because adult user groups are mainly considered in most common practices. This has led to the definition of projects, which, despite being more sensitive to the needs of the citizens, have turned out to be 'adult centric': i.e. they do not pay much attention to the wellbeing of younger people. Within this perspective, an urban transformation project was conceived as an opportunity to experiment with giving a different level of attention to future generations in contexts where the low level of schooling for women and the rigidity of social structures severely limits any possibility of social justice and expanded citizenship rights. As has been noted, decision-making processes in the Global South are generally less transgenerational and organised, while public participation and deliberation efforts are often perceived as 'lip service' (Yiftachel, 2006). However, development cooperation through the disciplines of urban-territorial planning can be called upon as an intermediary actor between beneficiary countries and partners by providing appropriate and timely research, reflection and intervention tools to address the more advanced and contemporary challenges of the city and territory (De Leo and Forester, 2017; Chitti and De Leo, 2021).[1]

Specifically, in the Re-generation Al-Zaytoun international cooperation project, the use of children's participation in the urban regeneration of a Cairo neighbourhood was intentionally and locally tested. The project's reference was the goal stated in 'UN-HABITAT's Urban Planning and Design' (UN-HABITAT, 2016a) regarding the use of spatial strategies through inclusive processes that consider human rights, gender, age and other identity categories to create a proactive framework for sustainable urbanization in international contexts (UNICEF, 2005; Paba, 2005; Paba and Pecoriello, 2006; De Leo, 2013). The work that was conducted concerned the design of urban spaces, considering the many different outlooks present in a richly multicultural and differentiated reality in which the children themselves move in and use spaces (private and collective) in ways and with approaches that are strongly linked to their culture of origin (Salama, 2013; Corbisiero, and Berritto, 2017). Therefore, the project was developed by flanking the international group's field analysis with a participatory process involving the youth and minorities living in the neighbourhood to:

- better understand the phenomena 'from the inside',
- offer solutions that followed a local logic as much as possible by responding to the needs of the inhabitants, and
- take into account existing conditions by overcoming the presumptions or 'clichés' Western planners often bring when working in other contexts.

In particular, the proposed project paid attention to the dynamics created by the use of the city by specific constituents and small situations that are sensitive to major transformations, proposing a regeneration strategy that starts from

---

[1]   Also considering that, as has been pointed out, 'the development of participatory planning experiences is also supported by the need to redefine a sort of social pact between citizens and institutions that is today visibly in crisis' (Brunod, 2007, p. 127).

a deep knowledge of the area and uses participatory practices right from the analysis phase.[2]

## 7.2    THE TERRITORIAL AND PLANNING CONTEXT

Cairo is located in a region where only 5 per cent of the land is inhabitable, and in the Greater Cairo Region, 40 per cent of the inhabitants live in informal neighbourhoods. These settlements grew out of a need for housing, and are now the structuring fabric of the city, with their own established internal economic structure.

Egypt has always undertaken policies to rehabilitate informal neighbourhoods. The three masterplans of 1956, 1970 and 1981 tried to delimit and contain the expansion of these areas, with little success. Indeed, between 1950 and the early 1960s, formal Cairo expanded mainly through land subdivision and building speculation, thus allowing the informal city to advance at double the speed and in total proximity to the formal city, in some cases creating mixed urban fabrics of hybrid settlement[3] (Madbouly and Lashin, 2003; Soliman, 2004; Sims, 2012; Abd Elrahman, 2016; Eid et al., 2014). Law 59/1979 introduced a new settlement policy, which allowed the construction of 18 new cities, including 10th Ramadan, Sadat City, Al Amiriya, City of 15th May, and 6th October.[4] These neighbourhoods were not able to satisfy residents in terms of quantity and quality of services, and the informal settlements continued to grow (Séjourné, 2009). Thus, inhabitants who had been uprooted from the places where they lived their daily lives would try to return to the capital, and accept living in informal situations that were more uncertain and dangerous than before. The redevelopments proposed by the government are often Western-inspired projects (such as gated communities)[5] that introduce

---

[2]    Even though the chapter has been shared by the authors, it is possible to attribute paragraph one to De Leo, paragraphs two and three to Calabrese and paragraph four to De Leo and Calabrese.

[3]    Ex-formal (hybrid) settlements: These settlements are residential units in formal areas, which have temporarily or permanently acquired degrees of informality. Unlike residential units in informal areas, this type of informality relates to individual dwelling units on a case-by-case basis, where some units in a formal neighbourhood or even an individual building are 'formal' and have remained largely so (Soliman, 2004, p. 22).

[4]    Data from Egypt's New Urban Communities Authority (NUCA) indicates that, on average, 30 per cent of the target population has settled in New Cities. There are a number of limitations with this data, but it does indicate that even by the government's own measures, the New Cities are facing significant challenges in achieving their targets. https://www.cesr.org/egypt-social-progress-indicators-urbanization/.

[5]    The gated communities in Egypt are Dreamland, Utopia, Beverly Hills e al Rehāb.

foreign models into the area (Sims et al., 2003; Bayat et al., 2004; Denis, 2016), and the rare cases of participatory planning – Manshiet Nasser and Bulaq Al-Dakrour – have not yielded the desired results (El-Shahat and El Khateeb, 2013).

From 2000 onwards, international actors have taken turns drafting and financing new instruments (GTZ-German Technical Cooperation, UN-HABITAT, Word Bank). In 1994, the ISDF-International Standard for Describing Functions developed a strategy for the redevelopment of informal neighbourhoods,[6] which still accounts for 80 per cent of government interventions. It demolishes houses and provides residents with new homes, usually in low-rent social housing, in areas remote from the original neighbourhood (Maldina and Tonnarelli, 2012; UN-HABITAT, 2016b). The remaining 20 per cent involves the improvement of informal neighbourhoods *in situ*, performing the necessary development and upgrading of the area itself without having to move residents to remote locations (Japan International Cooperation Agency (JICA), 2011; UN-HABITAT, 2011, 2015; PPS – Project for Public Space, UN-HABITAT, 2012). In the Vision of Egypt 2030 Plan, the government has planned the redevelopment of informal neighbourhoods through demolition and redesign, resulting in the displacement of the population. In the name of 'wellbeing', areas such as the Maspero Triangle and Majra Al Uyun, defined as *ashawayyat*,[7] are being demolished, and new mid- to high-end residences, administrative services and luxury facilities are being introduced. These renovation projects aim to provide the city with quality spaces and thus increase the wellbeing of its citizens. But this 'collective' wellbeing does not coincide with the individual's perception of wellbeing, thus accentuating dynamics of discontent.

The selected project area was the Zaytoun district (population density 40 407 inhabitants/sq km), located northeast of the historic centre of Cairo. The district borders the informal and poor settlements of Ain Shams and Matariyyah (population density 76 187 and 86 415 inhabitants/sq km) on one side and, on the other, the rich formal district of Heliopolis (population density

---

[6] The ISDF (International Standard for Describing Functions) strategy is divided into three implementation phases: from 1994 to 2004, providing these areas with minimum infrastructure (electricity, water and sewage supply, paving of roads); from 2004 to 2008, designing a functional ring capable of limiting sprawl; and from 2009 to the present, supporting local governments in building houses on a cost-recovery basis.

[7] *Ashwa'iyyat* is a plural form of *Ashwa'iyya*, meaning 'half-hazard'. The term has taken on a pejorative connotation and has become synonymous with 'slum' in UN official or popular language (Sims et al., 2003). The use of one term, *ashwa'iyyat*, to describe all informal areas in Cairo is highly problematic, due to its inability to capture the differences among informal housing structures, such as the quality of the building structures and the heterogeneity of their inhabitants (see also: O'Donnell, 2010).

14 753), now largely affected by forms of illegal building (Soliman, 2004). This is a territory composed of two different fabrics as well as opposite income brackets, in which a situation of semi-informality prevails concerning the economic, social and cultural exchanges that have developed over time among the different forms and structures. In addition, Al-Zaytoun is a link to commercial, administrative and religious services – a home to religious centres of different professions, which are central reference points for social life. These are areas that are not classified, but where segments of the middle class live, whose income and employment position play an important role in the services needed in the territory.

The surveys and the results of the activities carried out confirm that a network of commercial activities has developed in the neighbourhood, making the fronts 'interactive and interesting' (Gehl, 2013). The traditional and historical use of the street as a place for social and commercial exchange is no longer possible today due to the increasing use of cars. Reclaiming the street as places for people can strengthen the city in a variety of ways: economically, environmentally and socially. The neighbourhood is characterised by an undersized and at the same time out-of-scale road infrastructure compared to its surroundings. There are empty spaces in the neighbourhood that are informally used as car parks or as debris piles, and the few public green spaces charge an entry fee, making it impossible for the most vulnerable to use the park.

## 7.3    THE AL-ZAYTOUN RE-GENERATION PROJECT

In drafting the design proposal, the regeneration strategy started from networking with the deep knowledge of the territory held by the inhabitants, using a participatory approach that was introduced beginning with the analysis phase. The idea was to pay attention to the dynamics created by certain constituents using the city. The decision to adopt an open process had the aim of bringing out and composing readings and proposals that were more suitable for 'that specific' context: the combination of different techniques and strategies of participation (Giusti, 2001; Sclavi, 2014) was useful for having an overall vision that would guide the 'external' eye towards a deeper perception of social dynamics. In the same way, the choice to involve young people as active participants in the project helped to produce targeted and potentially positive design choices for a child-friendly and, consequently, highly accessible city (Pecoriello, 2007; Pecoriello et al., 2009).

It is important to add that the majority of the field research and related activities were conducted from the inside of a religious educational structure, which is crucial for reasons of organisation and management of available resources. This institution, located in the Zaytoun district, welcomes both local Egyptian youth and South Sudanese living in the nearby informal neighbourhoods, and is an important place in the district where different realities (ethnic, religious, class) meet. From this point of view, the project was, therefore, an experiment conducted explicitly with and for minorities. They were involved as local stakeholders both because of their greater accessibility and because they are the most vulnerable individuals who use the district. There are two minorities:

- the Egyptian Christian-Copts, who live in a predominantly Muslim territory, and
- the South-Sudanese, who live in Cairo as political refugees and are Catholic.

Observations of these two categories revealed cultural and relational differences both between them and the rest of the area's inhabitants. Coptic Egyptians, in fact, even if they are local, only have their own neighbourhood as a reference reality, in which they see and experience space and meeting places differently from Muslim Egyptian citizens. Without venturing into anthropological and religious discourses, it is interesting to note how religious differences produce a different way of conceiving quality and wellbeing in an urban space, and thus its present and future rules (Belli and De Leo, 2011). The South Sudanese, instead, live in a situation of precarious balance: they are refugees in a territory that considers them invisible, and they therefore mostly live in informal neighbourhoods (such as Ain Shams or Mattaryya), in unfinished buildings that are often rented at modest prices. However, they then go to Zaytoun daily, which they consider the preferred place for aggregation, assistance and trade.

These differences have led to a diversification of activities according to the sensibilities and socioeducational background of the different targets. What might have worked with South Sudanese children was considered inadequate for Egyptian ones. All of this must also be considered in light of the few tools available, and the significant language filter resulting from the linguistic differences characteristic of international cooperation projects. The participation process started with the analysis phase, from each participant's awareness and perception of the city (Gehl, 2014). The activities carried out were not only aimed at receiving information for a reading of the territory, but also at:

- introducing awareness of spatial and environmental perception,
- generating questions and reflections on space through a direct and collective approach,
- generating awareness of the services offered by the district, and
- identifying the flows, uses, spatial dynamics and difficulties that the city presents to children.

In sum, in the first phase the aim was to understand the district and the various problems linked to the different cultures present by applying participatory methodologies and techniques for young people; the second phase, saw the implementation of participatory activities involving the younger part of the neighbourhood inhabitants; then, in the third phase, all the data was processed for the elaboration of the masterplan. Specifically, the participation activities were as follows.

### 7.3.1    Interpreting Reality (Age: 6–12 Years)

A drawing activity was proposed to the South Sudanese children, asking them to represent what they normally observe on their way from home to the oratory. This served to involve them from the outset with their daily experiences, and to have a graphic representation of what wellbeing and quality of living and inhabiting the city meant for them, from an affective point of view as well. Levels of discomfort or wellbeing emerged from the interpretation of the signs and elements included in the drawings and the characterising factors of the neighbourhood represented by their view of spatial inequalities.

### 7.3.2    Making a Wish (Age: 6–12 Years)

The Egyptian children, considering their different level of competence with graphic representations, were asked to carry out a more interactive and dynamic activity, having to overcome this critical ability of graphic analysis influenced by stereotyped models. They were, therefore, asked to design a square together using a story (Fig. 7.1). The purpose of the story was to encourage the children to imagine a public space 'to their measure' and based on their wishes and needs. They reflected on the theme of spatial wellbeing, identifying all the elements that could be used to achieve it. Starting with a context very similar to the reality of the neighbourhood, the children, with the aim of chasing away a dragon, imagined a green space without cars and full of games. From this emerges an image of the kind of playground they would like, or the ways in which they would improve the city (Pecoriello, 2007; Pecoriello et al., 2009).

### 7.3.4    Mapping for Older Age Groups (Age: 14–20 Years)

The proposed activity was mapping, where the young people were able to deal with space and memory (Marchigiani et al., 2017). The result of the activity was a surprisingly detailed mapping of the central area of the neighbourhood. The density of use of the different areas of the neighbourhood (Fig. 7.2) can be seen from the results of this activity. It was noted that the girls reported a more detailed representation of the areas accessible to them. The boys, on the

*Figure 7.1     On the left, the drawings of the South Sudanese children (7–10 years old) that lead to precise points in the neighbourhood, developed through their perception of space. On the right, the Egyptian children's (6–10 years old) idea of a square*

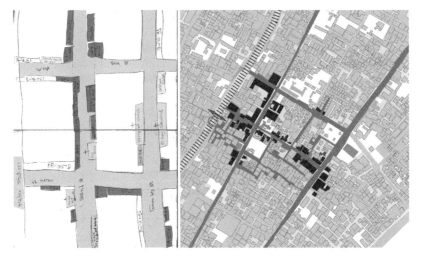

*Figure 7.2     The mapping activity (left) made it possible to identify and classify the services and flows of urban spaces in the neighbourhood*

other hand, gave a more global but also a more general view. Everything was deepened by an individual exchange of information.

### 7.3.5    At Children's Height (Age: 6–18 Years)

Concurrently with the on-site activity sessions, walks around the city were organized with some of the children and young people to discover the places where they live their daily lives. According to their own age, children look at the city from a different height and, thanks to this activity, they help planners to consider their points of view (from below). They were able to perceive the difficulties that they confront in the city, but also those spaces that are essential to them but neglected by adults. As part of this experience, the children were able to identify the use of public spaces and the most frequently used gathering points, assessing them according to quality and wellbeing criteria inspired by Jan Gehl's pedestrian landscape theme (Gehl, 2017).[8]

### 7.3.6    Outreach (Age: 18–30 Years)

It was possible to visit the homes of the young people who were not able to take part in the various activities, as well as some of the educators, and conduct semistructured interviews with them (Bobbio, 2004). This was a very useful process aimed at acquiring very detailed knowledge of the diversity of the cultures involved, precisely in order to understand how to define projects to guide the planning of new spaces and housing in relation to knowledge of current living conditions.

The awareness that the participants acquired during the activities was fundamental in recognising and reading the strengths, weaknesses, opportunities and threats inherent in the area. This provided an articulated representation of the Al-Zaytoun neighbourhood by highlighting the spatial problems, as well as those related to the social relations created in every street and corner of the neighbourhood. The understanding of the area gained through the activities was translated, in addition to the development of a meta-project, into a classification of the types of public spaces, streets and buildings in the neighbourhood, highlighting physical and social characteristics. Walking as a tool for listening and perceptual acquisition of space is fundamental not only for the participants

---

[8]    The 12 criteria are divided as follows: PROTECTION: 1. Protection from traffic and accidents; 2. Protection from unpleasant sensory experiences; 3. Feelings of safety; OPPORTUNITY: 4. Opportunities to walk; 5. Opportunities to stay; 6. Opportunities to sit; 7. Opportunities to see; 8. Opportunities to talk and listen; 9. Opportunities to play; COMFORT: 10. Scale; 11. Opportunities to take advantage of positive aspects of the climate; 12. Positive sensory experiences (Gehl, 2013, p. 279).

but also for the designer, who acquires the spatial knowledge transmitted by the participants, is guided by them and sees through their eyes.[9]

All the information gathered suggested three macro-themes regarding possible regeneration solutions for the neighbourhood, including:

1.  improvement of connections between the various transport systems to provide greater accessibility to the poorer classes,
2.  targeted interventions in the informal urban fabric to improve the quality of urban space and the built environment without relocating the resident population, and
3.  identification of possible public spaces, especially in the informal areas, and activation of participatory design processes for these areas to create spaces that are more aligned with the needs of citizens, especially the younger generation.

The macro-themes were translated into three project guidelines and developed into a coherent and unified master plan. These were developed at operational scales capable of responding promptly to the problems that emerged from the structured listening to the young participants. Thus, three urban guideline projects were created, to be further developed and implemented through subsequent moments of interaction and comparison with the inhabitants and young city-users. The three guidelines all aim to improve the quality of the residential and public space in the Zaytoun neighbourhood, especially for the informal areas, and considering its social capital.

## 7.4    CONCLUSIONS AND LESSONS LEARNED

In the context of international cooperation projects, it is more important than ever to:

1.  understand the inhabitants' idea of adequate quality of living and dwelling in the place, and
2.  involve local populations to avoid transformation processes that all too often increase disadvantages instead of reducing spatial inequalities.[10]

In this framework (Gouda, 2013; Chitti and De Leo, 2021), the useful elements of this international cooperation project regard its adoption of an approach that

---

[9]    For example, recreational activities take place outdoors but are strictly regulated by gender relations, and access to public parks (such as El-Tahr Park or El Kobba Park) is limited by entrance fees.

[10]    These two aspects are in line with the objectives of the New Urban Agenda (Habitat III) and Goal 11 of the 2030 Agenda for Sustainable Development.

was explicitly oriented towards understanding what the current living conditions are for the younger inhabitants and minorities who already live within the neighbourhood, in order to:

- define a transformation project with them, and
- improve the quality of the project without increasing but, on the contrary, reducing spatial inequalities.

In particular, the project involved interventions that it was essential to think of in terms of battling spatial inequalities by improving overall wellbeing, in accordance with the following aims:

1. promoting public mobility
2. letting the informal fabric breathe
3. sharing the care of public space.

These are described in detail in the following subsections.

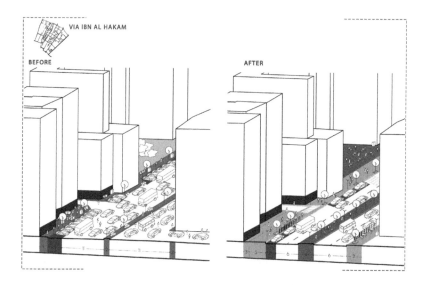

Figure 7.3     *Road sections of the existing conditions and the redistribution of the pavement-street ratio, with the aim of implementing the soft mobility network by reordering the road flows*

### 7.4.1    Promoting Public Mobility

Intervening on neighbourhood mobility is a mandatory step, needed to provide a solid foundation for other future upgrades. Understanding the perceptions of dangerousness, inaccessibility, and difficulty in enjoyment that children have while walking on the streets served to provide evaluation parameters for technically translating the problems of the street system. By highlighting the problems and social relationships created in each street, an abacus of the different street types in the neighbourhood was drawn up, from the freeway to the *zuqaq* (alley). Each typology encompasses homogeneous physical and social characteristics. This was also used in the participation activities for a careful evaluation of the different street types. The mobility actions in the neighbourhood consider the presence of informal transport and how it is used. Thus, the project proposes an alternative to the informal transport network present in the informal neighbourhoods of Cairo with the insertion of two bus rapid transit lines to connect with the inner city.[11] In addition, a road section project is proposed in connection with the theme of public spaces, to achieve a much more equitable pavement-to-road ratio (Fig. 7.3). This intervention aims to facilitate soft mobility and the use of the street as a common shared space by implementing quality public space and urban wellbeing.

### 7.4.2    Letting the Informal Fabric Breathe

The most complex part of the project was the intervention in the informal and non-informal urban fabric. The proposed interventions are all designed with the fixed requirement of not displacing the neighbourhood's inhabitants, and show attention to the local ways of doing, building and living (Hassan, 2012).

Buildings have been classified according to their condition and possible interventions, allowing the creation of a building census that can be used to apply a renovation process in stages and avoid creating mass relocations of the residents involved. In particular, specific interventions have been foreseen for each possible condition identified for the buildings in their current state (Fig. 7.4), specifically:

- unsafe building to be demolished in relation with the surrounding areas,
- open spaces to be safeguarded as common urban spaces close to public and mixed housing,
- low and solid buildings to be upgraded and raised, and

---

[11]    This system used in large metropolises, such as the example of Bogota (Colombia's Bus Rapid Transit), is an alternative solution to the metro infrastructure that is sustainable and economical (Turner et al., 2012).

- abandoned and unfinished buildings to be completed, in which families from demolished dwellings are to be placed.

This is all conceived within a unitary process aimed at improving the safety of the buildings and the quality of the urban space while avoiding relocating the resident population. For public housing, then, the overall solution proposed within this experimentation moves away from the scheme usually used in Egypt of isolated and abandoned public housing and proposes a more accurate and distributed location to create a social mix and not a further reclusion zone.

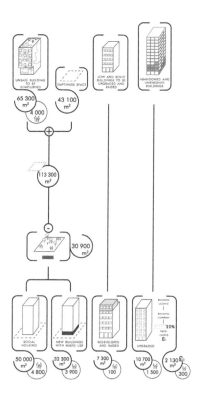

*Figure 7.4*      *Buildings classification scheme and possible solutions*

### 7.4.3    Sharing the Care of Public Space

The public spaces are key elements of the project. The success of an urban space becomes a central objective of the redevelopment and is linked to the ability to meet the needs and requirements of the citizens. The 'surgical' intervention approach in the informal fabric is important for activating a community empowerment process for community spaces that will be designed by the community for the community through the proposal of pocket spaces. New public spaces are proposed, especially in informal areas, through the recovery of urban space, as a corridor between blocks or as the result of selective demolition (Fig 7.5). This will serve to stimulate collective movements that in anticipation can activate a process of citizen management and maintenance of public spaces. The willingness to operate according to micro-interventions that minimise the inconveniences resulting from implementation defines

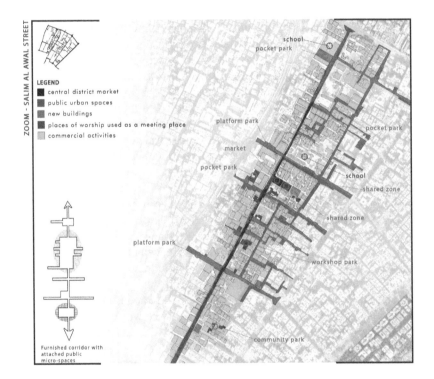

*Figure 7.5*    *Insight into one of the main axes of the neighbourhood: here the observation of positive spontaneous practices concerning the organization of urban space served as a guide for a strategy of public space closer to the needs of the users*

a light project that nevertheless has the ambition of having both a long term and a large-scale effect. After the identification and systematisation of public space, the design of these spaces is left to the community and local government. These constituencies, with the support of local authorities and development projects, can activate processes of community empowerment and space construction. These movements can also help with the care of urban space and the improvement of wellbeing. When people identify with a place, it becomes a common good, and they will work to maintain it.

Three guideline projects are a response to problems that have emerged (unregulated and chaotic mobility, noninclusive or absent public spaces and overcrowding of the urban fabric). They were shaped together with young stakeholders, starting from an awareness of the reality to create a proposal for change. This proposal encourages consideration of adaptive planning methodologies that help urban planners to learn to overcome contrasts, conflicts and even power imbalances by listening to the unequal, to the other. In fact, it is extremely important that the regeneration interventions in a neighbourhood create awareness among those who live there, activating the interest of the youngest both by implementing the educational aspect of the city towards a livelier and more collaborative city and by grasping the intrinsic characteristics of the territory to design a city tailored to the resident population. Specifically, as we have seen, the involvement of the younger generation led to the formulation of a strategy customised for the local population: keeping children's and minority rights in mind in planning processes can lead to solutions that are balanced between state 'governance', district diversity and sustainable development.

Moreover, issues about wellbeing emerged because this element is poorly analysed in today's urban planning practices, especially in large metropolises, where this concept is limited to areas designated by governments for a well-defined (wealthier) social class. Redevelopment practices usually demolish informal neighbourhoods and rebuild new modern-style neighbourhoods that are only accessible to higher income groups (Yousry, 2010; Hassan, 2012; Gouda, 2013). These new neighbourhoods nullify the essence of the place and create yet an inhospitable ghost town for residents. In this perspective, this project for Al-Zaytoun could be considered a proposal for renewing the planning policies being implemented in Egypt and in international cooperation practices today, which do not address these kinds of approaches and are still rooted in a more traditional vision of urban planning development (Alraouf, 2006). So, in this specific case, the role of the international cooperation project aims at assisting municipalities and supporting local development efforts according to different perspectives. Nonetheless, if the Egyptian government initiated a more inclusive urban policy, collaboration between local governments, universities and international cooperation could bring great benefits, such as needs assessments, environmental management, health, education, training, cultural and recreational activities by defining new and different urban scenarios that are capable of reflecting the demand for quality space.

This type of proposal calls upon the various actors involved to conceive and implement new urban scenarios, and to express a demand for wellbeing and the quality of space in neighbourhoods that are socioeconomically distressed and sit at the transition between the centre and the periphery. When we speak of a 'city for children', we are not thinking of the 'Amusement Park model', but of a city, as demonstrated here, which is accessible, sensitive and changing, and which shows attention to liveable space, to spaces for meeting, playing and gathering. It is an analysis that does not neglect the 'dark and grey' sides of planning and tries to question the messy interactions between planning policies, spaces and people (Yiftachel, 2015).

## REFERENCES

Abd Elrahman, A., and El-khateeb, S. (2016). Mapping Informal Areas in Egypt Between the Past Interventions and Next Urban Revolution. *Journal of Urban Research*, 21(1), 116–129.

Alraouf, A. A. (2006). Dubaization: The Emergence of New Urban Brand in the Middle East. *Journal of Cultural Exchange*-Kultur Austausch, 3, 25–31.

Bayat, A., Gilbert, A., and Bromley, R. (2004). *Urban informality: Transnational perspectives from the middle East, latin America, and south Asia.* Lexington Books pp.7–30.

Belli, A., and De Leo, D. (2011). Per una visibilità incondizionata. Ospitalità, città e moschee. *Crios*, 1(2), 57–66.

Bobbio, L. (2004). *A più voci. Amministrazioni pubbliche, imprese, associazioni e cittadini nei processi decisionali inclusivi.* ESI.

Brunod, M. (2007). Aspetti metodologici nella progettazione partecipata. *Spunti*, 9, 127–134.

Chitti, M., and De Leo, D. (2021). Contesti di cooperazione internazionale e circolazione delle idee nelle pratiche di pianificazione urbana tra profili professionali e possibili apprendimenti. Contesti di cooperazione internazionale e circolazione delle idee nelle pratiche di pianificazione urbana tra profili professionali e possibili apprendimenti. *ASUR*, pp.53–69.

Corbisiero, F., and Berritto, A. (2017). *I bambini inventano la città: partecipare per progettare.* Galdini, R., Marata, A.(a cura di). La città. Mimeo.

De Leo, D. (2013). *Planner in Palestina. Esperienze di ricerca e pianificazione del territorio e dello sviluppo nel conflitto: Esperienze di ricerca e pianificazione del territorio e dello sviluppo nel conflitto.* FrancoAngeli, Milano.

De Leo, D., and Forester, J. (2017). Reimagining planning: moving from reflective practice to deliberative practice – a first exploration in the Italian context. *Planning Theory & Practice*, 18(2), 202–216.

Denis, E. (2016). *Cairo as Neoliberal Capital? Diane Singerman and Paul Amar.* Cairo Cosmopolitan, American University in Cairo Press, pp.47–71.

Eid, Y., Khalifa, M. A., and Azouz, N. (2014). *Good Urban Governance of Informal Settlements in Metropolitan Areas: Case Study of the Informal Settlement of Ezzbet Al-Haggana, Cairo-Egypt.* Creating new resources, 3, 383–392.

El-Shahat, M., and El Khateeb, S. (2013). Empowering people in Egyptian informal areas by planning: towards an intelligent model of participatory planning. *The Journal of Urbanism*, 26(1), 1–11.

Gehl, J. (2013). *Cities for people*. Island press.

Gehl, J. (2014). *Istanbul – Public Space Public Life*, study conducted by Gehl Architects for EMBARQ Turkey.

Gehl, J. (2017). *Città per le persone*. Maggioli, Milano.

Giusti, M. (2001). Modelli partecipativi di interpretazione del territorio. In Magnaghi, A., a cura di, *Rappresentare i luoghi. Metodi e tecniche,* Alinea, Firenze.

Gouda, E. A. (2013). Urban Form Rehabilitation of the Informal Settlements in Egypt. *The Journal of Urbanism*, 1(26), 1–10.

Hassan, G. F. (2012). Regeneration as an approach for the development of informal settlements in Cairo metropolitan. *Alexandria Engineering Journal*, 51(3), 229–239.

Marchigiani, E., Basso, S., and Di Biagi, P. (2017). *Esperienze urbane. Spazi pubblici e città contemporanea*. EUT-Edizioni Università di Trieste (comitato scientifico di referaggio).

Maldina, S., and Tonnarelli, F. (2012). *Frozen Cairo – Un programma di riqualificazione per i quartieri storici in declino, il caso studio di Arab al Yassar*. Università degli studi di Ferrara.

Madbouly, M., and Lashin, A. (2003). *Housing Development in Informal Settlements in Cairo*. Unpublished Research for Urban Training Institute, Ministry of Housing.

O'Donnell, S. (2010). *Informal Housing in Cairo: Are Ashwa'iyyat Really the Problem?*

Paba, G. (2005). *I bambini costruttori di città e di ambiente*. l'Università 'Vivere la città di oggi. Progettare la città di domani'.

Paba, G., and Pecoriello, A. L. (2006). *La città bambina: esperienze di progettazione partecipata nelle scuole*. Masso delle Fate.

Pecoriello, A. L. (2007). Spazi di gioco e autocostruzione. In Poli, D. (a cura di)*, Il bambino educatore. Progettare con i bambini per migliorare la qualità urbana*. Alinea, Firenze, pp.115–135.

Pecoriello, A. L., Rispoli, F., Paba, G., and Perrone, C. (2009). *Partecipazione in Toscana: interpretazioni e racconti* (p. 218). Firenze University Press, Firenze.

PPS – Project for Public Space, UN-HABITAT, Placemaking and the Future of Cities (2012), https://www.pps.org/article/placemaking-and-the-future-of-cities.

Salama, H. H. (2013). Tahrir Square: A narrative of a public space. *ArchNet-IJAR: International Journal of Architectural Research*, 7(1), 128.

Sclavi, M. (2014). Avventure urbane. Progettare la città con gli abitanti.

Sims, D., Sejoume, M., and El Shorbagi, M. (2003). Cairo, Egypt. *Understanding urban slums*.

Sims, D. (2012). *Understanding Cairo: The logic of a city out of control*. Oxford University Press.

Séjourné, M. (2009). *The history of informal settlements. Cairo's informal areas between urban challenges and hidden potentials*. Cairo: GTZ Egypt and Participatory Development Programme in Urban Areas (PDP), 17–19.

Soliman, A. (2004). Tilting at Sphinxes: Locating urban informality in Egyptian cities. *Urban Informality: Transnational Perspectives from the Middle East, Latin America, and South Asia*, 171–208.

Turner, M., Kooshian, C., and Winkelman, S. (2012). Colombia's Bus Rapid Transit (BRT) Development and Expansion: A Case Study of Barriers and Critical Enablers of Colombia's BRT Systems.

UN-HABITAT. (2011). Cairo, a city in transition. International report. Mimeo.

UN-HABITAT. (2016a). Urban Planning and Design Labs: tools for integrated and participatory urban planning. https://unhabitat.org/urban-planning-and-design-labs -tools-for-integrated-and-participatory-urban-planning.

UN-HABITAT. (2016b). '*Egypt Housing Profile*' *David Sims and Hazem Abd-El Fattah.*

UN-HABITAT. (2015) *Legislative analysis to support sustainable approaches to city planning and extension in Egypt.*

UNICEF Innocenti Research Centre. CFC Secretariat. (2005). *Costruire città amiche delle bambine e dei bambini: nove passi per l'azione.* Comitato Italiano per l'Unicef.

Japan International Cooperation Agency (JICA) (2011) *Data Collection Survey Mission on Slum and Informal Area Development in the Greater Cairo Region*, Final Report.

Yiftachel, O. (2006). Essay: re-engaging planning theory? Towards 'south-eastern' perspectives. *Planning theory*, 5(3), 211–222.

Yiftachel, O. (2015). *Epilogue—from 'gray space' to equal 'metrozenship'? Reflections on urban citizenship.* International Journal of Urban and Regional Research, 39(4), 726–737.

Yousry, A. (2010). *The privatization of urban development in Cairo. Lessons Learned from the Development Experience of Al Rehab Gated Community*, Faculty of Urban and Regional Planning, Cairo University.

# 8. Behind left and right: disentangling the voting behaviour of radical parties in Europe

## Luise Koeppen, Dimitris Ballas, Arjen Edzes and Sierdjan Koster

## 8.1 INTRODUCTION

The last decade has seen a considerable rise of various types of radical and anti-establishment (perceived and/or self-proclaimed) parties, on both the left and right side of the political spectrum in Western democracies. In this context, there has been a rapidly increasing interest in voting behaviour as a geographic phenomenon highlighting relevant spatial patterns and cleavages. In particular, it has been argued that regions that have been defined by similar factors pointing to socio-economic inequalities and cultural divisions tend to reflect comparable voting behaviour and political preferences (Dijkstra et al., 2020; Los et al., 2017; Lee et al., 2018; McCann, 2018; Rodríguez-Pose, 2018; Norris and Inglehart, 2019; Rodríguez-Pose et al., 2020). To that end, the growing spatial separation has been linked to concepts and terms such as the 'geography of discontent' and the 'revenge of places that don't matter', developed, operationalised and analysed in several studies in the field of regional science and economic geography (McCann, 2020; Rodríguez-Pose, 2018; Rodríguez-Pose et al., 2020). Most recent studies outlining the 'geography of discontent' focus on analysing discontent at the aggregated regional or national level, relating it to regional aggregate measures, suggesting that factors of relative economic decline are associated with individual resentment and collective perceptions and feelings of being 'left-behind' resulting from neglected territorial inequalities (e.g. Dijkstra et al., 2020; Rodríguez-Pose, 2018). In addition, these studies analyse the support for radical or self-proclaimed anti-establishment parties (e.g. vote share of populist and/or so-called anti-systemic/elite parties) jointly, as they express (political) discontent. However, most of the studies to date perform analysis at aggregate area level, typically using vote share at regional level as the dependent variable and considering area-level determinants.

Overall, it can be argued that there is a long tradition in the social sciences of analysing various determinants that explain voting behaviour at the ecological area level, but there is still a relative paucity of studies that combine geographical (i.e. regional) and individual dimensions determining voting behaviour, especially in relation to the recent themes of geographies of discontent and 'the revenge of places that do not matter'. Among the notable exceptions is the work of Lenzi and Perrucca (2021) and Koeppen et al. (2021), who examine simultaneously the geographical area and individual level with the use of social survey microdata as well as regional data, reflecting the complexity of the broad spectrum encompassed as populism because of its diversity.

This chapter builds on these studies and, in particular, the recent work by Koeppen et al. (2021) that used European Social Survey data to consider the individual and spatial contextual determinants of voting for so-called anti-establishment political parties (APEP). The study presented by Koeppen et al. (2021) considers APEP as a group comprising both right- and left-wing parties as well as parties widely described as populist. In this chapter, we build on this by considering alternative groupings for right and left as well as additional explanatory variables. In addition, following that study, we adopt a multilevel methodological framework to further examine individual- and contextual (regional)-level determinants of voting for different groupings of parties that can be characterised as radical left or radical right. Further, our analysis aims to explore whether there is an association between voting for radical right and left parties and individuals' level of subjective wellbeing (SWB), and if so, whether there are differences between these two types of parties. To that end, we argue it is crucial to consider individual-level data in more detail and whether voting for radical right or left is explained by discontent that reflects the unhappiness of individuals living in 'places left behind'.

More specifically, this chapter contributes to the existing literature on the theme described as the 'geography of discontent' as expressed through voting behaviour, whereby we specifically distinguish between voting for radical right or left parties (Rodríguez-Pose, 2018; Dijkstra et al., 2020; McCann, 2020; Koeppen et al., 2021). As such, the question remains how to interpret the geographical variation of voting for radical right and left parties. Despite recent attempts in regional science to explain these voting patterns conceptualised as discontent in response to 'places left behind' (Dijkstra et al., 2020; Koeppen et al., 2021; McCann, 2020; Rodríguez-Pose, 2018), we consider these patterns as a protest behaviour providing indirect information about perceived unhappiness or discontent. Consequently, this gives rise to the question whether radical voting behaviour is driven by manifestations pertaining to individual and contextual effects (i.e. national, regional and local context-specific manifestations) of an overarching phenomenon, more precisely defined as a 'sense of emotional grievance or marginalisation' stimulated by the role of discrete emotions. Emotional appeals are often used in political rhetoric and circulated among the electorate. Thus, in order to understand the phenomena of radical parties, we argue that there is a need for more research aimed at examining individual emotional dynamics entailing anger, anxiety, sadness and related feelings. Given the gap in the literature, this study hereby provides important insights in that direction, by introducing the measurement of subjective well-being (SWB), in order to directly examine how SWB may affect individuals' propensity to vote for radical right or left parties, by including relevant contextual variables.

There is scientific evidence that subjective happiness matters in determining how people vote, especially when linked with political attitudes and social and geographical factors. Thereby, we use the broader concept of subjective wellbeing to capture the individuals' overall evaluations of life as well as the experience of negative or positive emotions (Diener et al., 1998). A growing literature confirms the links between political significance and subjective wellbeing (e.g. Frey and Stutzer, 2000). Given that the existing literature has associated subjective wellbeing as an important determinant with political participation (i.e. voting), yet, little is known about the link between the distinction of voting for radical right or left parties and subjective wellbeing.

Building on previous empirical analyses and methodological frameworks developed to study geographical and socio-economic determinants of subjective wellbeing (and, by extension, voting for radical right and left parties, for example, see Aslam and Corrado, 2012; Ballas and Tranmer, 2012; Ballas and Thanis, 2022), this chapter revisits the work of regional scientists and economic geographers briefly discussed above to address the following question:

> What are the regional and individual determinants of either voting for radical and/or populist right or left parties?

In order to address this question, we use a multilevel modelling approach to the analysis of the European Social Survey (ESS) data for the years 2010, 2012, 2014, 2016 and 2018. The remainder of this chapter is structured as follows. The next section reviews key relevant literature that underpins the research in this study and which is used to frame the methodological approach and analysis presented in the following sections. The third section describes the data sources, the variables of interest and the empirical design. The fourth section includes the main findings, which are discussed in the subsequent section and directly. The last section presents some concluding comments and reflections.

## 8.2 DEFINING AND ANALYSING RADICAL RIGHT AND LEFT PARTIES AND THE GEOGRAPHY OF DISCONTENT

This chapter builds on recent literature in regional science and economic geography, which highlights the crucial role of individual and regional characteristics in electoral geography by emphasising the relevance of recent work on the 'geographies of discontent' and the 'revenge of the places that don't matter' (Koeppen et al., 2021; Lenzi and Perucca, 2021). While the common denominator of these studies seems to be related to 'discontent', scholars have only recently started to highlight how territorial and individual characteristics, as well as their evolving situation, can affect voting behaviour across European regions (ibid.). However, most of the studies in regional science focus on the anti-establishment/anti-system parties, but, to our knowledge, have not previously investigated voting for radical parties, of both the right and left spectrum. Before considering relevant studies of the determinants of radical right and left parties, it is useful to provide a brief overview of relevant definitions and issues.

### 8.2.1  Radical Parties: Right and Left

Over recent years, radical parties, on both the right and left side of the political spectrum, have been gaining ground across Europe (Rooduijn et al., 2017). Today, in most European countries, the presence of at least one radical party has offered a considerable challenge to mainstream parties by impinging logics of party competition and shaping policy outcomes (see Rooduijn et al., 2017). Although there have been various explanatory approaches for the success of radical parties in the past (e.g. Rydgren, 2005, 2007; Rooduijn et al., 2017; Rooduijn and Burgoon, 2018; Van Hauwaert and Van Kessel, 2018), more recent scholarly work offers relatively limited insights into the determinants of both types of radical party families together – and, by extension, radicalism – as well as highlighting mostly territorial or individual characteristics (see, for example, Kriesi, 2014; Rooduijn and Burgoon, 2018). To understand determinants of radical right and left voting behaviour, both in terms of contextual as well as individuals' factors, it is important first to carefully delineate the radical party families.

Radical right parties can be considered as nationalist parties, as the ideological core of these parties is based on a combination of characteristics of nativism and authoritarianism (Mudde, 2007). More specifically, those parties emphasise that 'states should be inhabited exclusively by members of the native group ("the nation") and that non-native elements (persons and ideas) are fundamentally threatening to the homogeneous nation-state' (Mudde, 2007, p. 19). Moreover, what unites radical right parties is the desire to create an authoritarian system that is ordered according to the 'natural' and exist-ing differences in society, as well as a law-and-order system where deviant behaviour is punished (Mudde, 2007). For example, it entails strengthening the political interest of ethno-cultural unity, territorial integrity and sovereignty of the native population (Rydgren, 2005, 2007).

In contrast to radical right parties, radical left parties are typically rooted in a common communist tradition with persistent legacies (e.g. Leninist and/ or Trotskyist), criticising the capitalist system. Further, they are united by the aspiration to transform society by advocating 'root and branch' transformation of capitalism and neoliberal and market-oriented policies in order to take power from existing political and economic elites (March, 2011). The parties' main stated concerns are to promote socio-economic equality and rights, social welfare reforms, and strive to adopt an egalitarian and universalist agenda (March, 2011; March and Mudde, 2005). This is in line with their criticism of the 'neoliberal' character of globalisation and specifically European economic integration (ibid.). In other words, the radical left supports socialism, which is often combined with ideological features such as multiculturalism, ecologism, feminism, anti-imperialism or gender equality (March, 2011).

To this end, the two families depict important differences in their socio-economic and socio-cultural views, but we can anticipate that simul-taneously considering contextual and individual circumstances might well offer insights on similarities on voting for radical left and right parties. For example, central to the radical left is the general rejection of contemporary capitalism and its consequent socio-economic structure, while aiming to pursue an alternative economic welfare structure that includes major redis-tribution of resources (March, 2011). Contrary to this, central to the radical right are xenophobic and nativist attributes and its focus on the reshaping of the cultural dimensions, which are linked to issues on the restructuring of the integration-demarcation conflict. Nevertheless, both the radical right and left share parts of Euroscepticism, where economic anxieties and resistance to aus-terity measures are mobilised by the radical left against the project of European integration, while the radical right's central focus is driven by securing national identity and stimulating feelings of cultural threats (De Vries and Edwards, 2009). These conceptual criteria are translated into a list, the PopuList, by Rooduijn et al. (2019), which categorises proclaimed populist parties across various European countries into far right, far left and Eurosceptic parties. In this chapter, we adopt this list to define and analyse radical right and radical left parties (for more details, see Rooduijn et al., 2019) building on earlier work (Koeppen et al., 2021; also discussed in more detail in the next section) that analysed them as one single grouping described as APEP.

## 8.2.2 Determinants of Voting for Radical Right and Left Parties

The emergence of many self-proclaimed anti-establishment or anti-system parties in Europe has reshaped the political landscape. In the political science literature, radical right and left parties are considered among these parties (see Georgiadou and Mavropoulou, 2021; Bourdin and Tai, 2022). Thus, given the significant differences between radical right and left voting as highlighted in the previous section, it is important to consider the distinction between these two types of parties, aiming to better explain an emerging phenomenon – 'geography of discontent' – used to describe spatial patterns of anti-establishment or anti-system voting at regional and local levels (Rodríguez-Pose, 2018; Dijkstra et al., 2020; McCann, 2020; Rodríguez-Pose et al., 2020). Nevertheless, the literature on such types of parties is in most cases focusing either on the individual or regional level, with some exceptions considering both the individual and regional level simultaneously. For example, recent work by Rooduijn and Burgoon (2018) explore determinants of votes for radical right and left parties across Europe, or Vasilopoulos et al. (2021), who examine determinants on electoral support for the far right in France.

Concurrently, there have been some recent studies by economic geographers and regional scientists that have considered and analysed anti-establishment or anti-system voting focusing on both levels simultaneously. For example, building on this work, Koeppen et al. (2021) provided a comprehensive overview of the vote for self-proclaimed anti-establishment parties (APEP) – including radical right and left parties, among others – across 18 European member states. Using a multilevel modelling framework and by combining individual-level and contextual level data (i.e. age, employment status, social attitudes and regional GDP per inhabitant in PPS), the study demonstrated that the extent of voting for APEP is a result of individual and contextual (regional) level determinants, pointing to a 'places that do not matter' and 'people that do not matter' reasoning. As such, an important finding is that discontent as proxied by levels of individual happiness does not in itself affect the propensity to vote for APEPs. Moreover, when linked with socio-economic and demographic, political and cultural characteristics in addition to the mediating effect of the regional context, voting for APEPs is driven by both the individual and contextual (regional) level determinants. To this end, the authors conclude that understanding factors underlying feelings of discontent, and to capture more specifically particular party families, can be an especially significant empirical contribution. A similar argument is made by Lenzi and Perucca (2021), re-examining the rise of a geography of political discontent in the EU and by extension the relevant argument made in recent studies of a strong spatial association between anti-system voting, where regional economic and demographic decline, alongside poor occupational opportunities, suggest that mostly territorial socio-economic disparities within the EU are the origin of some of the most recent political events, such as Brexit. By disentangling the effect on individual and political discontent of different socio-economic disadvantage conditions at the interregional, intraregional and individual level, the authors confirm that a 'geography of discontent' exists across EU regions. Yet, their findings also highlight that intraregional inequalities matter to a great extent for individual discontent, while individual socio-economic disadvantaged conditions amplify further this negative effect.

When considering the concept of 'geography of discontent' more broadly and in the realm of social capital, there is increasing evidence on the correlation between adverse impacts of discontent (by extension, it could be argued, unhappiness) and anti-system voting (e.g. see Rodríguez-Pose et al., 2020). In other words, many of the issues that were originally expressed by Putnam (2000) are echoed in the underlying social capital phenomena, which are driving the 'geography of discontent'. For instance, this is reflected in the electoral success of Donald Trump in 2016, to the extent to which a large number of citizens in certain cohesive localities sensed that their communities are being 'left behind' by the impact of long-term socio-economic and population decline, rather than by widening interpersonal income (and wealth) inequalities. It has also been argued that the rise in social discontent that may be underpinning such election results could be considered to be an expression of high levels of social capital reinforced by the citizens' collective ability to speak out by choosing to 'golf' with Trump (Rodríguez-Pose et al., 2020). Consequently, in the realm of the 'geography of discontent', it can be argued that this may be the result of the discontent of people who live in declining regions and who demonstrate strong cohesiveness as a community, with rooted cultural and emotional ties to these regions.

Besides the relevance of socio-economic determinants highlighted in the territorial studies, scholars have also foregrounded the role of cultural grievances (Halikiopoulou and Vlandas 2020; Halikiopoulou, 2020), or else the 'cultural backlash thesis' (Norris and Inglehart, 2019). It is argued that the anti-establishment/anti-system vote can be understood as an authoritarian reaction from older, more conservative and traditionalist cohorts to cultural transformations and a shift toward more post-materialist values. Further, these cultural changes are perceived as threats to core norms, values and traditional identities and stir anger and resentment towards immigrants, globalisation and progressive cultural values (Halikiopoulou and Vlandas, 2020). In this context the work by Bhambra (2017) is also of relevance, arguing that the vote for Brexit had deep cultural identity roots and reflected delayed resentment about the loss of empire and the privileges and feeling of entitlement associated with it (see Dorling and Tomlinson, 2019).

### 8.2.3    Individual Discontent, Subjective Wellbeing and Voting

Following the discussion of relevant literature in the previous section, this chapter builds on relevant empirical work that makes links between subjective wellbeing (SWB) with political participation and ideology (e.g. Frey and Stutzer, 2000; Weitz-Shapiro and Winters, 2011). Rather than considering election outcomes, much of the research examines procedural aspects of voting and political participation (i.e. referendums) affecting subjective wellbeing (see Flavin and Keane, 2012; Liberini at al., 2019; Lorenzini, 2015; Miller, 2013). In contrast, Pierce et al. (2016) use evidence from the 2012 US Presidential election exploring the impact on subjective happiness when partisans win (Democrats) or lose (Republicans). Another example of relevant work is the research conducted by Herrin et al. (2018) examining how changes in community measures of wellbeing, and the change since 2012, affected electoral shifts that led to the outcome of the 2016 United States presidential election. The analysis suggested that US regions experiencing the largest shifts away from the incumbent party reported both lower levels of wellbeing and greater drops in wellbeing when compared with regions that did not shift, irrespective of income. In a recent study, Powdthavee et al. (2019) use subjective wellbeing measures as the outcome, examining the effect of the Brexit referendum on individuals' subsequent subjective wellbeing, particularly focusing on their overall life satisfaction and the impact on mental health.

As such, by building on previous relevant work on the analysis of electoral geography, in this study, subjective measures of wellbeing are employed, which we argue is an expression of discontent and protest and thus, a component and suitable measure of voters' life dissatisfactions/unhappiness. We thus associate subjective measures of wellbeing as a sense of individuals' general discontent. Instead of treating voting behaviour solely as an economic outcome, as suggested in the literature on political economy (see Lewis-Beck and Stegmaier, 2000), the interpretation of subjective wellbeing reflects the individual's overall evaluation of quality-of-life (i.e. life satisfaction) and, by extension, a component of subjective happiness (see Diener et al., 2018), both depending on economic as well as noneconomic factors (Flavin and Keane, 2012). Thereby, we aim to mirror the notion of voters' discontent, which potentially can be reflected in regional variations. Specifically, in this study, we examine the role of subjective measures of wellbeing (i.e. subjective happiness and life satisfaction) as determining factors of voting outcomes, alongside the comparison of geographical variations.

### 8.2.4   Building a Multilevel Modelling Approach to the Analysis of Radical Right and Left Parties and the Geography of Discontent

This chapter also foregrounds a conceptual and a methodological argument to consider spatial patterns in voting behaviour, which is explained by the combination of compositional and spatial contextual effects. Put differently, compositional effects are the result of non-random spatial concentrations of individuals structured by specific individual characteristics (e.g. age and education), which is associated with voting behaviour. In contrast, spatial contextual effects posit (also known as the 'neighbourhood effect') that individuals' voting decisions and political attitudes are influenced by their physical and social environment (e.g. high unemployment rate and/or other factors) regardless of individual characteristics, and as a result, similar individuals living in different places may vote for different parties (MacAllister et al., 2001; Johnston and Pattie, 2006). In addition, and in line with previous relevant work on methodological frameworks exploring the geography of happiness and wellbeing in Europe at times of economic crisis and political instability, especially in regions affected by austerity policies (Ballas and Thanis, 2022), it is also of interest to explore whether levels of subjective wellbeing can affect individual voting behaviour. As noted in the previous section, the emerging regional science literature has highlighted the fact that voting behaviour depends on territorial characteristics. More specifically, in this study we aim to directly examine how voting behaviour for radical right and left parties may be affected by individual-level characteristics pertaining to socio-economic circumstances, cultural and political attitudes, as well as subjective wellbeing. Put differently, individuals with similar individual attributes (i.e. gender, age) and socio-economic characteristics (education, income) might vote differently if that person reports higher levels of subjective wellbeing, even after controlling for regional contextual characteristics. As such, we posit that individuals with lower levels of subjective wellbeing tend to be more inclined to vote for radical right or radical left parties, when regional contextual characteristics are controlled for and applied in a multilevel model analysis.

Building on literature within quantitative social science (including Radcliff, 2001; Liberini et al., 2019, Ward et al., 2021), there is evidence that reversed feelings of happiness can contribute in explaining voting behaviour when controlling for other individual characteristics. Intuitively, it could be argued that emotions (i.e. anger, fear, anxiety or nostalgia) and by extension unhappiness may induce a stronger effect on the vote choice for anti-establishment parties (Vasilopoulos et al., 2019; Vasilopoulou and Wagner, 2020), but recently there has been the argument suggesting a paradox of happy people voting for ostensibly angry parties (see Forgas, 2019).

Of particular relevance here is the work of van Leeuwen et al. (2020) who demonstrated that, in the context of the Netherlands, both compositional and contextual circumstances in areas of demographic decline are especially significant drivers of voting for the PVV (Party for Freedom) and expression of discontent. In this chapter, we build on this work (as well as on Koeppen et al., 2021) by considering the impact of individual factors and regional contextual factors, such as the regional GDP per inhabitant in purchasing power standards (European Commission, 2022a) and unemployment rate (European Commission, 2022b), but also consider the countries' Gini coefficient (European Commission, 2022c). Put differently, it is of interest whether voting behaviour of individuals with similar characteristics tends to be affected by both compositional and contextual circumstances.

From a methodological perspective, in order to analyse the simultaneous impact of individual and contextual variables, hierarchical multilevel models are considered. By adding a geographical scale to examine regional differences, we advance the argument that, beyond individual level modelling methods, multilevel models have key advantages (Jones, 1997). It is of particular relevance to study geographical differences of political participation through explaining the interaction between those two (ibid). Therefore, we can group those determinants into those that contribute to the individual level and those that constitute regional contextual effects. In order to estimate the contextual and/or individual effects on individual voting behaviour, we need a suitable method allowing us to disentangle both effects. In essence, it is of particular interest to estimate if individuals would have voted differently, with particular socio-economic and contextual characteristics, also when explained by the levels of subjective wellbeing. Therefore, this study builds on the work in electoral geography that highlights the value of contextual analyses (Agnew, 1996) by adding an approach centred at the individual level (see Pattie and Johnston, 2000; Johnston and Pattie, 2006). Also of importance is the geographical scale to study electoral behaviour in order to capture possible contextual impacts (Weaver, 2014). The appropriate scale needs to be suitable to encompass regional impacts, political outcomes and social interaction effects. Given the present data limitations, we consider spatial units at the regional level for contextual characteristics, thereby accounting for the fact that policy-related variables are often considered at the national scale while this misses the driving mechanisms of the contextual effects measured.

## 8.3    DATA AND METHODS

### 8.3.1    Data Sources

We analyse pooled, cross-sectional individual-level data from the European Social Survey (ESS), which is an academically driven survey conducted across Europe since its establishment in 2001. It is conducted every two years at the individual level with newly selected, cross-sectional samples, covering a wide selection of questions providing useful information related to attitudes, beliefs and values as well as voting behaviour next to basic demographic characteristics (e.g. age, sex, education, etc.) (ESS Round 9: European Social Survey Round 9 Data, 2018; Kish and Frankel, 1974). This allows us to better examine changes in population prevalence of attributes (i.e. voting behaviour) whilst controlling for numerous observable factors. At every stage, respondents' selection involved a strict random probability sampling. All countries adopt the same questionnaire and methodological standards of the design and operation of the project, enhancing the comparability across countries (ibid.). In order to correct for unobserved bias in the data, the ESS recommends the application (by default) of post-stratification weights to specifically correct for differences in the probability of selection, sampling errors and possible nonresponse errors, thereby making the sample more representative, and takes makes it possible to adjust for differences in population size across countries (Kaminska, 2020). We focus upon data from the EU27 Member States plus the United Kingdom from five consecutive waves, covering the period 2010 – 2018 (round five, round six, round seven, round eight and nine). Given the time period of analysis covered, we can assume that an eight-year period is sufficient to detect voting patterns, especially following the beginning of the crisis (2008) as well as the post-crisis period and in regions as related to recent research vis-à-vis the 'geography of discontent' (e.g. Cramer, 2016; McCann, 2018; Dijkstra et al., 2020). In addition, since the data structure is clearly hierarchical, containing two distinct levels (i.e. regions and individuals), the time period of analysis is restricted to the covered years as for the individual-level data, the ESS multilevel data only starts from wave 4 in 2008 (Schnaudt et al., 2014). Furthermore, by necessity, the analyses on voting for radical right and left parties cover those European countries where the party families are present respectively. This implies that the empirical models run for the analysis include a partially different selection of countries.

Central to this study is information on levels of individual wellbeing, alongside information on socio-economic and demographic characteristics, as previous regional science literature on voting behaviour suggested (Liberini et al., 2019; Alabrese et al., 2019). The ESS provides insights into political behaviour, especially individuals' voting behaviour in the last election, while at the same time providing information on individuals' level of subjective wellbeing, which makes the survey suitable for the analysis. In order to explain radical voting, for both radical right and left parties, across European regions, we also include information on the spatial context. For this, we consider as the appropriate scale the European Nomenclature of Territorial Units for Statistics (NUTS) 2 level. This enables us to capture evident variation on individual voting behaviour and preferences within regions, as evidenced by Agnew (1987, 1996), postulating that the local context is considered as an important dimension in understanding voting behaviour. In other words, voters are influenced by their social and geographical environments as well as their own individual situation (Johnston and Pattie, 2014), allowing us to infer that the local place matters as a behavioural context. It should be noted however, that throughout the selected time period, there is no NUTS 2 level information available for Germany and the UK, and for Italy only in 2018 on GDP per inhabitant in purchasing power standards. Hence, for these countries and their missing information, we revert to the NUTS 1 level. The selected regional variables are based on the data provided by Eurostat, which have already been included with the ESS data. In addition, country dummy variables are included in order to control for unobserved country effects. The resulting model in our analysis consists of two levels, where individual responses are treated as level-one, the regional information (NUTS 2) are combined into level-two and the country dummy variables are treated as country fixed effects. In total, the dataset comprises data of 242 regions across 25 European countries (see Table 8.2 – null model) over a period of eight years. The number of individual obser-vations available is 196 291, although the final sample size for the analysis is 62 111 individuals at NUTS 1 and NUTS 2 level for radical right voting (58 270 for radical left voting), due to missing values for some of the key variables of interest.

The creation of radical right and left parties is based on the classifications according to the PopuList database (Rooduijn et al., 2019), where all parties are considered that have been classified as radical left and radical right parties. In addition, the PopuList's categorization of parties, specifically in our case radical right and left parties, is based on widely used coding, following the literature, including that by March and Mudde (2005), Mudde (2007), March (2011) and Rooduijn and Burgoon (2018), as well as Jolly et al. (2022).

### 8.3.2    Method

The modelling strategy applied aims to reflect the notion that voting behaviour is an individual decision taken within a regional and country context. Thus, given our conceptualization and the structure of the data, the most suitable modelling strategy is reflected when analysed with multilevel techniques (see Snijders and Bosker, 2012). In particular, this approach can be used when addressing multilevel processes, when individual data are nested within groups (i.e. neighbourhoods, districts and regions) and group-level characteristics are used to predict individual outcomes (Duch and Stevenson, 2017; Johnston et al., 2007; Snijders and Bosker, 1999). Moreover, multilevel models anticipate both between-individual variation and between-place variation, which improves the inference and interpretation of the coefficients of the model (Jones, 1997). In addition, multilevel models have an additional advantage to account for methodological details over more conventional models applying fixed effects for different levels and spatial units with the use of dummy variables.

To draw inferences about the relationship between measure of subjective wellbeing and a variety of individual-level socio-economic and demographic characteristics, most previous studies on the analysis of measures of subjective happiness and wellbeing are based on the use of microdata or studies aggregating levels of subjective happiness at the country level for comparison across countries. However, by adopting a multilevel modelling approach, Aslam and Corrado (2012) were among the first using ESS data for a regional level analysis of subjective wellbeing. Since then, this approach has received more attention in regional science, especially for the analysis of compositional and contextual determinants (and by extension subjective happiness) (Ballas, 2021; Ballas and Thanis, 2022), thereby accounting for the dependency of observations within groups, as well as taking into account variation due to various levels in the data (Ballas and Tranmer, 2012; Snijders and Bosker, 1999). More recently, in order to address such hierarchical processes with, for example, individuals nested within regions, Koeppen et al. (2021) model individual voting behaviour for APEP as a function of individual and regional characteristics, employing a two-level model with a binary dependent variable where individuals are nested in regions. Similarly, the authors highlight the advantage of multilevel modelling for assessing the effects of lower-level and higher-level variables simultaneously, while also accounting for the clustering of observations (i.e. dependency of observations) (see Snijders and Bosker, 1999). Building on this, and given the hierarchical structure of the data and the binary nature of the dependent variables for the baseline models, we apply multilevel logistic modelling by considering random intercepts, meaning that the intercepts between regions vary but the relationship between the explanatory variables and voting for radical parties is assumed to be the same in all regions. Additionally, in order to control for unobserved heterogeneity between countries, country-fixed effects are included.

#### 8.3.2.1  Dependent variables

We classify parties into party families developed by a consortium of scholars who have conducted extensive research on populism ('The PopuList Project', see Rooduijn et al., 2019). Our dependent variables voting behaviour were constructed based on the question 'What party did you vote for in the last national election of [country]?' The answers were then recoded into a dichotomous variable. Thus, the dependent variables in our baseline models are two binary variables (1 = voted for a radical right or a radical left party, respectively, 0 = denotes those individuals that voted for non-radical parties, including mainstream parties, such as conservative/liberal/Christian-democratic and/or social-democratic). For each indicator, we estimated a series of multilevel logit models with standard errors clustered by regions. To our knowledge, no studies have considered both party dimensions separately when analysing individual level characteristics and regional contextual effects on individual voting intentions, including a measure for feelings of discontent. It should be noted that only individuals who reported having voted in the country's most recent national election were included, excluding individuals who were not eligible to vote (i.e. under age 18). Further, we opted in particular for the ESS, as individuals are directly asked which party they voted for, enabling us to assume high validity for the outcome variables. However, potential shortcomings may involve that individuals chose not to have voted, do not remember the party voted for, refused to answer and/or absentees from the polling station, which eventually results in missing values and have thus been excluded from the analysis (Table 8.1 presents summary statistics for all the variables included in our analysis).

#### 8.3.2.2  Independent variables

Following the discussion and the literature reviewed in the previous sections, an important independent variable to analyse individual voting intentions is subjective wellbeing, in order to explain measures of the related constructs of overall quality-of-life evaluations and/or discontent and by extension feelings of anger or fear (see Koeppen et al., 2021). We use two different measures for it: subjective happiness and life satisfaction. These two measures have been found to be associated with political engagement, when controlling for other factors such as age or income (Liberini et al., 2019; Ward et al., 2021). Subjective happiness and life satisfaction are measured by a 10-point Likert scale (0–10) and recoded with (0) indicating 'Extremely unhappy/dissatisfied' and (10) referring to being 'Extremely happy/satisfied'. It should be noted that these variables were coded in reverse order to the original ones, meaning that higher categorical values of subjective happiness and life satisfaction imply worse perceived happiness and life satisfaction of the individual. The variables are included in the analysis separately.

*Table 8.1*    *Descriptive statistics*

| Continuous variables | N | Min. | Max. | Mean | St. Dev. |
|---|---|---|---|---|---|
| Subjective happiness | 195 244 | 0 | 10 | 2.8 | 2.0 |
| Life satisfaction | 195 461 | 0 | 10 | 3.1 | 2.2 |
| Pro-immigration attitudes | 174 071 | 0.5 | 7 | 3.8 | 0.9 |
| Traditionalist attitudes – traditions and customs | 194 747 | 1 | 6 | 2.6 | 0.88 |
| Traditionalist attitudes – cultural liberalism | 194 635 | 1 | 6 | 2.5 | 0.74 |
| Income (net household) | 155 050 | 1 | 10 | 5.2 | 2.8 |
| Economic insecurities | 194 500 | 0 | 10 | 3.6 | 2.9 |
| Level of religiosity | 194 475 | 0 | 10 | 4.5 | 3.1 |
| Attitudes Redistribution (dummy, ref: pro-redistribution) | 192 963 | 0 | 1 | 0.73 | 0.25 |
| Age | 190 388 | 18 | 114 | 50.6 | 18.0 |
| [NUTS2] GDP per inhabitant in PPS (in % of the EU28 average) | 196 291 | 27 | 234 | 99.1 | 38.0 |
| [NUTS2] Unemployment rates by age 15–75, all sexes in % | 196 243 | 1.3% | 37.0% | 9.0 | 4.8 |
| Gini coefficient | 196 291 | 20.9 | 39.6 | 29.595 | 3.636 |
| *Dummy variables* | *Frequency* | *Percent* | | | |
| Radical Right Vote (0 = mainstream party; 1= radical right party) | 108 446 | | | | |
| Mainstream party | 94 925 | 87.53 | | | |
| Radical right party | 13 521 | 12.47 | | | |
| Radical Left Vote (0 = mainstream party; 1= radical left party) | 102 800 | | | | |
| Mainstream party | 94 925 | 92.34 | | | |
| Radical left party | 7855 | 7.66 | | | |
| Gender (dummy, ref: men) | 196 228 | | | | |
| Male | 90 601 | 46.17 | | | |
| Female | 105 627 | 53.83 | | | |
| Level of Employment (ref: employed) | 196 291 | | | | |
| Employed | 94 946 | 48.60 | | | |
| Unemployed | 68 814 | 35.22 | | | |
| Economically inactive | 31 602 | 16.18 | | | |
| Highest level of education | 195 139 | | | | |
| Lower secondary education or less (low) | 56 999 | 29.21 | | | |
| Upper secondary education or advanced sub-degree (midlevel) | 72 332 | 37.07 | | | |
| Tertiary education (high) | 65 808 | 33.72 | | | |
| Oesch's five-class scheme | 138 724 | | | | |
| Higher-grade service class | 23 319 | 16.81 | | | |
| Lower-grade service class | 24 089 | 17.36 | | | |
| Small business owners | 15 258 | 11 | | | |
| Skilled workers | 46 074 | 33.21 | | | |
| Unskilled workers | 29 984 | 21.61 | | | |
| Marital status (dummy, ref: not married) | 191 496 | | | | |
| Married | 96 837 | 49.43 | | | |
| Not married | 94 659 | 50.57 | | | |

We also include individual attributes as well as additional individual-level controls, such as attitudinal variables. For example, existing literature studying voting behaviour suggests that, among others, the impact of unemployment, financial insecurities and income inequalities can be associated with political participation (Becker et al., 2018; Fetzer, 2019). Similarly, other studies focus on changing societal value structures in the context of voting behaviour, more specifically cultural grievances highlighting the 'cultural backlash' against perceived expansion of social-liberal values in society (Norris and Inglehart, 2019). We therefore control for these determinants by employing the following explanatory variables. Socio-economic insecurity is measured by constructing a scale that consists of three variables: 'if individuals are likely to be unem-ployed' (measured by means of the following categories representing (1) 'not at all likely' and (4) 'very likely'), if they are 'likely not have enough money' (measured by means of the several categories representing (1) 'not at all likely' and (4) 'very likely') and their 'feeling about the economic situation' (meas-ured by means of the five categories representing (1) 'very good' and (4) 'very difficult'). The newly created variable has been recoded and transformed, with (0) indicating that it is 'living comfortable' and (10) indicating that it is 'living difficult'. Cronbach's alpha is 0.64, indicating that the three items adequately measure the same latent dimension (Griethuijsen et al., 2014; Taber, 2018). An additional control for socioeconomic insecurity is defined by utilising Oesch's five-class scheme (Oesch, 2006), by constructing five binary class indicators out of the Oesch class scheme and assigning individuals to classes based on the occupation, which is meant to measure individuals' socio-economic back-ground.[1] In order to construct these variables from the codes provided by the ESS dataset, we rely on the scripts provided by Oesch (2006), which have been integrated into a single dataset and published on the ESS website (European Social Survey, 2022).

To measure the changing societal value structures, we also include several attitudinal variables capturing the individuals' importance to selected value statements. The 'pro-immigration' attitude of individuals has been assessed by constructing an exploratory factor analysis of six variables that were measured by the following propositions: *Allow immigrants of the same race; Allow immigrants of a different race; Allow immigrants from poor countries; Immigration is bad for the economy; Immigrants undermine our culture; Immigrants make the country a worse place to live.* We hence retrieved the factor of pro-immigrant sentiment (Cronbach's alpha is 0.84, see Table A.8.1). This factor scores low values for individuals with particularly strong

---

[1]    Higher-grade service class, lower-grade service class, small business owners, skilled workers, unskilled workers.

anti-immigration feelings and high values for voters favouring immigration. Further, we assessed for 'traditionalist' attitudes of individuals by composing two scales measuring (1) attitudes regarding traditions and customs, as well as (2) attitudes towards cultural liberalism. The first scale measures individuals' attitudes towards customs and traditions consists of the following five items: *Important to live in secure and safe surroundings; Important to do what is told and follow rules; Important that government is strong and ensures safety; Important to behave properly; Important to follow traditions and customs* (Cronbach's alpha is 0.71, see Table A.8.1). This index scores low values for individuals with particular attachment to customs and traditions, while high values are associated with voters who are indifferent towards customs and traditions. The second scale measures attitudes towards cultural liberalism by relying on the following propositions: *Gay men and lesbians should be free to live their own life as they wish; Ashamed if close family member gay or lesbian; Gay and lesbian couples right to adopt children* (Cronbach's alpha is 0.81, see Table A.8.1). This index scores low values for individuals with particularly strong anti-LGBT feelings and high values for voters supporting LGBT. As a final scale, we measure 'redistribution attitudes' by relying on the following question: *Should the government take measures to reduce differences in income levels?* The variable has been transformed and rescaled ranging from 0 to 1, where higher values (1) indicate support for redistribution.

### 8.3.2.3   Control variables

In addition, and in line with previous studies on subjective wellbeing and voting behaviour (as discussed in the previous section (2.2 and 2.3), we also include relevant individual level sociodemographic factors and control variables. For example, within the literature of social sciences analysing the links between subjective wellbeing and political participation, it has been established that voting for extremist/radical parties can be associated with older voters, low educational attainment, low life satisfaction and bad health (see, for example, Alabrese et al., 2019). We therefore include these variables by means of controls for individuals' gender, age, level of education and income as well as social class. Gender is operationalized as a dummy (1 female, 0 male). Moreover, the selection of all these explanatory variables was informed by the literature and the evidence reviewed by Koeppen et al. (2021). Educational level is measured by the seven-point ISCED classification, grouped into lower secondary education or less (low), upper secondary education or advanced sub-degree (midlevel) and tertiary education (high). We also assessed the level of employment by recoding the variable and grouping the variable by means of three categories, asking the respondent the main activity conducted in the past 7 days (1 = 'employed', 2 = 'not employed', 3 = 'economically inactive') (see Koeppen et al., 2021). The income variable refers to the country-specific net income decile of the individuals' household. Its values range from 1 (first decile) to 10 (tenth decile). We also control for marital status, by means of distinguishing if someone is living together with a husband, partner or cohabitant (= 1) and those who live alone (= 0). We also control for 'level of religiosity', which is operationalized by the variable subjective religiosity. Subjective religiosity is measured on a 10-point scale where (0) denotes 'secular' and (10) 'very religious'. In addition, we also include specific contextual-level data that are considered as important to measure the regional characteristics that are expected to be moderating the effects of individual-level characteristics and are in line with previous multilevel studies of happiness (Koeppen et al., 2021; Lenzi and Perucca, 2021; Ballas and Thanis, 2022). For example, the authors include measures for regional economic outlook, in terms of GDP per inhabitant in purchasing power standards and unemployment rate. The unemployment rate is measured by assessing the percentage of the civilian labour force unemployed (as a percentage of the total economically active population; Eurostat). We also include regional GDP per inhabitant in PPS (in percentage of the EU 27 – average) in our models. Following the discussion of Ballas and Thanis (2022), we also include the countries' Gini coefficient in order to measure socio-economic inequality, using data provided by Eurostat.

## 8.4    RESULTS

The previous sections provided the theoretical and methodological arguments for employing a multilevel modelling approach, which is in line with previous studies on multilevel modelling analysis (see also Aslam and Corrado, 2012; Koeppen et al., 2021; Ballas and Thanis, 2022). Before discussing the results of the multilevel modelling analysis, it is relevant to discuss the structure of the results section. As a first step, we will perform a multilevel (two-level) null model (see Table 8.2) where respondents are nested in NUTS 2 level regions and which includes a random intercept. Next, we consider demographic, socio-economic and attitudinal variables, as well as subjective wellbeing. Finally, the models are extended by adding regional characteristics. We end this section by considering robustness checks on life satisfaction.

### 8.4.1    Two-level Null Model

As already mentioned, the first step in our analysis involves the estimation of the proportion of overall variation in voting for a radical right or left party that is attributable to individuals and the variation that is attributable to regions. The intra-class correlation coefficients (ICC) of both null models, which include no covariates, support the choice to employ a multilevel logistic model, as it shows that 43 per cent of the variance in the individual's vote for radical right parties is located at the regional level and 46 per cent for radical left parties.

### 8.4.2    Subjective Wellbeing Measures, Demographic and Socio-economic Variables, and Social Attitudinal Variables

In Table A.8.2 in the Appendix to this chapter, we present the results of our baseline multilevel regression model and related individual demographic and socio-economic covariates, as well as the subjective wellbeing measures, crude controls for the national context and year dummies. When introducing individual-level variables, it is interesting to note that the two-level model intra-class correlation drops (compared to the null model) to 37 per cent (for those voting for radical right parties) and 44 per cent (for those voting for radical left parties). Additionally, when controlling for subjective happiness, the results are statistically significant and negatively associated with voting behaviour, both for radical right and left parties. Despite that, it is also interesting to note that the odds ratio for 'not employed' and 'economically inactive' (i.e. among others 'housework; looking after children; education') representing the variable 'occupational status' suggests a statistically significant negative association with voting for radical right parties. When comparing with voting for radical left parties, there is only a statistically significant negative association with being 'economically inactive'. As such, compared to those in employment, the odds for individuals being 'economically inactive' to vote for radical right parties is 0.784 and 0.878 for voting for radical left parties. Furthermore, individual income has a significant negative association with radical right (OR: 0.984) or radical left (OR: 0.934) voting. Similarly, this applies to age: for every unit increase, the odds of voting for radical right are 0.981 and for radical left 0.993, respectively. The odds ratio of gender show that women are less likely to vote for radical right (OR: 0.724) or radical left (OR: 0.887) parties compared to men.

We also include several attitudinal variables. More specifically, we control for attitudes pertaining to socio-economic insecurities as well as political and cultural attitudes. What is interesting to note, being of lower social class (Oesch's five-class scheme) and experiencing higher economic insecurities, are associated with a higher estimated probability of voting for radical right parties. These associations are statistically significant, with an odds ratio of 1.319 and 1.037, respectively. This partially aligns with voting for radical left parties. Experiencing higher economic insecurities is associated with a higher estimated probability of voting for radical left parties, while the association of being of lower social class is less pronounced and only slightly significant (OR: 1.150). Similarly, having a positive and welcoming attitude towards immigrants as well as 'experiencing immigrants as enriching to the country's

*Table 8.2     Two-level null model*

| Dependent variable: | Radical Left Vote | Radical Right Vote |
|---|---|---|
| Constant | -3.197***(0.115) | -2.295***(0.104) |
| Total N | 102 800 | 108 446 |
| Level-2 N | 242 | 242 |
| -2LL | -23 962.435 | -29 994.367 |
| ICC (NUTS2) | 0.466 (0.030) | 0.432 (0.025) |

*Note*:     *=p<0.1; **=p<0.05; ***= p<0.01. Standard errors in parentheses.

culture/life' is less associated with voting for radical right parties (OR: 1.853). When compared to voting for radical left parties, being positive and welcoming towards immigrants is associated with a higher probability to vote for radical left parties (OR: 0.816). It is also worth noting that being less open to cultural liberalism is associated with a higher estimated probability of voting for radical right parties (OR: 1.142), while being less in favour of customs and traditions is related with lower probabilities with voting for radical right parties (OR: 0.876). In this context, it is interesting to note that the association of being in favour of customs and traditions is less pronounced with voting for radical left parties (OR: 1.264). Intuitively, it can be assumed that this is related to the more progressive outlook relative to radical right parties. Likewise, the results for the variable representing someone's attitude toward income redistribution are also worth noting. The association is positive and slightly statistically significant, indicating that those individuals in favour of income redistribution are more likely to vote for radical right parties. Comparing the results to voting for radical left parties, it is interesting to note that the association is even more pronounced (OR: 9.769). In contrast to those individuals not in favour of income redistribution, the ones that agree are even more likely to vote for radical left parties. These results help to understand that examining voting behaviour for radical right and/or left parties can be misleading when only based on demographic and socio-economic issues, while underlying socio-cultural conditions and attitudes can add an additional layer in understanding individual voting behaviour for radical parties.

In addition, both models include country- and year-fixed effects. Germany serves as the reference country, where we find that individuals located in Hungary, Italy and Poland are more likely to vote for radical right parties, while individuals located in Cyprus, Czechia, Germany, Denmark, Spain, Finland, France, Greece, Ireland, Italy, the Netherlands, Portugal, Sweden, Slovenia and Slovakia are more likely to vote for radical left parties. This suggests that, controlling for several demographic and socio-economic or socio-cultural conditions and regional characteristics, unobserved country-specific characteristics (e.g. culture and/or history) may play a role in positively (or negatively) influencing individual voting behaviour for radical parties, either right or left. These findings seem to suggest that the electoral success of radical parties in Europe is not predominantly limited to peripheral European countries. Instead, it indicates that European voters are spread across the entire continent. In Table A.8.3 in the Appendix to this chapter, the extent of the regional characteristics is more explicitly addressed in understanding voting for radical right and radical left parties.

### 8.4.3   Subjective Wellbeing Measures, Demographic and Socio-economic Variables, Social Attitudinal Variables, and Regional Characteristics

In Table A.8.3 in the Appendix, we have added regional-level variables in order to describe whether voting for radical right or left parties can be a result of individual discontent and regional characteristics. As such, we include regional GDP per inhabitant in PPS (in percentage of the EU 28 average), an indicator of regional unemployment and the Gini coefficient measuring socio-economic inequality. Including the regional characteristics does not alter the effects of the individual-level characteristics. This might suggest that socio-cultural and political attitudinal variables, together with the demographic and socio-economic characteristics, trump regional socio-economic character-istics in explaining voting for radical parties. Additionally, it is interesting to note that two out of the three variables of regional characteristics (GDP per inhabitant in PPS and regional unemployment) are statistically significantly related to voting for a radical (and/or populist) right party, while there is no association with radical (and/or populist) left voting, which questions the role of regional socio-economic indicators in understanding voting for radical left parties. This assumption is further strengthened since the association between voting for radical left parties and the attitudinal variables remain largely unchanged: 'Experiencing immigrants as enriching to the country's culture/ life' reduces the odds of voting for radical left parties. Similarly, the variable representing the attitude towards income redistribution remains strongly pronounced with voting for radical left parties. Comparing these results to voting for radical right parties, we see that the attitudinal variables also remain largely unchanged, while including regional level characteristics, we can discern regional effects. In regions with higher levels of GDP, individuals are, on average, less likely to vote for radical right parties, whereas in regions with high levels of unemployment (compared to regions with lower levels of unemployment), voting behaviour for radical right parties is less pronounced. These results suggest that the relevant spatial context for voting behaviour might rather be at smaller geographical scales, as suggested in previous literature (e.g. Johnston et al., 2007), rather than by the NUTS 2 regional socio-economic circumstances. In this regard, it is also relevant to note here that the null model intra-class correlation was 43 per cent (for radical right parties) dropping to 7.8 per cent when introducing individual and contextual covariates and after country- and year-fixed effects. Similarly, the null model intra-class correlation was 46 per cent (for radical left parties) dropping to 13.5 per cent when introducing individual and contextual covariates and after country- and year-fixed effects. As such, another assumption can be that 7.8 per cent (or else 13.5 per cent) of the probability to vote for a radical party is explained by between-regional differences and 92.2 per cent (or else 86.5 per cent) is explained by within-regional differences. Put differently, individual characteristics explain voting for radical parties better. It is also noteworthy that the results for the country fixed-effects remain robust to the inclusion of the regional socio-economic characteristics, suggesting that if socio-cultural conditions (i.e. anti-immigration attitudes, cultural liberalism or redistribution attitudes) in a country are unfavourable, these are the ones that remedy unfavourable national economic conditions.

Overall, in understanding voting for radical parties, our results consistently underline the relevance of both individual characteristics, specifically including individual socio-cultural beliefs and attitudes, and contextual characteristics, in particular pertaining to country-level variations. Indeed, regions yield important information, as individuals living in the same region may share common socio-economic, political and cultural characteristics, alongside individual characteristics, determining voting for radical right or left parties. Yet, our results do not show robust evidence for regional socio-economic characteristics explaining voting patterns for radical parties well. An interesting result is that subjective unhappiness could be a predictor of voting for radical parties, after controlling for other individual-level or regional-level characteristics (i.e. levels of income, unemployment rates). In the next section, we then further examine the robustness of our findings between subjective happiness and voting behaviour.

### 8.4.4    Robustness Checks and Extensions

As outlined in the previous section, and as an extension to the analysis on subjective happiness as a determinant to further understand political behaviour, we consider the link between life satisfaction and voting for radical parties. Hence, to assess the robustness of our findings, we have executed some robustness checks by specifically considering as another subjective wellbeing measure 'life satisfaction'. The detailed results of these checks can be found in the Appendix (Tables A.8.2 and A.8.3). Here, we will present a brief overview of the main results. It is noteworthy that life satisfaction (Table A.8.2, column 4) is only statistically significant with voting for radical left parties – there is no significant association between voting for radical right parties and individuals' level of life satisfaction. Despite that, the results of the individual demographic and socio-economic characteristics remain largely unchanged. Yet, interestingly, the odds ratio for the variable representing 'occupational status' seems to have a statistically significant negative association with voting for radical right parties and being 'economically inactive' (OR: 0.789), while the variable is less pronounced with voting for the radical left. Furthermore, in Table A.8.2, the effects of the various attitudinal variables are displayed. As such, individuals experiencing economic insecurities, being more anti-immigration and less in favour of cultural liberalism, are more likely to vote for the radical right. Likewise, it seems that individuals being less in favour of customs and traditions but more in favour of redistribution are more likely to vote for radical left parties. Again, in Table A.8.3, we add regional socio-economic characteristics: regional GDP per inhabitant in PPS (in percentage of the EU 28 average), an indicator of regional unemployment rate and the Gini coefficient measuring socio-economic inequality. It seems that after including these indicators the effects of the individual-level characteristics remain largely unaltered. Similarly to the results of the models that include the variable representing subjective happiness, it seems that socio-economic characteristics are not significantly related to radical left voting, while there is an association with voting for radical right parties (Table A.8.3) when including the measure of life satisfaction. As such, in addition to individual attitudes, we cannot find a clear sign of regional effects, which questions the role of the relevant spatial context of socio-economic characteristics for voting behaviour again – as suggested in previous literature. The results for the country- and year-fixed effects remain robust to the inclusion of the attitudinal and regional socio-economic characteristics.

Overall, our findings suggest that the relationship between subjective happiness and life satisfaction on the one hand and voting behaviour on the other hand are not restricted to a unique and specific dimension of subjective wellbeing. Moreover, it seems generalizable across multiple dimensions of wellbeing.

## 8.5    CONCLUDING COMMENTS

The work presented in this chapter builds upon previous relevant research aimed at understanding the individual as well as geographical determinants of voting for anti-establishment/anti-system parties, investigated as radical right and left parties, with the focus on a multilevel modelling approach to the analysis of the 'geographies of discontent'. Hereby, we also engage with recent work in the emerging regional science literature by economic geographers (Los et al., 2017; Rodríguez-Pose, 2018; Dijkstra et al., 2020; McCann,

2018, 2020). In our analysis, we took into account both individual- and regional-level indicators from selected and participating European countries (wave 2010 to wave 2018). Before controlling for any individual or regional explanatory variables, we can detect a reasonable variation (43 per cent) of radical right voting and (46 per cent) of radical left voting that is attributable to regional-level characteristics. However, when we consider individual explanatory variables (including age, employment status, socio-cultural attitudes) as well as regional-level characteristics in the analysis, such as regional GDP per inhabitant in PPS, regional long-term unemployment and the Gini coefficient, this variation drops to 7.8 per cent and 13.5 per cent for radical right and left parties, respectively.

Although individual demographic and socio-economic, as well as socio-cultural and political attitudinal characteristics, are of importance, our analysis revealed that this only partly determines individual voting behaviour for radical right and radical left parties. According to our analysis, voting for radical right or left parties is also a result of lower levels of subjective wellbeing (i.e. subjective happiness and life satisfaction), which is partially in line with recent work by Koeppen et al. (2021) and Lenzi and Perucca (2021). Particularly, even though the results of the variables representing socio-cultural and political attitudes indicate that individuals vote for radical right or left parties because they are potentially socio-economically or politically dissatisfied, it can still implicate a general discontent with life. In other words, a 'generalised' decline in individuals' subjective wellbeing – and not merely political discontent with governments and institutions – may be playing a role. It is also noteworthy that, not just individual-level determinants are significant, but so are contextual effects, particularly unobserved country characteristics. When explicitly accounting for regional socio-economic characteristics, unexplained regional-level variability remains relatively high, suggesting that both contextual and compositional effects explain voting behaviour for radical right and left parties (e.g. van Leeuwen et al., 2020).

Overall, the results suggest that voting for radical right parties is determined by measures of economic insecurity and cultural factors, while voting for radical left parties tends to be more defined by attitudes about inequality. A potential driving mechanism behind voting for radical right or left parties could be related to group dynamics and configurations of local and national spatial environments in influencing a person's overall wellbeing. Moreover, the work presented in this chapter provides a strong argument for further analysis of 'geography of discontent' and 'revenge of the places that don't matter' (Rodríguez-Pose 2018, McCann, 2020; Dijkstra et al., 2020; Rodríguez-Pose et al., 2020) from the perspective of collective perceptions of group and place identities and feelings of belonging, where individuals perceive territorial inequalities as threats to their own happiness and that of their fellow citizens.

In this context, further research can also explore in more detail the extent to which the cohesiveness of communities, and by extension, the underlying social capital phenomena, may be related to the 'geography of discontent' (building on relevant work by Rodríguez-Pose et al., 2020).

The research we presented also benefitted from and built on relevant work in political sciences, particularly for defining and analysing radical parties (e.g. Rooduijn et al., 2019). It further builds on the extensive analysis on voting for radical right or left parties (Rydgren, 2005, 2007; Kriesi, 2014; Rooduijn et al., 2017; Rooduijn and Burgoon, 2018; Van Hauwaert and Van Kessel, 2018). Similarly, in the analysis, we considered the relevance of lower levels of subjective wellbeing as important explanatory variables for individual discontent. Thereby, we build on existing work on political participation and subjective wellbeing (e.g. Koeppen et al., 2021), as well as considered previous work on multilevel modelling (e.g. Ballas and Tranmer, 2012; Ballas and Thanis, 2022). An important contribution of our study is the finding that lower levels of subjective wellbeing seem to affect the propensity to vote for radical right or left parties. This assumption is further strengthened by the fact that, when linked with socio-cultural and political attitudes and at the same time accounting for regional socio-economic characteristics, voting for radical right or left parties is driven mainly by individual determinants.

Nevertheless, it is important to note that, although the analysis suggests that the probability to vote for radical right or left parties can be attributed mostly to socio-cultural and political attitudinal characteristics, there is also a need to consider the potential to analyse possible interactions between individual-level attributes and regional-level variables. For example, our analysis demonstrates that individuals having a positive and welcoming attitude towards immigrants as well as experiencing immigrants as 'enriching to the country's culture/life' are more likely to vote for radical left parties, while it is the exact opposite for individuals voting for radical right parties. However, it can be argued that the extent to which an individual is in favour (or not in favour) of immigration and cultural diversity may be to a great extent related to the social environment and personal networks. As such, wider cultural geographical considerations pertaining to particular social and economic groups ('social classes') supporting radical parties, which could involve the composition of neighbourhoods or households and its effects on voting behaviour, are of interest because, as emphasised in the literature on electoral geography, 'people who talk together vote together' (Pattie and Johnston, 2000). In addition, a possible methodological extension that could be explored and incorporated in future studies would be to consider multilevel models that include 'random slopes', underpinning the assumption that the relationship between voting for radical parties and the explanatory variables could vary spatially. Another relevant aspect to consider is, given the degree of electoral volatility, allowing a pooling of all the voting choices – such as for mainstream parties, for radical right, for radical left, and for abstaining from voting. This would allow a more specific focus, not only on one particular party family and/or party ideologies; moreover, it provides further insights in investigating the role of discontent in voting behaviour. Hence, a tentative interpretation can be that individuals can be dissatisfied with mainstream politics, while at the same time rejecting anti-establishment parties.

From a policy perspective, this study underlines the importance and need for institutions, not just at the national but also at the supranational level across the EU, in order to incorporate other factors than just economics in policy evaluations (e.g. Algan et al., 2017; Liberini et al., 2019; Norris and Inglehart, 2019). Specifically, since the wellbeing of European citizens may be playing a significant role in shaping and promoting democracy, policymakers need to remain vigilant. It can be argued that this might be to some extent consistent with the work of Van Hauwaert and Van Kessel (2018), which emphasises the need to further examine whether subjective wellbeing measures determine specific radical attitudes and divides that are independent of socio-economic and cultural drivers. The modelling strategy that we applied in this chapter can be extended to further consider more dimensions of individual and aggregated sources of grievances and discontent. In this context, the measurement and inclusion of measures of social capital indicators and long-term economic hardship (i.e. unemployment) and population decline may be particularly insightful (also in the light of recent work by Rodríguez-Pose et al., 2020; Crowley and Walsh, 2021). In addition, although the data at our disposal is extremely relevant and useful for the analysis of voting behaviour and its determinants, including individual and contextual factors pertaining to measures of subjective wellbeing and socio-economic and cultural factors, a limitation of our analysis is the structure of the data, since it is of cross-sectional nature and the survey is conducted biannually. In addition, due to the survey's sampling strategy, not all EU countries take part in all waves, yielding another important limitation.

Overall, the analysis and the overall methodological framework presented in this chapter can potentially be built upon to offer new innovative ways to further explore and provide an answer to the puzzle of understanding individual voting preferences, particularly when it comes to voting for radical parties. The findings we present in this study are not only important in themselves but can also lead to further exploration and open up discussions on the topic of the 'geography of discontent' and other avenues for future research in regional sciences. In particular, there is still ample room for detailed micro-level analysis to further specify more socio-economic and demographic conditions under which certain 'social classes' are stimulated to vote for radical and/or populist parties. Similarly, more comprehensive analysis at the party level provides room for more thorough elaboration on theoretical and empirical links between policies pertaining to socio-economic and cultural issues, helping to understand radical party discourse and political strategies.

## ACKNOWLEDGEMENTS

The authors are grateful for the public data provided by the European Social Survey (ESS). The authors are also grateful to the editors for their constructive comments. Thanks are due to participants at the STATEC Well-Being Conference – Luxembourg and the 61st ERSA Congress in Pécs for useful comments and suggestions.

All responsibility for the analysis and interpretation of the data presented in this chapter lies with the authors.

## REFERENCES

Agnew, J. A. (1987). Place and Politics: The Geographical Mediation of State and Society (1st ed.). Routledge. https://doi.org/10.4324/9781315756585.

Agnew, J.A. (1996). Mapping politics: how context counts in electoral geography , Political Geography, 15, 2, p. 129–146. DOI : 10.1016/0962-6298(95)00076-3.

Alabrese, E., Becker, S. O., Fetzer, T., and Novy, D. (2019). Who voted for Brexit? Individual and regional data combined. *European Journal of Political Economy*, 56, 132–150. https://doi.org/10.1016/j.ejpoleco.2018.08.002.

Algan, Y., Guriev, S., Papaioannou, E., Passari, E. (2017). The European trust crisis and the rise of populism. Brookings Papers on Economic Activity, 309–382.

Aslam, A. and Corrado, L. (2012). The geography of well-being. *Journal of Economic Geography*, 12(3), 627–649.

Ballas, D. (2021). The economic geography of happiness. In Zimmermann, K. F. (Eds.) *Handbook of labor, human resources and population economics*. Springer. https://doi.org/10.1007/978-3-319-57365-6_188-1.

Ballas, D. and Tranmer, M. (2012). Happy people or happy places? A multi-level modelling approach to the analysis of happiness and well-being. *International Regional Science Review*, 35, 70–102.

Ballas, D. and Thanis, I. (2022). Exploring the Geography of Subjective Happiness in Europe During the Years of the Economic Crisis: A Multilevel Modelling Approach. *Soc Indic Res*. https://doi.org/10.1007/s11205-021-02874-6.

Becker, S., Fetzer, T. and Novy, D. (2018). Erratum to: Who voted for Brexit? A comprehensive district-level analysis, *Economic Policy*, 33(93), 179–180, https://doi.org/10.1093/epolic/eix017.

Bhambra, G. K. (2017). Brexit, Trump, and 'methodological whiteness': on the misrecognition of race and class. The British Journal of Sociology, 68, 214–232. https://doi.org/10.1111/1468-4446.12317.

Bourdin, S. and Tai, J. (2022). Abstentionist Voting – Between Disengagement and Protestation in Neglected Areas: A Spatial Analysis of The Paris Metropolis. *International Regional Science Review*, 45(3), 1050–1056. https://doi.org/10.1177/01600176211034131.

Cramer, K. J. (2016). The Politics of Resentment: Rural Consciousness in Wisconsin and the Rise of Scott Walker. Chicago: University of Chicago Press.

Crowley, F. and Walsh, E. (2021). Tolerance, social capital, and life satisfaction: a multilevel model from transition countries in the European Union, Review of Social Economy, DOI: 10.1080/00346764.2021.1957994.

De Vries, C. E. and Edwards, E. E. (2009). Taking Europe To Its Extremes: Extremist Parties and Public Euroscepticism. *Party Politics*, 15(1), 5–28. https://doi.org/10.1177/1354068808097889.

Diener E., Sapyta J. J. and Suh E. M. (1998). Subjective well-being is essential to well-being. Psychol. Inq. 9, 33–37.

Diener E., Lucas, R. E. and Oishi, S. (2018). Advances and Open Questions in the Science of Subjective Well-Being. *Collabra: Psychology*, 4(1), 15. Doi: https://doi.org/10.1525/ollabra.115.

Dijkstra, L., Poelman, H. and Rodríguez-Pose. A. (2020) The geography of EU discontent. *Regional Studies*, 54(6), 737–753.

Dorling, D., and Tomlinson, S. (2019). Rule Britannia: Brexit and the end of empire. London: Biteback Publishing. https://www.bitebackpublishing.com/books/rule-britannia.

Duch, R. M. and Stevenson, R. (2017). Context and the economic vote: A multi-level analysis. *Political Analysis*, 13(4), 387–409.

European Commission. (2022a). Eurostat data browser, Regional gross domestic product (PPS per inhabitant in % of the EU27 (from 2020) average) by NUTS 2 regions. Statistical office of the European union. https://ec.europa.eu/eurostat/databrowser/view/TGS00006/default/table?lang=en&category=na10.nama10.nama_10reg.nama_10r_gdp.

European Commission. (2022b). Eurostat data browser, Unemployment rates by sex, age, educational attainment level and NUTS 2 regions (%). Statistical office of the European union. https://ec.europa.eu/eurostat/databrowser/view/LFST_R_LFU3RT/default/table?lang=en&category=labour.employ.lfst.lfst_r.lfst_r_lfu.

European Commission. (2022c). Eurostat data browser, Gini coefficient of equivalised disposable income. Statistical office of the European union. https://ec.europa.eu/eurostat/databrowser/product/page/tessi190.

European Social Survey Cumulative File, ESS 5–9 (2010–2018). Data file edition 1.0. NSD – Norwegian Centre for Research Data, Norway – Data Archive and distributor of ESS data for ESS ERIC. https://ess-search.nsd.no/.

Fetzer, T. (2019). 'Did Austerity Cause Brexit?' *American Economic Review*, 109(11), 3849–386.

European Social Survey. (2022). https://www.europeansocialsurvey.org/learning/shared_user_resources.html.

Flavin, P. and Keane, M. J. (2012). Life satisfaction and political participation: Evidence from the United States. *Journal of Happiness Studies*, 13(1), 63–78.

Forgas, J. P. (2019). Happy Believers and Sad Skeptics? Affective Influences on Gullibility. *Current Directions in Psychological Science*, 28(3), 306–313. https://doi.org/10.1177/0963721419834543.

Frey, B. S. and Stutzer, A. (2000), Happiness, Economy and Institutions. *The Economic Journal*, 110, 918–938. https://doi.org/10.1111/1468-0297.00570.

Georgiadou, V. and Mavropoulou, J. (2021). Anti-Establishment Parties in Government, *Southeastern Europe*, 45(1), 19–47. Doi: https://doi.org/10.30965/18763332-45010003.

Griethuijsen, R. A. L. F., Eijck, M. W., Haste, H., Brok, P. J., Skinner, N. C., Mansour, N. (2014). Global patterns in students' views of science and interest in science. *Research in Science Education,* 45(4), 581–603. DOI: 10.1007/s11165-014-9438-6.

Halikiopoulou, D. (2020). Economic Crisis, Poor Governance and the Rise of Populism: The Case of Greece, Intereconomics, ISSN 1613–964X, Springer, Heidelberg, 55(1), pp. 34–37, https://doi.org/10.1007/s10272-020-0866-4.

Halikiopoulou, D. and Vlandas, T. (2020). When economic and cultural interests align: the anti-immigration voter coalitions driving far right party success in Europe. *European Political Science Review*, 12(4), 427–448.

Herrin, J., Witters, D., Roy, B., Riley, C., Liu, D. and Krumholz, H. M. (2018). Population well-being and electoral shifts. *PloS ONE*, 13, e0193401.

Johnston, R. and Pattie, C. (2006). 'Bringing Geography In', Putting Voters in their Place: Geography and Elections in Great Britain, Oxford Geographical and Environmental Studies Series; online edn, Oxford Academic, 3 Oct. 2011), https://doi.org/10.1093/acprof:oso/9780199268047.003.0002.

Johnston, R. and Pattie, C. (2014). *Money and electoral politics: Local parties and funding at general elections*. Policy Press.

Johnston, R., Jones, K., Propper, C. and Burgess, S. (2007), Region, Local Context, and Voting at the 1997 General Election in England. *American Journal of Political Science*, 51, 640–654. https://doi.org/10.1111/j.1540-5907.2007.00272.x.

Jolly, S., Bakker, R., Hooghe, L., Marks, G., Polk, J., Rovny, J., Steenbergen, M. and Vachudova, M. A. (2022). Chapel Hill Expert Survey trend file, 1999–2019. *Electoral Studies*, 75, 102420.

Jones, K. (1997). 'Multilevel Approaches to Modelling Contextuality: From Nuisance to Substance in the Analysis of Voting Behaviour', in G. P. Westert and R. N. Verhoeff (eds.). Places and people: Multilevel modelling in geographical research. Utrecht: The Royal Dutch Geographical Society, pp. 19–43.

Kaminska, O. (2020). Guide to Using Weights and Sample Design Indicators with ESS Data Institute for Social and Economic Research, University of Essex. V1.1.

Kish, L., and Frankel, M. R. (1974). Inference from Complex Samples. *Journal of the Royal Statistical Society. Series B (Methodological)*, 36(1), 1–37. http://www.jstor.org/stable/2984767.

Koeppen, L., Ballas, D., Edzes, A., and Koster, S. (2021). Places that don't matter or people that don't matter?: A multilevel modelling approach to the analysis of geographies of discontent. *Regional Science Policy and Practice, 13*, 221–245.

Kriesi, H. (2014). The Populist Challenge, West European Politics, 37(2), 361–378, DOI: 10.1080/01402382.2014.887879.

Lee, N., Morris, K. and Kemeny, T. (2018). Immobility and the Brexit vote. *Cambridge Journal of Regions, Economy and Society*, 11(1), 143–163. DOI:10.1093/cjres/rsx027.

Lenzi, C. and Perucca, G. (2021). People or Places that Don't Matter? Individual and Contextual Determinants of the Geography of Discontent. *Economic Geography* 97(5), 415–445.

Lewis-Beck, M. S., and Stegmaier, M. (2000). Economic Determinants of Electoral Outcomes. *Annual Review of Political Science*, 3(1), 183–219. http://dx.doi.org/10.1146/annurev.polisci.3.1.183.

Liberini, F., Oswald, A., Proto, E. and Redoano, M. (2019). Was Brexit Triggered by the Old and Unhappy? Or by Financial Feelings? *Journal of Economic Behavior and Organization*, 161(1), 287–302.

Lorenzini, J. (2015). Subjective well-being and political participation: A comparison of unemployed and employed youth. *Journal of Happiness Studies*, 16(2), 381–404.

Los, B., McCann, P., Springford, J. and Thissen, M. (2017). The mismatch between local voting and the local economic consequences of Brexit, *Regional Studies*, 51(5), 786–799, DOI: 10.1080/00343404.2017.1287350.

MacAllister, I., Johnston, R. J., Pattie, C. J., Tunstall, H., Dorling D. F. L. and Rossiter. D. J. (2001). Class dealignment and the neighbourhood effect: Miller revisited. *British Journal of Political Science*, 31, 41–59.

March, L. and Mudde, C. (2005). What's left of the radical left? The European radical left after 1989: Decline and mutation. *Comparative European Politics*, 3, 23–49.

March, L. (2011). *Radical left parties in Europe*. Abingdon, UK: Routledge.

McCann. P. (2018). The trade, geography and regional implications of Brexit. *Papers in Regional Science*, 97(1), 3–8. https://doi.org/10.1111/pirs.12352.

McCann. P. (2020). Perceptions of regional inequality and the geography of discontent: insights from the UK. *Regional Studies*, 54(2), 256–267.

Miller, M. K. (2013). For the Win! The Effect of Professional Sports Records on Mayoral Elections. *Social Science Quarterly*, 94(1), 59–78. https://doi.org/10.1111/j.1540-6237.2012.00898.x.

Mudde, C. (2007). *Populist Radical Right Parties in Europe*. Cambridge: Cambridge University Press. DOI:10.1017/CBO9780511492037.

Norris, P. and Inglehart, R. (2019). *Cultural Backlash: Trump, Brexit, and Authoritarian Populism*. Cambridge: Cambridge University Press. DOI:10.1017/9781108595841.

Oesch, D. (2006). Coming to Grips with a Changing Class Structure: An Analysis of Employment Stratification in Britain, Germany, Sweden and Switzerland. *International Sociology*, 21(2), 263–288. https://doi.org/10.1177/0268580906061379.

Pattie, C. and Johnston, R. (2000). '"People Who Talk Together Vote Together": An Exploration of Contextual Effects in Great Britain.' *Annals of the Association of American Geographers*, 90(1), 41–66.

Pierce, L., Roggers, T. and Snyder, J. A. (2016) Losing hurts: The happiness impact of partisan electoral loss. *Journal of Experimental Political Science*, 3, 44–59.

Powdthavee, N., Plagnol, A., Frijters, P. and Clark, A. (2019). Who Got the Brexit Blues? The Effect of Brexit on Subjective Well-being in the UK. *Economica*, 86: 471–494.

Putnam, R. D. (2000) *Bowling Alone: The Collapse and Revival of American Community*. New York: Simon & Schuster.

Radcliff, B. (2001). Politics, Markets, and Life Satisfaction: The Political Economy of Human Happiness. *The American Political Science Review*, 95(4), 939–952. http://www.jstor.org/stable/3117723.

Rodríguez-Pose, A. (2018). The revenge of the places that don't matter (and what to do about it), *Cambridge Journal of Regions, Economy and Society*, 11(1), 189–209, https://doi.org/10.1093/cjres/rsx024.

Rodríguez-Pose, A., Lee, N., and Lipp, C. (2020). Golfing with Trump: Social capital, decline, inequality, and the rise of populism in the US. *Papers in Evolutionary Economic Geography (PEEG) 2038, Utrecht University, Department of Human Geography and Spatial Planning, Group Economic Geography.* https://ideas-repec-org.proxy-ub.rug.nl/p/egu/wpaper/2038.html. Accessed October 5, 2020.

Rooduijn, M., and Burgoon, B. (2018). The Paradox of Well-being: Do Unfavorable Socioeconomic and Sociocultural Contexts Deepen or Dampen Radical Left and Right Voting Among the Less Well-Off? *Comparative Political Studies*, 51(13), 1720–1753. https://doi.org/10.1177/0010414017720707.

Rooduijn, M., Burgoon, B., van Elsas, E. J. and van de Werfhorst, H. G. (2017). Radical distinction: Support for radical left and radical right parties in Europe. *European Union Politics*, 18(4), 536–559. https://doi.org/10.1177/1465116517718091.

Rooduijn, M., van Kessel, S., Froio, C., Pirro, A., De Lange, S., Halikiopoulou, D., Lewis, P., Mudde, C. and Taggart, P. (2019) *The PopuList: an overview of populist, far right, far left and Eurosceptic parties in Europe.* www.popu-list.org.

Rydgren, J. (2005). Is extreme right-wing populism contagious: Explaining the emergence of a new party family. European Journal of Political Research, 44, 413–437.

Rydgren, J. (2007). The sociology of the radical right. *Annual Review of Sociology*, 33, 241–262. https://doi.org/10.1146/annurev.soc.33.040406.131752.

Schnaudt, C., Weinhardt, M., Fitzgerald, R. and Liebig, S. (2014). The European Social Survey: Contents, Design, and Research Potential. *Journal of Contextual Economics – Schmollers Jahrbuch*, 134(4), 487–506. https://doi.org/10.3790/schm.134.4.487.

Snijders, T. A. B., and Bosker, R. J. (1999). *Multilevel Analysis: An Introduction to Basic and Advanced Multilevel Modeling*. SAGE.

Snijders, T., and Bosker, R. (2012). *Multilevel Analysis: An Introduction to Basic and Advanced Multilevel Modeling*. London: Sage Publishers.

Taber, K. S. (2018). The Use of Cronbach's Alpha When Developing and Reporting Research Instruments in Science Education. *Res Sci Educ*, 48, 1273–1296. https://doi.org/10.1007/s11165–016–9602–2.

Van Hauwaert, S. M. and Van Kessel, S. (2018), Beyond protest and discontent: A cross-national analysis of the effect of populist attitudes and issue positions on populist party support. *European Journal of Political Research*, 57, 68–92. https://doi.org/10.1111/1475-6765.12216.

Van Leeuwen, E. S., Halleck Vega, S., and Hogenboom, V. (2020). 'Does Population Decline Lead to a "Populist Voting Mark-Up"? A Case Study of The Netherlands.' *Regional Science Policy & Practice*, 13, 279–301.

Vasilopoulos, P., Marcus, G. E., Valentino, N. A. and Foucault, M. (2019). Fear, anger and voting for the far right: Evidence from the November 13, 2015 Paris terror attacks. *Political Psychology*, 40, 679–704.

Vasilopoulos, P., McAvay, H. and Brouard, S. Residential Context and Voting for the Far Right: The Impact of Immigration and Unemployment on the 2017 French Presidential Election. *Polit Behav*, (2021). https://doi.org/10.1007/s11109-021-09676-z.

Vasilopoulou, S. and Wagner, M. (2022). Emotions and domestic vote choice, *Journal of Elections, Public Opinion and Parties*, 32(3), 635–654, DOI: 10.1080/17457289.2020.1857388.

Ward, G., De Neve, J.-E., Ungar, L. H., and Eichstaedt, J. C. (2021). (Un)happiness and voting in U.S. presidential elections. *Journal of Personality and Social Psychology*, 120(2), 370–383. https://doi.org/10.1037/pspi0000249.

Weaver, R. (2014). Contextual influences on political behavior in cities: Toward urban electoral geography. *Geography Compass*, 8(12), 874–891.

Weitz-Shapiro, R. and Winters, M. S. (2011). The link between voting and life satisfaction in Latin America. *Latin American Politics and Society*, 53(4), 101–126.

# APPENDIX 8

*Table A.8.1    Factor rotation output for factor with eigenvalues > 1*

| Variable | Factor1 |
| --- | --- |
| Immigration Attitudes – Allow many/few immigrants of same race/ethnic group as majority | 0.7292 |
| Immigration Attitudes – Allow many/few immigrants of different race/ethnic group from majority | 0.8455 |
| Immigration Attitudes – Allow many/few immigrants from poorer countries outside Europe | 0.792 |
| Immigration Attitudes – Immigration bad or good for country's economy | 0.7389 |
| Immigration Attitudes – Country's cultural life undermined or enriched by immigrants | 0.7515 |
| Immigration Attitudes – Immigrants make country worse or better place to live | 0.7620 |

*Notes*:
Rotated factor loadings and unique variances using principal component factor and orthogonal varimax rotation (Kaiser off)
The scale variables measuring individuals' attitudes towards customs and traditions, as well as attitudes towards cultural liberalism have been created following the below data manipulation:
eigen customs_traditions = rowmean(imptrad impsafe ipfrule ipstrgv ipbhprp);
eigen LGBT = rowmean(freehms hmsfmlsh hmsacld);
lab var customs_traditions 'scale items cover tradition_customs';
lab var LGBT 'scale items cover gay/lesbian'.

*Table A.8.2     Voting behaviour as dependent on wellbeing measures, demographic, attitudinal and socioeconomic variables*

| | Radical Right vote | Radical Left vote | Radical Right vote | Radical Left vote |
|---|---|---|---|---|
| Fixed effects | 1 | 2 | 3 | 4 |
| Intercept | 0.004***(0.003) | 0.003***(0.006) | 0.004***(0.003) | 0.003***(0.005) |
| Gender (ref: men) | 0.724***(0.022) | 0.887***(0.031) | 0.725***(0.022) | 0.888***(0.031) |
| Age | 0.981***(0.001) | 0.993***(0.001) | 0.982***(0.001) | 0.993***(0.001) |
| Married (ref: not married) | 0.958 (0.032) | 0.898***(0.035) | 0.949 (0.031) | 0.896***(0.034) |
| Income | 0.984**(0.007) | 0.934***(0.008) | 0.983**(0.007) | 0.936***(0.008) |
| Level of Education (ref. low) | | | | |
| Middle | 0.943 (0.038) | 0.884**(0.047) | 0.944 (0.038) | 0.880**(0.047) |
| High | 0.647***(0.032) | 1.004 (0.056) | 0.647***(0.032) | 1.004 (0.056) |
| Level of Employment (ref. Employed) | | | | |
| Not employed | 0.870***(0.037) | 1.001 (0.047) | 0.870***(0.037) | 0.990 (0.047) |
| Economically inactive | 0.784***(0.045) | 0.878**(0.053) | 0.781***(0.045) | 0.891*(0.054) |
| Subjective Happiness (reversed) | 1.027***(0.009) | 1.075***(0.012) | . | |
| Life Satisfaction (reversed) | | | 1.004 (0.008) | 1.114***(0.008) |
| Oesch's five-class scheme (ref.: Higher-grade service class) | | | | |
| Lower-grade service class | 1.007 (0.053) | 1.032 (0.054) | 1.012 (0.054) | 1.030 (0.054) |
| Small business owners | 1.160**(0.069) | 0.724***(0.052) | 1.175***(0.070) | 0.727***(0.052) |
| Skilled workers | 1.320***(0.068) | 1.075 (0.058) | 1.320***(0.068) | 1.076 (0.058) |
| Unskilled workers | 1.319***(0.077) | 1.150**(0.074) | 1.325***(0.078) | 1.143**(0.074) |
| Pro-Immigration attitude | 1.853***(0.023) | 0.816***(0.012) | 1.854***(0.023) | 0.810***(0.012) |
| Attitudes redistribution | 1.148**(0.070) | 9.769***(0.859) | 1.152**(0.070) | 9.553***(0.840) |
| Economic insecurities | 1.037***(0.008) | 1.052***(0.009) | 1.042***(0.008) | 1.034***(0.009) |
| Traditions and customs | 0.876***(0.031) | 1.264***(0.047) | 0.877***(0.031) | 1.265***(0.047) |
| Cultural liberalism – LGBT | 1.142***(0.032) | 0.949 (0.029) | 1.147***(0.032) | 0.953 (0.030) |
| Level of religiosity | 1.013**(0.006) | 0.884***(0.006) | 1.012**(0.006) | 0.885***(0.006) |
| Year (ref: 2010) | | | | |
| 2012 | 2.217 (1.288) | 13.979 (22.830) | 2.206 (1.283) | 14.274 (23.309) |
| 2014 | 3.436**(1.995) | 16.275*(26.560) | 3.417**(1.986) | 16.443*(26.850) |

|  | Radical Right vote | Radical Left vote | Radical Right vote | Radical Left vote |
|---|---|---|---|---|
| Fixed effects | 1 | 2 | 3 | 4 |
| 2016 | 4.261**(2.475) | 15.415 (25.176) | 4.234**(2.461) | 15.831*(25.851) |
| 2018 | 6.513***(3.783) | 18.066*(29.504) | 6.456***(3.753) | 18.490*(30.193) |
| Country (ref. GER) |  |  |  |  |
| AT | 2.084***(0.060) | 0.149***(0.066) | 2.081***(0.471) | 0.154***(0.068) |
| BE | 0.467***(0.094) | 0.269***(0.087) | 0.464***(0.108) | 0.272***(0.088) |
| BG | 0.554*(0.081) | 1 (empty) | 0.562*(0.186) | 1 (empty) |
| CY | 0.125 (0.038) | 8.755***(7.206) | 0.125 (0.168) | 8.967***(7.378) |
| CZ | 0.258***(0.108) | 1.360 (0.456) | 0.260***(0.072) | 1.381 (0.463) |
| DK | 2.847***(0.414) | 4.115***(1.591) | 2.824***(0.772) | 4.304***(1.663) |
| EE | 0.579 (0.173) | 1 (empty) | 0.577 (0.353) | 1 (empty) |
| ES | 0.422***(0.049) | 1.525 (0.397) | 0.419***(0.085) | 1.494 (0.389) |
| FI | 3.616***(0.532) | 0.881***(0.375) | 3.559***(1.006) | 0.914 (0.389) |
| FR | 2.423***(0.235) | 1.022 (0.227) | 2.426***(0.372) | 0.957 (0.213) |
| GB | 0.894 (0.100) | 0.016***(0.007) | 0.894 (0.172) | 0.016***(0.006) |
| GR | 1 (empty) | 83.315**(190.901) | 1 (empty) | 75.292*(172.230) |
| HR | 0.606 (0.150) | 1 (empty) | 0.612 (0.307) | 1 (empty) |
| HU | 40.804***(5.404) | 0.170***(0.101) | 41.490***(10.077) | 0.163***(0.097) |
| IE | 1 (empty) | 1.526 (0.623) | 1 (empty) | 1.498 (0.611) |
| IT | 8.795***(0.907) | 0.869 (0.227) | 8.757***(1.488) | 0.870 (0.227) |
| LT | 1.314 (0.339) | 0.006**(0.013) | 1.337 (0.700) | 0.005**(0.013) |
| LV | 1.439 (0.513) | 0.073 (0.133) | 1.427 (1.047) | 0.070 (0.128) |
| NL | 2.410***(0.279) | 1.594***(0.464) | 2.401***(0.484) | 1.618 (0.471) |
| PL | 14.432***(1.546) | 0.020***(0.010) | 14.515***(2.617) | 0.020***(0.010) |
| PT | 0.096***(0.022) | 1.870***(0.730) | 0.096***(0.044) | 1.760 (0.687) |
| SE | 2.038***(0.259) | 0.813***(0.266) | 2.037***(0.468) | 0.827 (0.271) |
| SI | 3.975***(0.788) | 0.658 (0.410) | 3.992***(1.569) | 0.636 (0.397) |
| SK | 0.813 (0.140) | 1 (empty) | 0.824 (0.275) | 1 (empty) |
| Random effects |  |  |  |  |
| NUTS2-variance (level-2) | 0.214 | 0.520 | 0.217 | 0.520 |
| ICC (NUTS2) | 0.061 (0.007) | 0.136 (0.016) | 0.062 (0.007) | 0.136 (0.016) |
| Log likelihood | -16302.801 | -12734.796 | -16325.999 | -12689.866 |
| Wald Chi-Square (df) | 4990.08 (45) | 2394.28 (43) | 4959.74 (45) | 2468.18 (43) |
| Level-2 N | 216 | 209 | 216 | 209 |
| Total N | 62,111 | 58,270 | 62,121 | 58,267 |

*Note:*        *=p<0.1; **=p<0.05; ***= p<0.01. Odd ratios displayed. Standard errors in parentheses. For the interpretation of the attitudinal variables, see the description in Section 8.3.2.

*Table A.8.3*  *Voting behaviour as dependent on wellbeing measures, demographic, attitudinal, socioeconomic variables and regional characteristics*

| | Radical Right vote | Radical Left vote | Radical Right vote | Radical Left vote |
|---|---|---|---|---|
| Fixed effects | 1 | 2 | 3 | 4 |
| Intercept | 0.004***(0.002) | 0.004***(0.006) | 0.004***(0.002) | 0.003***(0.005) |
| Gender (ref: men) | 0.719***(0.022) | 0.888***(0.031) | 0.720***(0.022) | 0.888***(0.031) |
| Age | 0.981***(0.001) | 0.992***(0.001) | 0.982***(0.001) | 0.993***(0.001) |
| Married (ref: not married) | 0.961 (0.032) | 0.898***(0.035) | 0.951 (0.032) | 0.896***(0.034) |
| Income | 0.984**(0.007) | 0.934***(0.008) | 0.984**(0.007) | 0.936***(0.008) |
| Level of education (ref. low) | | | | |
| Middle | 0.935 (0.038) | 0.883**(0.047) | 0.937 (0.035) | 0.879**(0.047) |
| High | 0.643***(0.032) | 1.003 (0.057) | 0.644***(0.027) | 1.003 (0.057) |
| Level of employment (ref. employed) | | | | |
| Not employed | 0.879***(0.038) | 1.002 (0.047) | 0.880***(0.038) | 0.999 (0.047) |
| Economically inactive | 0.792***(0.045) | 0.878**(0.053) | 0.789***(0.045) | 0.892*(0.054) |
| Subjective happiness (reversed) | 1.028***(0.009) | 1.075***(0.012) | | |
| Life Satisfaction (reversed) | | | 1.004 (0.008) | 1.114***(0.010) |
| Oesch's five-class scheme (ref.: Higher-grade service class) | | | | |
| Lower-grade service class | 1.007 (0.053) | 1.032 (0.054) | 1.012 (0.054) | 1.030 (0.054) |
| Small business owners | 1.156**(0.069) | 0.723***(0.052) | 1.171***(0.070) | 0.727***(0.052) |
| Skilled workers | 1.312***(0.068) | 1.074 (0.058) | 1.312***(0.068) | 1.075 (0.058) |
| Unskilled workers | 1.311***(0.077) | 1.149**(0.074) | 1.318***(0.078) | 1.142**(0.074) |
| Pro-immigration attitude | 1.857***(0.023) | 0.816***(0.012) | 1.858***(0.023) | 0.810***(0.012) |
| Attitudes redistribution | 1.161**(0.070) | 9.774***(0.860) | 1.165**(0.071) | 9.560***(0.841) |
| Economic insecurities | 1.039***(0.008) | 1.052***(0.009) | 1.045***(0.008) | 1.034***(0.009) |
| Traditions and customs | 0.875***(0.031) | 1.264***(0.047) | 0.876***(0.030) | 1.266***(0.048) |
| Cultural liberalism – LGBT | 1.139***(0.032) | 0.949 (0.029) | 1.144***(0.032) | 0.953 (0.030) |
| Level of religiosity | 1.013**(0.006) | 0.884***(0.006) | 1.012**(0.006) | 0.885***(0.006) |
| [NUTS2] GDP per inhabitant in PPS (in % of the EU28 average) | 0.994***(0.002) | 0.998 (0.002) | 0.994***(0.002) | 0.998 (0.002) |
| [NUTS2] Unemployment rates by age 15–75, all sexes in % | 0.893***(0.011) | 0.997 (0.011) | 0.894***(0.011) | 0.996 (0.011) |
| GINI | 0.975 (0.018) | 0.984 (0.024) | 0.977 (0.018) | 0.986 (0.024) |

| | Radical Right vote | Radical Left vote | Radical Right vote | Radical Left vote |
|---|---|---|---|---|
| Fixed effects | 1 | 2 | 3 | 4 |
| Year (ref: 2010) | | | | |
| 2012 | 2.231 (1.299) | 14.017 (22.893) | 2.221 (1.294) | 14.330*(23.401) |
| 2014 | 3.373**(1.963) | 16.526 (26.992) | 3.356**(1.955) | 16.692*(27.260) |
| 2016 | 3.555**(2.070) | 15.510 (25.332) | 3.534**(2.059) | 15.892*(25.954) |
| 2018 | 4.448**(2.595) | 18.045*(29.480) | 4.417**(2.580) | 18.388*(30.037) |
| Country (ref. GER) | | | | |
| AT | 2.125***(0.542) | 0.147***(0.066) | 2.131***(0.545) | 0.153***(0.068) |
| BE | 0.491***(0.131) | 0.252***(0.086) | 0.492***(0.131) | 0.258***(0.087) |
| BG | 0.642 (0.253) | 1 (empty) | 0.646 (0.255) | 1 (empty) |
| CY | 0.183 (0.251) | 8.351**(6.862) | 0.183 (0.251) | 8.583***(7.050) |
| CZ | 0.171***(0.054) | 1.156 (0.419) | 0.174***(0.055) | 1.183 (0.428) |
| DK | 3.071***(0.938) | 3.951***(1.542) | 3.058 (0.937) | 4.157***(1.621) |
| EE | 0.601 (0.400) | 1 (empty) | 0.600 (0.400) | 1 (empty) |
| ES | 2.023***(0.547) | 1.580 (0.482) | 1.989***(0.539) | 1.559 (0.476) |
| FI | 4.423***(1.448) | 0.811 (0.356) | 4.381***(1.440) | 0.851 (0.374) |
| FR | 3.229***(0.581) | 0.958 (0.222) | 3.237***(0.585) | 0.901 (0.208) |
| GB | 0.859 (0.189) | 0.016***(0.007) | 0.857 (0.189) | 0.016***(0.006) |
| GR | 1 (empty) | 86.009**(196.945) | 1 (empty) | 77.625*(177.496) |
| HR | 0.762 (0.416) | 1 (empty) | 0.772 (0.422) | 1 (empty) |
| HU | 35.621***(10.321) | 0.146***(0.088) | 36.508***(10.616) | 0.140***(0.085) |
| IE | 1 (empty) | 1.729 (0.738) | 1 (empty) | 1.712 (0.731) |
| IT | 17.317***(3.526) | 0.885 (0.243) | 17.167***(3.508) | 0.885 (0.243) |
| LT | 1.787 (1.058) | 0.006**(0.013) | 1.804 (1.072) | 0.005**(0.013) |
| LV | 1.927 (1.513) | 0.072 (0.132) | 1.898 (1.494) | 0.069 (0.126) |
| NL | 2.429***(0.564) | 1.521 (0.459) | 2.433***(0.566) | 1.555 (0.469) |
| PL | 12.731***(2.865) | 0.018***(0.009) | 12.866***(2.906) | 0.017***(0.009) |
| PT | 0.145***(0.072) | 1.819 (0.737) | 0.144***(0.072) | 1.708 (0.692) |
| SE | 2.416***(0.633) | 0.775 (0.261) | 2.425 (0.637) | 0.795 (0.267) |
| SI | 3.691***(1.668) | 0.555 (0.356) | 3.749***(1.700) | 0.544 (0.349) |
| SK | 0.790 (0.316) | 1 (empty) | 0.814 (0.326) | 1 (empty) |
| Random effects | | | | |
| NUTS2-variance (level-2) | 0.275 | 0.514 | 0.277 | 0.513 |
| ICC (NUTS2) | 0.077 (0.010) | 0.135 (0.016) | 0.078 (0.010) | 0.135 (0.016) |
| Log likelihood | -16245.342 | -12733.934 | -16269.428 | -12689.013 |
| Wald Chi-Square (df) | 4908.29 (48) | 2397.43 (46) | 4881.25 (48) | 2471.21 (46) |
| Level-2 N | 216 | 209 | 216 | 209 |
| Total N | 62,111 | 58,270 | 62,121 | 58,267 |

*Note*:     *=p<0.1; **=p<0.05; ***= p<0.01. Odd ratios displayed. Standard errors in parentheses. For the interpretation of the attitudinal variables, see the description in Section 8.3.2.

# 9. Spatial justice: the contemporary uncertainties of the French model

## Interview with Daniel Behar, Geographer, Lab Urba – Ecole d'Urbanisme de Paris

### Daniel Behar and Valeria Fedeli

**Q.** Prof. Behar, from your experience in both theory and practice, during these years you have been observing growing inequalities in the French context, as well as a shift in the policy approach, basically consisting of a crisis in the French principle of inequality, which has long inspired the model of public action. What are the reasons and consequence of this crisis?

**A.** France and its territories are today particularly concerned by the issue of spatial justice. In the eyes of the French, the principle of equality occupies a central place within the national motto 'liberty, equality, fraternity'. But above all, France has long chosen to project this republican principle on the ground, considering that equality between citizens depends on equality between territories (Estèbe, 2015). Long centred on politics and institutions – from the egalitarian paving of the 36 000 municipalities to their national representation within the Senate – in the post-war period, this conception of social and territorial equality created a model of public action: 'French-style regional planning' focused on the search for balance among territories. While evolving strongly with decentralization, this model of territorial action lasted until the end of the last century. It has since entered a crisis – less in terms of efficiency than of legitimacy – under the impact of globalization. Beyond a now explicit reference to this principle of 'territorial equality', this crisis is manifested today by political and strategic uncertainty as to its application in public policies.

This model has changed through time and has undergone two different phases.

The first phase can be defined the Regional planning period, inspired by what we could define a 'justice through balance' approach.

In the expanding France of the 1960s, the State gave itself a dual mission: on the one hand, to support growth, through a national policy of investment and infrastructure that brought together industry resources (essentially, at that time, labour); on the other hand, the reduction of territorial imbalances, through better distribution of functions and factors of production.

Induction by growth and compensation for the inequalities it generates: the State, i.e. DATAR,[1] the Planning Commission and the Ministry of Infrastructure, formed part of this dual logic. They organised a centralised government from a local one that needed modernising, relying mainly on the classic state instrumentation of rules and standards, which are symbolized in the long term by the procedures invented by the framework land law of 1967 (Master Plan of Development and Urban Planning – SDAU – and Land Use Plans – POS). Their combined action established a hierarchical conception of the French territory. The hierarchy of territories was manifested by a territorial division of labour and functions. Large cities, regional metropolises, medium-sized towns, small towns, rural communities: each of these spaces was assigned its own functions: decisions, research, intermediate commands, skilled production, low-skilled production.

This hierarchical territory also had to be balanced: on the outskirts of Paris, the new towns played a role of counterweight to the city-centre and a link the bordering regions; these *métropoles d'équilibres* [TN: literally 'balance cities', designed to counterbalance the pre-eminence of Paris] were equipped with infrastructure intended to make them secondary poles that, in turn, had to influence their surroundings. Finally, the balance required the decentralization of production activities and opening up the territory through infrastructure. The territorial scales were nested like Russian dolls, each benefiting from the influence of the higher level and playing this role in turn vis-à-vis the lower levels; at each level, finally, there was a similar organisation and balance in functions: this was the ideal territory proposed by modernist Gaullism. From this perspective, land-use planning – here we refer to the whole country – constituted in a way the condition for the implementation of a 'societal project', one that we will later qualify as a Fordist compromise of the *Trentes Glorieuses*.

The conception that underlies this emerging policy is indeed that of the search for equality between places. The watchword that expressed it perfectly – and that persists even today – is 'balance' between territories. It was, within a vision that is both organic – everyone has their own specialised function – and hierarchical – the pyramid of the 'urban framework' – a question of national territory, of minimizing the gaps between the places occupied by each of the local spaces of which it is made up.

To do this, the State mainly put in place three types of instruments. The first concerned standards and regulations: with exhaustive and nested regional

---

[1]    Delegation for regional planning and regional action.

planning, the State defined in a manner of speaking the place of each territory within the national arrangement. On this basis, the State could deploy its privileged instrument of direct action: the programming of infrastructures and facilities that constituted the first lever to guarantee this reduction of the gaps between places. The last instrument was then indirect action to ensure the redistribution and equalization of the means available to the territories.

This is where zoning comes in. This was therefore an exclusively distributive function. In this national regional planning policy, the zoning was designed with a large-mesh grid. In a way, it covered almost all of the national territory: on the one hand, in a logic of 'restriction' of resources – the approval system put in place to limit the establishment of activities in the Paris region – and on the other, with a view to distributing strengthened resources to promote an optimal spatial distribution of industrial development, with the extremely wide zoning covered by the 'special facilities premium' (1960). The systems would evolve over time, for example with the establishment of the 'regional development premium' (1972), but the purpose of guiding the distribution of activities in the territory according to a large-mesh zoning grid remained. This widespread use of zoning was later integrated with targeting that was both finer and more limited, focused on the territories requiring industrial reconversion (mines and steel industry), which demanded maximum equalisation effort.

The second period is the period of Decentralisation, inspired by the motto 'from equal places to equal opportunities'.

By the end of the 1960s, the modernist reason of the enlightened technocrats was a source of annoyance among many: the local notables resisted with all their might. They won this fight in the 1969 referendum, which saw a majority vote in favour of 'no' to regionalisation. The elective territories rebelled against the centre.

However, beyond this political revolt, the 1970s opened another front: territorial dynamics. The old industrial towns continued to sink into crisis, the countryside continued to empty; under modern architecture, villages and towns appeared endowed with their own dynamics that a national scheme was unable to oversee. The political slogan 'Living and working locally' was based on a socio-economic reality.

The State gradually lowered its head, abandoning its overall vision and making way for other actors. It no longer purported to dictate its law: it proposed contracts. It started in 1973 with the 'country contracts'. These were followed by medium-sized city contracts, offered to municipalities by DATAR itself. The decentralisation laws, from 1982, completed, in legal terms, this ten-year political evolution: the territories rose, on an equal footing with the State, to the rank of actors in regional planning.

Whilst the State continued to use the old planning tools (POS, SDAU, etc.), it gradually abandoned its initial mission. In the 1960s, the State purported to lead growth and the search for social and spatial equality. During the 1970s, and even more so in the 1980s, the State conceded development to the territories and limited itself to tasks of compensation and solidarity. The function of the territorial issue vis-à-vis public action was reversed. The Territory was the condition for the implementation of a social project. From the 1980s, local territories became in a way both the problem (see the large social housing complexes or industrial regions in crisis) and the solution for the sectoral policies of the State (housing, health, education, etc.). They were expected to be a lever for modernising public action. This would be evoked by the recurring injunction to 'the territorialisation of public action'.

The map of 'lived territories', published by DATAR in the mid-1990s, illustrated this division of tasks: the hierarchical pyramid of the 1960s was replaced by that of 'meshed polycentrism', which offered an egalitarian vision of a continental France criss-crossed with networks symbolizing the interdependencies between cities and countryside (Jean and Vanier, 2008).

Thus, in the early 2000s, regional planning appeared to have been stabilized by a new doctrine. The State ensured solidarity between territories (through significant transfers, which accounted for approximately 70 per cent of the financial resources of local authorities) and equal access to services; the territories, organised into villages and agglomerations, together with local State services, were given responsibility for local development – urban and rural. The contractual instrument became the rule of visible relations between the State and the local authorities, co-producers of the territories.

The new doctrine was expressed by the formula: 'one territory, one project, one contract'. This motto also became the general rule of inter-territorial relations: the general councils and regional councils in turn adopted the contractual formula to frame the subsidies they paid to cities and the countryside. In the early 2000s, regional planning experienced a new golden age of unlimited contractualisation.

The political reversal resulting from decentralisation became part of a situation perceived as an economic and social crisis whose effects were concentrated in space. This meant a double challenge for the State. On the one hand, it had to specify its actions in the face of the rising power of local authorities. Focusing on providing a targeted response to the localised effects of the crisis helped achieve this objective. Simultaneously, because this disengagement of a certain number of industrial, rural or urban territories marked in a certain way the failure of its ambition to reduce territorial inequalities from above and exhaustively, the mobilisation of local territories appeared a possible alternative.

Indeed, a new conception of equality between territories was emerging. This conception was based on the capacity of each territory for self-development, with the sum of these local developments having to constitute in some way national development. The shift from the organic and hierarchical representation of the national territory to that of polycentrism explicitly formalised this reference to equality through local development. The role of the State then consisted of supporting these dynamics by contributing to the establishment of local projects through the territorialisation of its policies. It was then up to the State – by means of contracts – to legitimise and reward this ability of the local authorities to develop a viable project.

The caesura of decentralisation not only marks a shift in the exercise of power over the territories between the State and the local authorities. It has the corollary of changing the conception of spatial justice and hence of the expected functions of zoning. To describe the function of zoning in these two successive conceptions of equality between territories, we propose employing the analytical framework established for another plan: social justice (Dubet, 2010). We sustain that there are two major conceptual models of public action aimed at social justice. One – equal places – focuses on the structure of the positions occupied by individuals and aims to reduce the inequalities between these positions. The second model – equal opportunities – takes greater account of the individual ability to engage in social competition and therefore aims to reduce the obstacles preventing fair competition.

It is with reference to this model of equal opportunities that the instrument of zoning assumes its full meaning and full scope. For each territory to have its opportunity, to be able to develop and participate in national development, we need to compensate for the handicaps from which some suffer in order to reinstate them in the overall logic. To ensure this function of getting all the territories 'back in the race', zoning would thus be deployed according to three successive methods. The distributive zoning from the previous period was extended, particularly in terms of economic development through the establishment of the regional planning grant (PAT) in 1981. But this system of direct aid to job creation, constrained by the reduction of State resources and the rules of the European Union, would lose its geographical scope and its equalizing capacity. Under the influence of these European policies, and in particular the establishment of structural funds, the mode of use of zoning would evolve during the 1980s to comply with the principle of eligibility. This was less a question of over-funding in direct aid than of an opening of rights to specific financing for projects by the territories thus targeted. Therefore, for territories covered by zoning, as for territories covered by common law, the local dynamic is decisive. Finally, the last method, undoubtedly the most radical, was established in principle by the 1995 law on regional planning: the zoning of tax or social derogation. This principle is systematized and concerns both economic development (PAT zoning), rural territories (ZRRs, 'rural revitalization zones') and social housing districts (ZUSs, 'sensitive urban zones'). However, the exceptional and at first sight mechanical nature of these derogation provisions cannot be interpreted as a renunciation of the overall 'developmentalist' logic. On the contrary, the derogation aims to reinforce this logic. Thus, almost everywhere, and particularly in the case of urban policy, tax and social derogations do not make territorial contractualisation disappear; they contribute to it.

In other words, zoning, with the diversity of its modes of implementation, constitutes the exceptional mechanism guaranteeing the inclusion of all territories in an overall logic of equal opportunities through local development.

**Q.** To what extent does the French case present general elements for reflection when coming to terms with policy design and the attempt to support spatial justice and wellbeing? Are there new interpretative models able to inspire policymaking? In your recent work you have been highlighting a risk of misrepresentation, which could sound familiar to scholars and policymakers in other contexts.

**A.** Since the start of the century, this long history of the search for greater spatial justice has been greatly destabilised.

Throughout the first twenty years of decentralisation, the political and academic debate on the relevance and effectiveness of the French model and its reversal focused on an unprecedented figure of socio-spatial inequalities: the disengagement of large suburban housing estates inherited from the *Trente Glorieuses*. As Jacques Chirac, then candidate for the Presidency of the Republic in 1995, put it, 'in certain dilapidated suburbs of large cities, entire areas are outside the law'. The flipside of growth and metropolisation, the urban divide overlaid the social fracture (Bourdieu, 1993). Faced with this unprecedented divide, the modernising city policy implemented by the State was insufficient (Tissot, 2007). The invoked principle of 'positive territorial discrimination' (Council of State, 1997) remains virtual. A veritable 'Marshall plan for the suburbs' was required.

At the start of the century, the challenges created by the scale of globalisation engaged the public authorities; should more emphasis be placed on the territories contributing to the competitiveness of France in the world, that is to say the major cities and particularly the global French city, the Great Paris (Gilli and Offner, 2009)? Simultaneously, the question of spatial justice was shifting and radically changing in nature. The question of the urban divide, within the cities, was followed by that of the territorial divide between the major cities and the rest of the territory. Therefore, that which has historically formed the basis of the French model of spatial justice for two centuries was put back on the political agenda. The notion of 'peripheral France' would thus emerge very quickly in the public debate (Guilluy, 2015). This term refers to a process of unprecedented geographical dissociation between the places of production of wealth – the major cities – and the territories (all the other areas) of life of the working classes. This new representation of the social and spatial issue and inequalities would structure the debate within the political sphere and have a lasting impact on public opinion, in particular during the 'yellow vest protests' in 2018, which appeared as the expression even of this territorial divide. From then on, 'peripheral France' entered the common language and became a category that describes reality.

The situation is actually paradoxical. While public opinion thus seems to highlight the perception of widening inequalities and the appearance of a territorial divide, most observers agree on a very different observation.

First, they note the weaker growth of social inequalities in France, compared to other European countries (Rousselon and Viennot, 2020). This is explained in particular by the power of the redistribution mechanisms. The second shared observation is that national public policies have largely contributed to limiting the rise in inequalities between territories. For the contemporary period, this is due to the effects of the public and private circulation of income, which is greater than the unequal creation of wealth among territories (Davezies, 2021). The effects of the public redistribution of resources are confirmed over an even longer period (Bonnet et al., 2021). There is then a very sharp drop in inter-departmental inequalities in average taxable income over a century, as well as a contribution that is significant – but variable over time – of income tax to the reduction in these inter-departmental inequalities.

Finally, while spatial inequalities are an indisputable reality, it is impossible to describe them according to a single geographical divide (Delpirou, 2017). There are multiple different social and territorial contrasts, and the biggest social inconsistencies are instead intra-urban.

**Q.** How then do we explain the success of what can be likened to a 'self-fulfilling prophecy'? Should we see in it a sign of the difference between reality as objectified by scientists and as it is experienced by society? Can this apparent contradiction be a significant question for experts as well as policymakers?

**A.** We can make an additional hypothesis. Its success is not based on its ability to describe reality, even viewed subjectively. It moves rather in the opposite direction of the ability to break free in order to reconstitute a vanished reality. This vanished reality is the reality that had been established in collective representations through a framework inspired in a rudimentary way by Marxist approaches: the territory is 'the *projection on the ground of social relations*' (Lefebvre, 1968). Each type of space corresponds to a social reality. And the equation is reversible: 'Tell me where you live, I'll tell you who you are.'

Today, this territorial order is fading or even disappearing. In our mobile society, all social groups, rich and poor alike, belong to multiple territories, every day and throughout their life cycles. This behaviour rearranges the territories and merges them through a generalised 'hopping' from one to another.

So, in Seine-Saint-Denis, so-called 'sensitive' districts are shared by mobile populations for whom the neighbourhood is a pressure-free zone and populations under house arrest for whom it is a trap (Estèbe, 2018). And in many municipalities in the same department, 'gentrified' districts and 'ghettos' are found side by side. At the other end of France, when Occitanie welcomes more than 100 000 new residents per year, it attracts both households on an upward trajectory and vulnerable groups in search of less difficult living conditions. Therefore, inequalities are everywhere. Ways of life are blurring the cards, recomposing territorial categories. The yellow vests are not rural or semi-urban, they are both residents of semi-urban areas, users or employees of the services of the average city and former residents or current consumers of the major cities. Because they are thus themselves the actors of this blurring of maps and categories, they will seize this simple representation that is offered to them: peripheral France. It gives everyone the ability to identify their place and identify with it: 'We are peripheral France.' Better still, it offers society as a whole – via its territorial reflection – the chance to show itself, beyond its complexity. Thus the collective thrill caused by the representation of a France cut in two is paradoxically reassuring: there remains a legible territorial order in a universe whose understanding escapes us.

This shift is evident in large cities and metropolitan areas (increasing mobility between home and work, generalisation of recreational mobility, etc.). This does not, however, place metropolitan cities and peripheral France in opposition in the style *'anywhere/somewhere'* (Goodhart, 2017), quite the contrary. Those living in less dense and rural areas are even more multi-territorial and frequent 'hoppers'. The yellow vest protests do not reflect the geography of the losing or 'abandoned' territories: this geography of the territories socially weakened or less well treated by public action crosses the spatial categories; according to the indicator chosen, the relative or absolute weight considered, all types of urban or rural territories are concerned. On the other hand, from a territorial point of view, the crisis highlights more a form of 'spatial suffering of the French' (Latour, 2010) and the disarray of the 'lost': those who, through their own practices, muddle the territorial landmarks and undermine a certain 'territorial order' (Behar, 2018). Far from being part of an inherited territorial order, evoked by the figure of the village community, the multiple portraits of the yellow vests, in their diversity, describe the same form of relationships with territories, in the archipelago, of households, often with couples who both work, permanently navigating between the places where they live (rural or semi-urban), work (average cities) and frequent for leisure or shopping (metropolitan areas). We are all from both 'somewhere' and 'everywhere', with the fear of feeling we are from 'nowhere'.

**Q.** How does one respond to the rise in power of this kind of representation of a widening of the territorial divide and to this crisis of meaning of spatial justice policies? How and to what extent can the reference to territorial cohesion still be consistent and relevant?

**A.** Since 2010, all successive French governments have been largely fascinated by this binary interpretation. Some (on the right) saw it as a form of electoral springboard, while it makes others (on the left) feel guilty for having abandoned the people in favour of metropolitan social groups.

The first response – a reflex one might say – was to state as if it were a magic formula that which had hitherto been implicit, because it was obvious. Thus, in 2012, upon his election, President Hollande created a Ministry of Territorial Equality. This was followed by the establishment of a General Commission for Territorial Equality (CGET), the publication of an expert report (Laurent, 2012) and a flurry of related instruments.[2]

This reactivation of the principle of territorial equality was rapidly revealed to be illusory and required a paradigmatic overhaul.

In 2017, an overhaul of the spatial justice model was therefore proposed, in a perspective more aligned with the European reference framework, of cohesion between territories. A Minister for Territorial Cohesion was appointed and a National Agency for Territorial Cohesion (ANCT) was created.

The notion of 'territorial cohesion' has followed a rather complex genealogy. This concept has been greatly popularized by the European Commission and its services in charge of defining regional policies. While in France, the notion of 'cohesion' is perceived as a mark of European influence, many analysts of Community policies have pointed out, since the 2000s, the significant French influence is in its affirmation (Faludi, 2004). The Lisbon Treaty of 2009 adds 'territorial cohesion' to the objectives of the European Union. This notion therefore makes a strong comeback in France. What, then, does its use mean and how can it be distinguished from the previous notion of territorial equality?

The notion of 'equality of territories' highlights the idea that at each level of the territorial framework (hamlet, village, town, small town, medium-sized town, metropolis, etc.) corresponds to a 'right to' a certain number of facilities or services. Equality is thus achieved by a 'good spatial ordering' of facilities, attributes and services according to the size of the towns or cities. Overall, the objective is to reduce, as far as possible, the gaps between the territories, whether these be the gaps between their positions (equal places) or between their trajectories (equal opportunities).

The notion of 'territorial cohesion' highlights what 'holds together' a territory: within it, each party must participate, according to their characteristics,

---

[2]    See, for example, the Regional Plan for Sustainable Development and Territorial Equality (SRADDET) in 2015.

in facilitating access to a service or resource. Let's take an example: for the cultural planning of the territory, the approach by equality consists of defining the characteristic for each link in the territorial framework (a metropolis must have an opera, a prefecture, a theatre); the approach by cohesion consists of thinking about the contribution of each part of the territory to access to works (the opera is located in the main city, a rural festival is held there twice a year, high schools in medium-sized towns are twinned with metropolitan facilities, etc.). The notion of territorial equality emphasizes the urban framework and the desirable hierarchy of their attributes; the notion of cohesion focuses on the territorial systems and the cooperation to be built between its components.

This paradigmatic shift can give rise to debate (Demaye-Simoni, 2022). For critics of the notion of cohesion, 'equality' is the pursuit of the spatial ideal of the welfare State, supplementing everyone's social rights with a form of territorial right to the provision of a service, while 'cohesion' would be the cover for the withdrawal of the State, highlighting the benefit of horizontal solidarity between territories through the incapacity to ensure vertical solidarity from the State.

But above all, at this stage, the notion of territorial cohesion remains without an operational variation in terms of public policies, all the more so since 'the yellow vest crisis' in 2018 confined it to the rhetorical register of protests, in order to replace it with a different logic of appeasing a society losing its territorial bearings.

Since 2018, the State seems to have given up on reducing spatial injustices, and aims above all to reassure the populations of the territories for whom the expression 'peripheral France' has offered a form of identification of their 'spatial suffering'. This requires a categorical, exhaustive treatment of all territories, with the exception of metropolitan areas.

A 'Town Centre Action' programme was set up for medium-sized towns, then a 'Small Towns of Tomorrow' programme targeting local towns, to which are added the 'Industrial Territories' programme or a 'Mountain Future' plan. In each of these cases, no territorial differentiation, in terms of the objective difficulties of one territory compared to another, is implemented. The entire stratum concerned is taken into account. Thus the 'Small Towns of Tomorrow' programme brings together all municipalities with a population of less than 20 000 serving a central function (more than 1600 municipalities).

The political priority appears to be in a way the need to respond to the feeling of abandonment and the need for recognition. Lost territories give way to forgotten territories (Epstein and Kirszbaum, 2016).

If the categories of territory that are the subject of these programmes fail to benefit – due to their number in particular – from a change in the sectoral policies of the State in their favour, they nevertheless obtain specific resources in terms of public engineering.

This greatly contributes to the expected appeasement effect, particularly vis-à-vis the representatives of these territories, the local elected officials. Thus, while for decades there has been a slow withdrawal of State public services from these territories (treasuries, postal agencies, etc.), every canton (over 2500) in France is provided with a 'Maison France Services', that is to say, a one-stop service point for most of the major State public services.

Thus, considering each category of territory in a homogeneous manner, without differentiating, for example, between the small, weakened towns of eastern France and the more attractive towns in western France, or between those isolated with respect to others that fall under metropolitan influence, prevents us from tackling effectively the phenomena of territorial disengagement. This categorical treatment is all the less effective given that territorial fragilities today essentially relate to the nature and intensity of the interdependencies between territories (Vanier, 2015).

In other words, the problem today is the wide gap between the display of the willingness to transform (cohesion) the model of territorial public action and the practice, which is limited to the appeasement of the local political sphere (elected officials).

This appease/transform dilemma is particularly sensitive at the level of national policies, piloted by the State. It is much less so at the level of local policies. In fact, local authorities today tend to mobilize the vertical solidarity policies of the State to initiate horizontal, more cooperative approaches, aimed at improving solidarity between individual territories. Examples of such practices are increasing in number, in particular, around environmental issues for which cohesion consists in establishing reciprocal relations between production territories and consumption territories (water, energy, food, etc.).

So, the open question is now if the imperative of green transition will make it possible in the years to come – because of the unprecedented territorial inequalities that it highlights – to install effectively a new reference system for spatial justice in France, based on the notion of cohesion among territories.

## REFERENCES

Behar D. (2018) La France des ronds-points enterre la France des territoires. Libération 11 décembre 2018.

Bonnet, F., d'Albis, H. & Sotura, A. (2021) Income Inequality across French Departments over the Last 100 Years. Economie et Statistique / Economics and Statistics, 526-527, 49–69.

Bourdieu P. (1993) *La misère du monde* ed du Seuil Paris.

Conseil d'Etat (1997) *Rapport public 1996 sur le principe d'égalité* Documentation française.

Davezies L.. (2021) *L'Etat a toujours soutenu les territoires* ed du Seuil. Paris.

Delpirou A. (2017) L'élection, la carte et le territoire : le succès en trompe-l'œil de la géographie, *Géoconfluences* https://geoconfluences.ens-lyon.fr/actualites/eclairage/election-geographie-medias.

Demaye-Simoni P. dir, (2022*) La cohésion des territoires. De nouveaux mots pour panser les maux* Berger Levrault.

Dubet F. (2010) *Les places et les chances. Repenser la justice sociale,* Ed. Seuil, collection La république des idées, Paris, 120.

Epstein R., Kirszbaum T. (2016) Territoires perdus versus territoires oubliés : les deux discours de la fracture. Urbanisme, Publications d'architecture et d'urbanisme, 2016, Vraies et fausses fractures, pp.57–59.

Estèbe P. (2015) L'égalité des territoires, une passion française. PUF.

Estèbe P. (2018). Seine-Saint-Denis : le sas et la nasse. *Tous urbains*, 22, 34–43.

Faludi A. (2004) Territorial Cohesion: Old (French) Wine in New Bottles?, Urban Studies, vol. 41, no 7 pp. 1349–1365.

Gilli F., Offner, J. (2009) *Paris, métropole hors les murs: Aménager et gouverner un Grand Paris*. Presses de Sciences Po.

Goodhart D. (2017) *The road to somewhere. The populist revolt and the future of politics,* Hurst Publishers.

Guilluy C. (2015*) La France périphérique: Comment on a sacrifié les classes populaires*. Flammarion.

Jean Y. et Vanier M. (2008) *La France : aménager les territoires*, Armand Colin, collection U.

Latour B., (2010) La mondialisation fait-elle un monde habitable ?, Territoires 2040, Prospective périurbaine et autres fabriques de territoires, Revue d'étude et de prospective n° 2, Datar, 2010, pp. 9–18, http://www.bruno-latour.fr/node/68.

Laurent E. (dir.) (2012) *Vers l'égalité des territoires*, Paris, La Documentation française, 2012.

Lefebvre H. (1968) Le Droit à la ville, Paris Anthropos.

Rousselon J., Viennot M. (2020) Inégalités primaires, redistribution : comment la France se situe en Europe. *La note d'analyse de France Stratégie*, 97, 1–16.

Tissot S. (2007*) L'Etat et les quartiers. Genèse d'une catégorie de l'action publique.* Ed du seuil Paris.

Vanier M., (2015) *Demain les territoires. Capitalisme réticulaire et espace politique*. Paris Hermann.

# Index